FOIL

FOIL

The ~~Freedom~~ Law and the Future
of Public ~~Access~~ Information
in ~~Upstate~~ New York

Brett Orzechowski

SYRACUSE UNIVERSITY PRESS

∞ The paper used in this publication meets the minimum requirements
of the American National Standard for Information Sciences—Permanence
of Paper for Printed Library Materials, ANSI Z39.48-1992.

For a listing of books published and distributed by Syracuse University Press,
visit www.SyracuseUniversityPress.syr.edu.

ISBN: 978-0-8156-3572-7 (hardcover)
978-0-8156-3590-1 (paperback)
978-0-8156-5438-4 (e-book)

Library of Congress Cataloging-in-Publication Data
Names: Orzechowski, Brett, author.
Title: FOIL : the law and the future of public information
in New York / Brett Orzechowski.
Description: Syracuse : Syracuse University Press, 2018. |
Includes bibliographical references and index.
Identifiers: LCCN 2017061241 (print) | LCCN 2018000392 (ebook) |
ISBN 9780815654384 (ebook) | ISBN 9780815635727 (hardcover : alk. paper) |
ISBN 9780815635901 (pbk. : alk. paper)
Subjects: LCSH: Freedom of information—New York (State) | Public records—
Law and legislation—New York (State) | Public records—Access control—
New York (State) | Government information—New York (State)
Classification: LCC KFN5827 (ebook) | LCC KFN5827 .O79 2018 (print) |
DDC 342.74708/53—dc23
LC record available at https://lccn.loc.gov/2017061241

Contents

Acknowledgments   *vii*

Part One. **History and Changes in Media**

1. A Brief History of New Yorkers' Right to Know   *3*
2. Legacy Media: Choices and Challenge   *24*
3. Digital Media: Access and Denial   *38*

Part Two. **The Law and Legislation**

4. Article 78: Last Resort, First Step   *57*
5. Exemption, Ethics, and the Joint Commission
on Public Ethics   *72*
6. The Legislature: Two FOIL Bills, One Veto   *90*

Part Three. **Local**

7. Policy: Police Cameras and the Public   *107*
8. Public-Information Officers: Boards and the Bored   *117*
9. The Business of FOIL   *127*

Part Four. **More Information: Citizens, Advocacy, and Data**

10. The Citizen: George and Helen of Troy   *139*
11. Watchdogs: Transparency and Civil Liberties   *149*
12. Data: Numbers In, Some Numbers Out   *164*

Part Five. **More Perspective, Looking into the Future**

13. State and Fed: Different Levels, Same Issues   *179*
14. Transparency: Defining the Future of "Open"   *194*
15. The Administration   *210*
16. FOIL Analysis and Review: In Their Words   *227*

APPENDIX A: *The Freedom of Information Law*   *243*
APPENDIX B: *The Freedom of Information Act*   *259*
APPENDIX C: *Notable FOIL Cases*   *281*
APPENDIX D: *Sample FOIL Requests*   *293*
Notes   *299*
Index   *325*

Acknowledgments

In New York's politically charged state capital, remaining neutral is a remarkable feat. Bob Freeman's job is to interpret the Freedom of Information Law, and his pragmatic view didn't change when I walked into his office in May 2016 to pitch to him the idea of writing a book on FOIL. During the year I researched this book, I attended some of the nearly eighty talks Freeman gives annually to civic groups, journalists, school districts, and government agencies. He drives around New York State every year to deliver one of the more candid performances you will see from a government employee. When I asked for interpretation of certain aspects of the law, he offered a number of solutions or applicable court cases. When I asked for names of subject-matter experts, he didn't flinch. So for all of this I owe him an immeasurable debt of gratitude.

I would also be remiss if I didn't show my fullest appreciation for the seventy-four individuals I interviewed on and off the record who shared their anecdotes and perspectives on FOIL. They represent about 75 percent of the total number people I reached out to with a request, and they confirmed my belief that FOIL is an important topic. I thank all of them for their time and guidance.

I also thank Syracuse University Press and acquisitions editor Alison Shay, who has become one of the most invaluable persons involved in this project. They took a chance on a first-time author and offered honest and essential feedback through the entire process. For a press that at times focuses on New York State matters, this book is a natural fit, but the time and care Alison took to ensure that the closest thing to perfection has been produced makes me wonder how editors have the patience to do this dozens of times each year. It takes a unique person and organization to carry out such a process.

As an extension, I also thank the reviewers from the media and legal communities who took the extra time and care to comb over every word of this manuscript from its earliest and roughest iteration to what you see here. Since this book serves as a guide for those in the journalism, government, legal, and academic communities—in addition to almost twenty million New Yorkers—the concept needed to resonate with multiple audiences. The reviewers offered detailed suggestions and commentary on certain sections. For this, I am indebted to them and to all the people at Syracuse University Press. The process made a stronger final product.

Also, projects like this can never be carried out without family. While I was growing up, conversations around the dinner table would begin with talk about the day, the Mets and Knicks, and sometimes the law. When you grow up with a father who is an attorney, conversations sometimes feel like inquisitions—you are sometimes asked the same question five different ways before one answer is (maybe) satisfactory. Decades later, when you're writing a book that involves deeper legal investigation, it's probably best to have in your corner a father like Stan Orzechowski, who was a trustworthy guide through the world of some complex legal constructs and who in the end always wanted to make sure it was right. I also cannot thank him enough for instilling in me the temerity to ask "why." It's one of the best questions to ask but never to be asked.

I researched and wrote this book during one of the more transitional periods of my life. I left the media industry, reentered academia, moved back to New York State, and extended our little family. With an infant cradled in one arm and a preschooler swinging off the other, my wife, Jodie, calmly offered her perspective on the process and then on the importance of achieving a work–life balance. With humor and blunt feedback, she offered sage advice and guidance over these years. I'm lucky to have her as a wife and even more fortunate to be her husband.

Last, I want to acknowledge the tens of thousands New Yorkers who have exercised their legal rights over the decades in their search for the truth and information. Yes, the Committee on Open Government has issued more than twenty-five thousand advisory opinions, but this figure does not include the number of FOIL requests or appeals that have been submitted to government agencies since the 1970s. When used correctly and responsibly by both citizens and the government, a law can be truly effective. Systems and laws are often imperfect. People challenge their existence, but at the same time citizens will always remain vigilant. In a way, this is part of any New Yorker's DNA composition, and as we continue into an age when information becomes a commodity more and more each day, it is important to remember that this is our law—and very much our right to know.

Part One

History and Changes in Media

1

A Brief History
of New Yorkers'
Right to Know

NEW YORK PUBLIC OFFICERS LAW, ARTICLE 6
SECTIONS 84-90
FREEDOM OF INFORMATION LAW

§84. Legislative declaration.
The legislature hereby finds that a free society is maintained when
government is responsive and responsible to the public, and when
the public is aware of governmental actions. The more open a
government is with its citizenry, the greater the understanding and
participation of the public in government.

As state and local government services increase and public problems
become more sophisticated and complex and therefore harder to
solve, and with the resultant increase in revenues and expenditures,
it is incumbent upon the state and its localities to extend public
accountability wherever and whenever feasible.

The people's right to know the process of governmental decision-
making and to review the documents and statistics leading to determinations is basic to our society. Access to such information should
not be thwarted by shrouding it with the cloak of secrecy or confidentiality. The legislature therefore declares that government is the
public's business and that the public, individually and collectively

3

and represented by a free press, should have access to the records of government in accordance with the provisions of this article.

———

The Committee on Open Government (COOG) shares office space with other New York State public agencies, but beyond the hanging landscape prints and rows of file cabinets are distinct reminders of its accomplishments—awards from various media and community associations, decades of meticulously kept physical records of thousands of advisory opinions, and a framed cartoon from the *Buffalo News* illustrator Daniel Zakroczemski. The artwork includes a journalist and a man with a dark suit and tape over his mouth flanking a capitol building. American author Robert Heinlein's words balance the bottom of the page: "Secrecy is the beginning of tyranny."

For Bob Freeman, the choice to hang Zakroczemski's art was easy. Freeman, the committee's executive director, thought the political cartoon adds a "touch" to the three-person office. Beyond the illustration and the sunlight that sometimes splits the Albany skyline and spills into the expansive sixth-floor windows on the Washington Avenue space, the office's style undeniably suggests government.

This space is not the committee's first home. It has moved four times in Albany, but only one person has occupied the committee's office since 1974. From that point, Freeman's job has been to offer interpretation of New York's Freedom of Information Law (FOIL) and Open Meetings Law (OML), which has been on the books since January 1, 1977. A year later to the day, the current version of FOIL was enacted, which subsequently, by all legal accounts, strengthened the statute first passed four years earlier. The office also offers interpretation of the Personal Privacy Protection Law (PPPL) which pertains to personal information collected and maintained by state agencies. The law, passed in 1984, requires agencies to meet standards of fair information practices regarding the collection, maintenance, use, and disclosure of personal information. Overall, for nearly forty years the office that Freeman oversees has had one purpose—to interpret these three laws for any member of the public and in the process to hold government accountable.

The reason for the office's longevity—and, as an extension, Freeman's—is often supported by a fact that no one disputes: in 2016, the office penned its twenty-five thousandth advisory legal opinion on public-information cases. Those opinions, signed by Freeman or any of his assistant executive directors over the years, are sent to the FOIL petitioner and any one of the ten thousand New York State–based government agencies from which the information was requested, whether the Suffolk County Police Department, the Town of Clarkstown, or the Metropolitan Transit Authority. The contents of each opinion are clear: this is the law; this is the section of the law that the FOIL query addresses; this is how the law is interpreted. To close, each opinion is declarative in its purpose: this is only an opinion; the petitioner can take it or leave it. There is no enforcement, but the document carries strong, supporting weight.

Even with a concept such as proactive disclosure, which with technological advancements allows smaller and larger agencies to post public information online in digital formats in a timely manner, cases of denial are becoming more common throughout all levels of local and state government, including from the highest level, the executive branch. In some cases, when a New York government agency denies a public-information request, the story becomes very public. Otherwise, the petitioner expects to receive the requested information if the letter is filed correctly, is definitive in its intent, and is clear of any of the law's exemptions.

For every FOIL request for property-tax records of a local company in a Rochester suburb or the results of water-quality testing in rural Hamilton County, there is a request for information regarding a larger, state-wide matter such as the Fort Schuyler Management Corporation (FSMC), which is affiliated with the State University of New York (SUNY) Polytechnic Institute. New York governor Andrew M. Cuomo's administration refers to FSMC, which serves as the economic catalyst for predominantly nanotechnology development across the state, as a private corporation based on its nonprofit, 501(c)(3) status. In some public accounts, news outlets referred to FSMC as "quasi-public."[1] But, according to COOG, because FSMC is an economic extension of the state public-university system, any document associated with FSMC should be made public for inspection.[2] The administration suggests otherwise, which has led to an ongoing public and legal debate about the future of government business in New York State under the current Cuomo administration and, from some perspectives, a larger discussion about FOIL's present and future power.

The way COOG interprets the law, the term "quasi-public" is a misnomer, and the process by which the current administration requested construction and development bids for the Buffalo Billion project, via FSMC, should be open to public inspection.[3] Jim Heaney, a longtime investigative reporter with the *Buffalo News* and now with the nonprofit, independent *Investigative Post*, first filed a FOIL request on July 30, 2014, to inspect the inner workings of the process and contract bids.[4] The government denied Heaney's request, claiming FSMC is a private nonprofit.

Heaney and WGRZ, the Buffalo CBS affiliate and *Investigative Post* partner, began a legal proceeding against FSMC on May 18, 2015, and filed an Article 78 petition allowed by New York Civil Practice Law and Rules, which, for many FOIL petitioners, is the last resort for seeing a request through and the first step of what can potentially be a costly and time-consuming legal endeavor through the court system.[5] They asked that a state Supreme Court judge rule on whether FSMC was subject to FOIL. In response, the offices of Alain E. Kaloyeros, whom Governor Cuomo appointed president and CEO of SUNY Polytechnic and oversaw the business of FSMC, quietly posted the contract proposals online, making the bid documents public. This action removed grounds for suing, and the Article 78 lawsuit was withdrawn on July 17, 2015.[6]

The FSMC case offers a glimpse into the growing elasticity by which some state government agencies conduct business and their perception of public access to information. The case also underscores the cyclical nature of government and how one family's role in Albany has come full circle for COOG, which is housed under the New York Department of State. As the state government is structured, at the start of the New York State legislative session in 2017, the secretary of state, Rossana Rosado, answered to Governor Andrew Cuomo. In March 1976, when Freeman was officially appointed executive director, he worked under then secretary of state and future governor Mario Cuomo, Andrew's father. Now Governor Andrew Cuomo is the seventh governor to sign Freeman's paycheck.

The relationship between COOG and the executive branch is also unique—COOG serves as a government watchdog even though it is a government agency. When New York governor Malcolm Wilson approved legislation to enact New York State's first Freedom of Information Law on May 29, 1974, the office was known as the Committee on Public Access to Records (COPAR) and was housed, by law, in the Office of General Services.[7] (COPAR officially changed its name to the Committee on Open Government in 1981 because of its responsibility to interpret the OML, which deals with meetings of government bodies.) It was understood in the wake of Watergate that the office would serve as the independent voice to interpret access to all public-records matters but would not enforce the law. Later, as the secretary of state for Wilson's successor, Hugh Carey, Mario Cuomo told Freeman that his office's legal opinion might sometimes be unpopular with people in the governor's administration but that interpreting the law was his primary responsibility. "Cuomo, above all, at least in my opinion, was an attorney. He believed in the law," Freeman said. "If he thought I was completely correct on the law, he was completely supportive."[8]

Since then, Freeman tells audiences that he does not have a boss and that his only client is the law. As a government employee, he serves the people of New York, meaning that if a citizen or state official calls the office, most often he or she has a direct line to Freeman, who is registered as Independent to dispel any thoughts of political allegiance. Freeman also retired for a weekend in 2012 in order to collect a New York State pension; however, he still works full-time, collecting only the difference between his last year's salary and the pension, which also saves taxpayers' money.

The office can be in a precarious position whenever the budget is discussed. For twenty years, COOG served a Democratic governor, until 1995, when Governor George Pataki, a Republican, took office. At the time, there was some discussion about COOG's role, but ultimately it was perceived that an independent voice added another layer of checks and balances uncommon in other states. Since COOG had two decades of building a strong reputation in Albany, longtime legislators, the media, and the citizens of New York would view removing this nonpartisan office for perceived political reasons as an undesirable decision.

To add another layer of complexity, when the majority of states were adopting public-access and public-information laws forty years ago, only a few ethical questions arose about the role of an independent office in daily government functions. Laws to create such offices were desired when the public sentiment for full transparency was high, but enough public trust existed in state legislators to add a nonpartisan element to governance. Now, Freeman and many national freedom of information (FOI) advocates believe that significant trust issues exist across all levels of government and that the creation of an independent office on the state level could be scrutinized as a major conflict of interest, raising further ethical concerns.

In the process, many agencies like New York's COOG established in other states during the 1970s and 1980s were either dissolved or folded into other offices over time, trimmed by growing fiscal concerns, abolished for political reasons, or replaced by outside legal and advocacy organizations or independent attorneys who specialize in public-records matters. As of early 2017, New York was only one of two states (Connecticut is the other) in the country that houses an office like COOG that offers expertise on its public-information law, albeit with a unique structure—its attorneys are employed by the state, so that they are serving as both public servants and government watchdogs.

If you are a county official, you can call the office. If you are a citizen, you can call the same extension. If you are a reporter in New York State or New York City, chances are you have COOG's phone number. In 2016, the office fielded almost 3,900 phone calls and responded to 1,400 written inquiries.[9] This volume began to grow that year during the spring when New York City mayor Bill de Blasio, the city's former public advocate and proponent of open records—a fact he touted during the mayoral election in 2014—referred to Jonathan Rosen, a cofounder of the public-relations firm BerlinRosen, as an "agent of the city" and so claimed that the email correspondence between him and Rosen was not subject to FOIL.

This claim caught the attention of the media, especially NY1 reporter Grace Rauh, whose initial FOIL request for these records was denied in May 2016.[10] All New York City media outlets, including the *New York Times*, the *New York Daily News*, and the *New York Post*, continued to follow the story through the summer of 2016 as de Blasio's approval ratings dropped, but it was the *Village Voice* and its legal representation that called for an advisory opinion from Freeman and COOG. The *Voice* also submitted a FOIL request, asking for "all records of communication" between de Blasio and a number of people from January 1, 2014, through May 23, 2016, but the request was denied.

On August 3, 2016, a freshly signed advisory opinion on this matter sat on Freeman's desk. Sleeves rolled up to the elbows and Windsor knot firmly still in place, Freeman included in the opinion all the past FOIL cases that apply to the matter. It's a lengthier opinion, running just more than three pages, but concludes in customary COOG fashion:

> In an effort to enhance the intent and understanding of FOIL and encourage a change in the stance taken by the Office of the Mayor, a copy of this opinion will be sent to Henry T. Berger, the Mayor's attorney and Records Appeals Officer.
>
> I hope that I have been of assistance.[11]

The de Blasio administration had a choice—continue to deny the FOIL request or fulfill it. If the records were still denied, the *Village Voice* also had a choice—let the matter go or file an Article 78 lawsuit, triggering the start of the court process.

Freeman noted that from the public's perspective the situation did not look good either way, but he knew the story would not disappear.[12] More media outlets joined the pursuit, and on September 7, 2016, NY1 and the *New York Post* filed an Article 78 lawsuit against the mayor for refusal to release the emails in question.[13] More than two months later, on the night before Thanksgiving, the de Blasio administration provided more than fifteen thousand pages of heavily redacted documents that further outlined the relationship between government and the private sector and that suggested Rosen was involved in matters of policy and public-relations maneuvering.[14]

There was more, even though two weeks later de Blasio said future email exchanges with Rosen would be made public by request. As a response, the media company's lawyers filed an additional request on December 7, 2016, to obtain the past exchanges.[15] A subsequent additional denial of this request now spiraled into a very public matter.

Finally, on March 23, 2017, Manhattan Supreme Court judge Joan Lobis issued a thirteen-page ruling siding with NY1 and the *New York Post*. In the ruling, Lobis stated that "correspondence between the mayor and Rosen, who has not been formally retained by the mayor or any other city agency, is not exempt from disclosure under the inter-agency or intra-agency deliberative privilege under FOIL."[16] The ruling came down ten months after the initial FOIL request was filed, and the administration would later appeal.

The de Blasio case exemplifies a larger issue regarding the law's interpretation, which remains at the core of contentious and now often political struggles for information. The law was never intended to become a political device, but more examples are surfacing that contradict the original legislative mandate.

This book's exploration of the law, highlighted by noted regional and state cases and obscure quests for the truth—all bound by

FOIL—serves as a tour of a law that continues to affect every New York State resident. As demonstrated by case law, news stories, legal documentation, and scholarly examinations, FOIL remains a powerful public panacea in unlocking information even though the statute is challenged more than ever. Boundaries continue to bend against the constituencies that the statute is intended for, pushed by unforeseen social forces and government intervention. Nevertheless, the law remains steadfast in its support of the larger question: What would happen if the government disclosed information?

The Beginning

Freeman said local government officials from the state's sixty-two counties and the smaller municipal offices—villages and towns—contact COOG the most, although official data on this point do not exist. He estimated that each year 30 percent of calls are from local government but that just as many people from the general public dial his number—for the simple reason that legal resources are not readily available, nor do they have access to in-house counsel. About 15 to 20 percent of the calls are from news media, and the remaining are from attorneys and various others across the country and the world.[17] If you Google the name "Committee on Open Government" or the abbreviation COOG, you will find that only one search result appears. In 1974, search-engine optimization did not exist.

State agencies do not call COOG as often anymore. They rely on an extensive and growing case-law library of FOIL opinions that can mostly be found online, or they have in-house counsel that occasionally contacts Freeman's office. Larger municipalities across the state, including New York City, have corporation counsel or teams of attorneys. The other percentages of who contacts COOG, Freeman said, have remained consistent since the day he joined the office. As the law was drafted, neither its impact nor the constituencies it would directly affect were known, but those who originally crafted the language believed the law to be nonexclusive. The prevailing sentiment across the country in the 1970s, as the Watergate investigation was unfolding and eventually closed, was that an independent office could—and perhaps should—exist.

On February 1, 1973, Assemblyman Donald Taylor, a Republican from the 111th District in Watertown, introduced a bill to amend the Public Officers Law in relation to public access to records of state and local agencies.[18] At the time, Taylor was chairman of the New York State Assembly Committee on Governmental Operations. He was joined by Senator Ralph J. Marino, another Republican from Oyster Bay on Long Island (5th District), who chaired the New York State Senate Subcommittee on the Right of Privacy.[19] He would later become the first Long Islander to serve as Senate majority leader in Albany.[20] The 1973 legislative session ended, and full passage of the bill would have to wait another year.

Together, Taylor and Marino helped push through bill A-3247 and S-5205, which was signed into law by Governor Wilson as chapter 578 of the *Laws of 1974* weeks before the session ended.[21] Before enactment of the Freedom of Information Law, there was no general public right of access to government records or meetings of government bodies. (The same is true for the OML passed in 1977; there was no precedent.) The language echoed the federal Freedom of Information Act (FOIA), which passed in 1966, but was specific to New York. Among a number of statutes, the law stated that all records in possession of an agency and municipality are subject to the mandates of the law, whether the records were filed after September 1, 1974, when FOIL went into effect, or not.[22]

As New York moved forward, the federal government slightly sputtered with amendments to the FOIA. Just a month after New York's FOIL went into effect, President Gerald Ford vetoed the proposed FOIA amendments in Washington at a time when Congress was serious about establishing a reasonable public right-to-know measure along with stronger amendments to the law.[23] Ultimately, the veto was overridden by Congress—a rare occurrence. (According to the US Senate archives, Ford is the second-most vetoed US president, tied with Harry S. Truman at twelve. The most vetoes by a sitting president overridden by Congress were fifteen by Andrew Johnson immediately after the Civil War. From 1789 through Barack Obama's administration, only 111 vetoes were overridden by Congress.)

At the same time in New York, new agencies were being created as a result of the 1974 legislative session, including COPAR. The reshuffling of personnel took an approach different from the one taken by contemporary government. The office consisted of attorneys and staff on loan from other agencies: an attorney from a state office, another who served as a local-government liaison, and another involved with school districts.

This personnel menagerie was necessary given the widespread impact of FOIL, which stretched into every local and state agency, but attorneys did not stay long with COPAR. In just a few months, during the summer and autumn of 1974, the committee prepared and distributed a one-page questionnaire to all state and local units of government to assess compliance with FOIL.[24] All twenty state departments on the executive level adopted or drafted resolutions, and 85 percent of the remaining state agencies (including authorities and commissions) adopted or drafted regulations.[25]

The implementation was swift, with little opposition on the state level. The bipartisan measure, which was sponsored by Republicans in the Senate and Assembly, was serviceable, but many viewed the law as weak with respect to a few select words. Instead of stating everything is available "except," the law said the following information "is available to the exclusion of everything else," meaning rights of access were limited.

Nevertheless, the first iteration of the law worked on the strength behind the endorsement of Assemblyman Taylor and Senator Marino. Media organizations also trumpeted the creation of the law. In July 1974, two months after Governor Wilson signed the first FOIL bill, a government-appointed task force, COPAR, was created.[26] Included on the committee were Elie Abel, dean of the Graduate School of Journalism at Columbia University, and T. Elmer Bogardus, the publisher of the Eagle Newspapers in Cazenovia, outside of Syracuse.[27] Its tasks were to evaluate the current FOIL and its impact and to lend guidance through another degree of oversight.

The New York State legislation may have been similar to the federal FOIA, but a number of stakeholders were directly involved in the drafting of the state law. The task force included media representation and government officials, who often relied on legal counsel. One attorney was Louis Contiguglia, who served as counsel to the Majority Leader's Office in the New York State Senate from 1972 to 1978 and took the lead with Senator Marino in championing the bill that became FOIL.

Arguably, no state government felt the repercussions of Watergate as much as New York after President Ford tapped Governor Nelson Rockefeller to serve as his vice president. Since by that point Rockefeller had served New York as governor since 1959, Malcolm Wilson's only year in office (1973–74) worked as an extension of his predecessor's administration, with support by a few Rockefeller Republican holdovers, who aligned with the former governor and considered themselves moderates. Along with others in the Republican Party, Contiguglia felt a shift across the state and country in terms of party affiliation. The movement wasn't sudden. It had been percolating for some time, and the reverberations are still felt to this day.

During the New York State Constitutional Convention of 1967, Contiguglia served as counsel to the Minority Committee on Local Government and Home Rule. He noticed that the Constitutional Convention was stacked with legislators as opposed to citizens, an alarming shift in attendance and a frowned-upon practice. Contiguglia, now in his mideighties and still practicing law in Auburn, New York, knew that a shift would continue, but bipartisan work in Albany led by Republicans could still be accomplished—albeit by a different strategy. "If you were going to get meaningful feedback on any issue from citizens, we were in the minority, and we sort of knew this going forward," Contiguglia said. "What was proposed during that convention is that as Republicans we decided to work on individual amendments one at a time, which would require passage by the legislature, not by public referendum. We felt FOIL was one of those really meaningful laws. I think everyone felt it was very important. I knew it was."[28]

Strengthening FOIL

As Assemblyman Taylor introduced new legislation on the floor in Albany during the 1973 legislative session, Freeman was finishing law school at New York University. He moved to Albany in November 1973 to work at a private law firm, but he couldn't stand representing people based on their ability to pay. He heard of an opening at the New York State Department of Social Services and switched to the public sector.

Freeman was new to state government and found himself on the lowest level of any governmental depth chart and at an empty desk in the Office of Counsel. His immediate superior was an attorney who was frustrated with a number of developments in state government. Freeman remembered no one wanted to sit near Felix Infausto, a temperamental but fair attorney, but the desk next to him now belonged to Freeman.

Infausto assigned what Freeman believed to be relatively simple tasks: he had Freeman read the *New York Law Journal* and the *New York Times* and locate judicial decisions that had anything to do with the Department of Social Services. Infausto called Freeman into his office one day and praised him for his thoroughness in reading the *Journal*. In a reasonable but not defiant manner, Freeman told Infausto the exercise was silly. No one talked to Infausto that way, but the conversation earned Freeman some respect.

Infausto would begin calling Freeman into his office and confiding in the young attorney. His colleagues thought it was odd, but Freeman was never uncomfortable with being a confidant. In May 1974, a new law passed, and the governor's office began calling various state agencies to lend attorneys and staff to get a new office off the ground. COPAR's first executive director, Lou Tomson, called Freeman to ask if he would like to work in the new agency. Freeman asked about the nature of the position, and Tomson told him he would be dealing with the Freedom of Information Law. The young attorney said he knew nothing about the legislation, but Tomson assured him no else did either.

Freeman was lent to COPAR in August 1974, just before FOIL went into effect, and within a few months Hugh Carey became governor and appointed a new secretary of state who had never served in government but had made his reputation by fighting city hall from Queens—Mario Cuomo. As a result of a budget transfer, not by law, COPAR was moved to the New York Department of State. The new position also offered new challenges on the state and federal levels, and Freeman found himself in an interesting position when he gave his first advisory opinion. The office began receiving calls and letters asking for opinions on FOIL requests, and the first one that landed on Freeman's desk focused on student records. On August 21, 1974, a month after Freeman began at COPAR, President Ford signed the Family Educational Rights and Privacy Act (FERPA), which grants access to education records to parents of minor students, who acquire those rights at eighteen years of age, but prohibits disclosure to the public.[29] "Often you cannot give a correct answer unless you look at two or three statutes in combination with one another. But the timing of this one just verified that this job would be a challenge at a really interesting time with little or no precedent," Freeman said. "Ultimately, it was an easy decision. How can I possibly offer an opinion on FOIL that is in conflict with a federal statute, the law of the land?"[30]

Eventually, during the spring of 1975, every attorney lent to COPAR returned to his or her original agency, except Freeman. His boss, Tomson, was a holdover from the Rockefeller administration and had COPAR running efficiently, but, according to Freeman, he had a small flaw—he was terrified of dealing with the news media. Just as Infausto had assigned Freeman to read the *New York Law Journal*, Tomson assigned Freeman to pick up the phone whether it was the *New York Times* or the *Palladium Times* calling. Freeman listened to the concerns of citizens and the media alike, developing an understanding of FOIL's new impact. By late 1975, Tomson left his position as executive director of COPAR, and the Department of Social Services requested Freeman's return. Freeman was still interested in COPAR, however, and Secretary of State Cuomo offered him a position there, with a big raise. Freeman liked the work and stayed for an annual salary of $17,500. He now had the title of executive director of COPAR.

Even before Freeman was appointed, he had worked closely with Elie Abel, COPAR's chairman, to find avenues to strengthen the passage of FOIL in 1974. (COPAR began as a committee and evolved into an agency.) Still young and a newcomer to state government, Freeman needed to find ways to talk to key legislative players in the Senate and Assembly. If he wanted to talk to the Senate majority leader, he couldn't get a meeting, but Abel, who had developed a long working relationship with key legislators during his years with the *New York Times* and NBC, could make one phone call and get through.

The same held true for William "Bill" Bookman, who served as president of the New York State Society of Newspaper Editors' committee on legislative matters and consulted Governor Wilson during the original drafting of the bill.[31] He would later become chairman of COOG and would consult legislators in the original writing of the OML.[32] At the society's annual meeting in 1976, Freeman spoke at Bookman's request and expressed the same sentiment—FOIL existed, but it remained a weak piece of legislation.

From the time Freeman was appointed COPAR's executive director until November 1976, he worked with Abel and Bookman to propose several modifications to FOIL. They then sent a memorandum entitled "Problems and Solutions" to state and local agencies with copies of the proposed amendments.[33] Through the 1977 legislative session, discussions focused on the proposal, especially the language dealing with access. Freeman and others examined the federal law and weighed its pros and cons. They took stock of the type of requests and appeals trickling into the office. Overall, a law that would tilt the power to New York citizens was the desired outcome.

COPAR drafted a clear definition of the term "record." It also proposed language that addressed its primary concern, which also existed concerning the FOIA. Now, instead of stating that "the following items are available," the New York law would state that all public records are "available except." The committee believed this amendment would allow clearer interpretation of FOIL by both the public and legal entities.

In addition, as amendments were being discussed in Albany, legal decisions that would continue to have an impact on FOIL for decades were being handed down in courtrooms across the state. In November 1976, Burke v. Yudelson involved the "any person" principle (who can use the law) and Zuckerman v. New York State Board of Parole, established that state agency regulations cannot be more restrictive than FOIL.[34]

A year later Dunlea v. Goldmark set the definition of statistical or factual tabulations or data; Sheehan v. City of Binghamton made police blotters available for public inspection; and Westchester Rockland v. Mosczydlowski stated that records used in litigation were exempt from FOIL only if they were prepared solely for litigation.[35]

As these rulings would set the course for four decades of FOIL litigation, COPAR managed to convince lawmakers to repeal the original law, and in June 1977 a completely revised FOIL was enacted based on the "Problems and Solutions" proposal. The new law was signed by Governor Hugh Carey and went into effect on January 1, 1978.[36]

Challenges to the Present

In FOIL's forty-year existence, the tenor of the state and federal government has gradually changed. Rampant skepticism still exists, but unforeseen challenges that involve privacy and security have greatly altered the public landscape, most notably the events of September 11, 2001. Coupled with contemporary issues such as law enforcement and body cameras, digital transmission of government discussions, the New York Secure Ammunition and Firearms Enforcement (SAFE) Act in the wake of the Newtown shootings, and the continued push for what constitute open data from agencies, the past twenty years of FOIL have been more challenging than the first twenty, when precedents were being established across the state.

Amendments have been added to FOIL over time to reflect a changing society, but none has been as full as the repeal and new passage of the law in 1977. The seven sections of FOIL have remained largely intact, with sections 87 and 89 experiencing the most growth and revision—and for good reason. Section 87 outlines access to agency records, and section 89 defines general provisions relating to access records and certain cases. The latter section also details COOG's role.

As the legislative session ended in Albany on June 18, 2016, eleven proposed bills in the Senate and Assembly addressed FOIL-related issues. The two most notable focused on attorney and retrieval fees and the time a government agency can take to appeal a court order decision to release information. Earlier versions of similar measures reached an impasse when Governor Cuomo vetoed two FOIL bills in the early hours of December 12, 2015.[37] One bill would allow judges to award attorneys' fees to individuals who win cases against agencies that deny information. The other limited to two months the time an agency can delay a court-order release of information while drafting an appeal. In his veto message, Governor Cuomo stated his belief that the transparency bills should extend beyond the executive branch to include the legislative branch.[38] In the same veto message, he shared his intentions for comprehensive FOIL reform the next legislative session.

However, he signed an executive order the next day to expedite the appeals process for local agencies, but the attorneys' fees bill remained untouched.[39] At the root of these bills are the most contemporary FOIL and free-press issues. A significant challenge facing news organizations, aside from fluctuating business models mainly for newspapers as they transition into the digital age, is the ability to pursue legal recourse after a FOIL denial because of the potential for mounting legal fees. These concerns are not mutually exclusive of one another, but provisions in the law that focus on the amount of time to fulfill a request and the amount of time to respond to a request have become some government agencies' most significant reasons for delay or denial.

With the knowledge that either a citizen or news organization may not have the resources to pay tens of thousands of dollars in legal fees to bring an access-to-records case to court, some responses to initial requests outline the cost associated to retrieve some information. If the records request requires digital retrieval, some agencies cite the provision that because the retrieval requires specialization, particularly through information technology specialists, they will charge the petitioner for these services. Ultimately, this tactic deters an individual or an organization from pursuing a request or appeal.

Aside from the thirty-day appeal window if the request for information is denied, the two most common time provisions are found in section 89, "General provisions relating to access to records; certain cases, 3(a)" (see appendix A):

The Acknowledgement
Each entity subject to the provisions of this article, within five business days of the receipt of a written request for a record reasonably described, shall make such record available to the person requesting it, deny such request in writing or furnish a written acknowledgment of the receipt of such request and a statement of the approximate date.
The Answer
If an agency determines to grant a request in whole or in part, and if circumstances prevent disclosure to the person requesting the record or records within twenty business days from the date of the acknowledgement of the receipt of the request, the agency shall state, in writing, both the reason for the inability to grant the request within twenty business days and a date certain within a reasonable period, depending on the circumstances, when the request will be granted in whole or in part.

There are also appeal processes, with the government agency required to answer an appeal of a denial in ten business days. The give-and-take interplay between agency and petitioner is commonly referred to at COOG as "access delayed, access denied," and it's a growing point of contention for media organizations, watchdog groups, and citizens requesting perceived controversial records.

Conversely, just as the process of requesting information has become a legal challenge for petitioners such as citizens and the media, at other levels of government it has emerged primarily as a resource issue because of the growing volume of such requests. For example, a rural county clerk could be the FOI or public-records officer for an agency, responsible for receiving FOIL requests and serving as the point of contact for the public. This person may also have the ability to approve or deny a request and in the process may also redact certain information in the requested documents or data that may breach laws exempted by FOIL, such as FERPA or the Health Insurance Portability and Accountability Act (HIPAA). On the other end of the spectrum, larger agencies may have FOI officers who are also attorneys or an entire office or team of attorneys working on public-information concerns.

Ultimately, no universal solution exists for fulfilling a request for information in a certain timeframe, and the language associated with fulfilling a request "in a timely manner" is open to interpretation. The rural county clerk usually runs an office by himself or herself and is also assigned other duties, so a three-hundred-page public document that has been requested may also need to be inspected to make sure the request complies with other laws, which could take weeks.

Some offices use this reasoning to take time to fulfill a request, whereas others, regardless of office size or jurisdiction, use this provision simply to delay fulfilling a request or just to ignore it. This dilemma remains one of the most prevailing issues regarding the law, even as state agencies release more information online. As a result, FOIL requests have not declined; in fact, they have increased across the board at every level of government, and current frustration is directed toward the top. As the current media landscape changes and legal recourse is no longer the first or even a viable option for some news organizations, Governor Cuomo's administration has offered a conflicting view on FOIL, not so much in words but by action. As noted earlier, just after vetoing two FOIL bills in December 2015, he signed an executive order to expedite the FOIL appeals process. At the same time, the FSMC exists as an economic arm of SUNY Polytechnic, but the administration claims it is a private company, exempt from FOIL.

Many of today's issues never existed in 1977. Now they are very much paramount because of digital advancement and a changing political, media, and societal landscape. "These news organizations are struggling financially, and they don't have the money for FOIL battles, save for Hearst, the *New York Times*, or Gannett, who can fight them, and the primary violator of FOIL is the Cuomo administration, which is ironic on so many levels," said Diane Kennedy, the president of the New York News Publishers Association. "With this administration, everything is transactional, and we have nothing to offer [Cuomo]. The law is fine and loose enough to cover technological changes, but I don't think the language is the problem; lack of enforcement is, in addition to the ability to watch government."[40]

Kennedy first arrived at the organization now known as the New York News Publishers Association in 1990 and became president in 1993, representing more than fifty news organizations in New York State, from the *New York Times* to the *Glens Falls Post-Star* to the *Wellsville Daily Reporter*. As a reporter for the *Troy Record* in the 1980s, she was introduced to FOIL and OML by way of her beat. She covered small-city government in Watervliet and found herself locked out of city board meetings. As a young reporter, she was not informed of board decisions. Someone suggested she call COOG.

After speaking with Freeman, Kennedy began putting her ear against the door when the city board went into executive session. She had every right to, according to the OML. Stories soon began appearing in the *Troy Record* about the inner workings of the Watervliet government, and the city board wondered where she received her information. At the next meeting, a board member happened to open the door as Kennedy was leaning against it, and she fell into the room. The board began complying more with the law, but it also moved its meetings to a more secure location.

This secrecy enraged Kennedy, and she took this thinking to her position at the New York News Publishers Association. Among other roles, she lobbies the legislature on all media matters, especially FOIL. The issue concerning attorneys' fees was paramount, and now that Kennedy has been in the state capitol for more than a quarter century, she knows that once a bill is vetoed, the Senate and Assembly won't revisit the proposed legislation unless something significant happens.

This is often the case in New York and across the country. At the same time, the past decade has ushered in a heightened sense of distrust, and even though proactive disclosure has become more common, an insatiable appetite for more information continues to grow. Databases detailing public-employee compensation, online viewing of highway department agreements and school district superintendents' contracts, and text message exchanges—all disclosed and made public through FOIL requests—are now common.

FOIL has become increasingly essential in the pursuit of public information even as contemporary complexities such as technological advancements, dwindling government resources, and bureaucratic obstacles continue to challenge its reach and power as the definition of transparency remains vastly different for public officials, legal experts, journalists, and citizens. Over four decades, FOIL has been amended to address some issues, but system-wide inconsistencies— mixed with wider contempt—have slowly tipped a law designed for public access in the favor of government, thus creating a critical inflection point for the law.

2

Legacy Media

Choices and Challenge

A colleague of Brendan Lyons approached him one day in 2008 at the *Albany Times Union* with an inquiry that most would deem fleeting but to a journalist begged a follow-up call and a walk around the city.

Lyons's colleague lived across the street from the Albany County Family Court building and noticed a man parking his car illegally in front of the colleague's apartment every day, and each time the man did it, a ticket appeared on his car. The colleague wondered how someone could afford to pay a forty-dollar fine every day. Lyons asked the *Times Union* attorneys at its parent company, Hearst, to research whether picking up a parking ticket and inspecting it is a crime. They told him no—he would not be obstructing justice; if anything, he would only infuriate the police department. Lyons then asked the colleague if he could take a photo of the ticket and send it to him. When he received the photo, he noticed something odd—on the ticket, the line that detailed how many days were needed to pay the fine read "0." Lyons asked a law enforcement source about this, and the source told him about no-fine "ghost" tickets, noting that if Lyons looked closely, he would see a bull's-eye sticker on some cars.

A general curiosity then turned into a chase. Lyons remembered telling his investigation editor Bob Port that this was going to be the little story that could. The story began unfolding in 2008 in the early months of the Great Recession and at a time when traditional newspaper companies continued to plan for the inevitable transition to digital, which has proven to be a major disruption to their longtime business model. Some newsrooms across the country were beginning to feel the pull of a changing economic climate and shuffled departments and beats. Those same newsrooms had endured a smattering of layoffs in the previous decade, but nothing like what would come in the next eight years.[1]

The *Times Union* is similar to most midsize metro newspapers across the country, especially those that have to balance coverage between a city, a region, and a state capitol. The Hearst-owned newspaper has never shied away from controversial stories, and its award-winning journalism has reverberated across the state for decades. When it comes to exercising the Freedom of Information Law, the *Times Union* continues to remain resolute as traditional dailies on every level have had to make the difficult choice of pushing a FOIL request to court or allowing the pursuit of information to end. As the industry entered 2017, advertising revenue and the number of subscribers continued to wane, budgets tightened, layoffs continued, and resources remained scarce.[2] The list of concerns also included the necessary resources to challenge higher levels of government, which usually means a lengthy legal process and higher attorneys' fees.

Some newspapers that once employed in-house counsel or kept on retainer a law firm specializing in media matters no longer have that luxury. When it comes to FOIL, the economic realities for legacy media organizations are often cited as the main reason why government transparency continues to be opaque.[3] Fewer journalists mean fewer accountability questions and stories. Fewer resources mean less of an incentive and support to pursue challenging stories. "The TU [*Times Union*], in general, with the backing of some fantastic First Amendment attorneys in New York City, supports us. We do sue. We do challenge FOIL and go to court, and the other side knows this," Lyons said. "Do you know how rare that is now and how much leverage a reporter has with that?"[4]

Lyons continued to walk the parking tickets story backward from 2008, describing how a hunch eventually turned into a FOIL request and the discovery of a lengthier, unforeseen trend. He did not use FOIL either as the first step in obtaining public information or as the means of last resort; he used the statute to hold public officials accountable, which has long remained a mantra of news organizations globally. This philosophy remains embedded in theory, Lyons said, but not as often in practice.

As he began finding more no-fine "ghost" tickets downtown, Lyons asked more questions of his sources in law enforcement. He eventually found that the Albany Police Officers Union gave out little bull's-eye stickers, following a process that an old cement plant used for security purposes—affixing stickers to trucks when they left the plant and then returned through the front gate. If a car was parked illegally but had a bull's-eye, its owner would be issued a no-fine "ghost" ticket. This, Lyons later found, had been a practice since the early 1980s.[5]

Lyons worked the story for weeks, and one day in early November 2008 he brought along a photographer to look for tickets along Broadway in Albany. They passed a deli owned by an Albany police officer and found no-fine "ghost" tickets up and down the street. A man passed them, looked at them oddly, and walked into the deli. The owner, then pedaled his bike down the street and found Lyons. Almost a decade later, Lyons clearly remembered the conversation. The officer asked the pair what they were doing. After Lyons told him the matter was of a proprietary nature and asked if they had committed a crime, the officer told them no, but he would still let the chief of police know what they were doing.[6]

Albany Police chief James W. Tuffey had led the department since 2005 but had spent ten years as the police union president from 1985 to 1995, until he first retired as a detective. Tuffey later returned as chief at the request of Albany mayor Jerry Jennings. At the time, the relationship between Lyons and the department was acrimonious at best. After encountering the deli owner, Lyons knew the story had to be rushed, so he raced back to the newspaper's office north of the city but drove through the parking lot of police headquarters first so that he could count the number of private vehicles outside of headquarters with bull's-eye stickers: he found a dozen. He then called Tuffey.

Tuffey told Lyons he did not know what Lyons was talking about. Even after the journalist told him to walk downstairs and count the stickers on cars, Tuffey, as Lyons recalled, still feigned ignorance. Lyons had enough to run the story on November 15, 2008, prompting an outcry from citizens and others in city government. The Albany Common Council held a series of hearings as part of its five-month investigation and invoked its subpoena power for the first time in a century to call city personnel to testify.[7]

It was found that not only did Tuffey know about the bull's-eye sticker system when he was president of the police union, but he had in fact started it. The city treasurer, Betty Barnette, whose office oversaw the Parking Violations Bureau, which processed all tickets, testified that she had no knowledge of the system. After the hearings and the subsequent Common Council report was issued on August 3, 2009, New York State comptroller Thomas P. DiNapoli's office conducted an audit of the system and found the city had issued at least 57,420 no-fine "ghost" tickets between 2001 and 2009 and had dismissed another 30,857 that had fines. Even though the audit could not produce an exact tally, millions of dollars were presumed to be lost because of the system.[8]

The Common Council's report resulted in the rewriting of city laws and some reform, but Tuffey and Barnette remained employed. Lyons knew the system extended beyond a few top officials, so in April 2009 he submitted a FOIL request for all no-fine "ghost" tickets issued in the city of Albany during a sixteen-month span.[9] His FOIL request was denied, as was the subsequent appeal when the city claimed the dismissed tickets were the equivalent of sealed criminal records.[10] The Hearst attorneys took the city to court through an Article 78 proceeding. Before the case went to the New York Supreme Court, and after a year of fighting the FOIL request, the city released the records. Hearst then filed a lawsuit in the New York Supreme Court, Appellate Division, Third Judicial Department, to recoup the legal fees it had incurred.

Lyons received boxes full of tickets, all in paper, and found decades-long, system-wide abuse. When he connected tickets to specific plates, he found tickets issued to Barnette and the head of business improvement in Albany as well as to hundreds of other vehicles and people tied to law enforcement. Lyons found that the police union had kept a ledger listing all persons who had received the bull's-eye stickers and that they had been given out to officers, bar owners, girlfriends, wives, and citizens who worked at the courthouse. In addition to the bull's-eye stickers, a VIP section had been included in the police department's computer records, so that when a meter officer, unaware of the process, ran a registration for infractions using a handheld computer, those in the VIP section would get a pass.

Tuffey would later resign in 2009 after it was found he used a racial slur during an investigation.[11] Barnette lost her re-election bid owing in large part to the public's perception of her credibility as a result of the parking-ticket stories.[12] Ultimately, on April 2, 2012, the Appellate Division unanimously awarded $70,000 to Hearst and the *Times Union* for legal fees, a fine that was to be taken from the city's general fund.[13]

The no-fine "ghost" ticket story did not end the challenge that Lyons, the *Times Union*, and Hearst face when extracting records from law enforcement agencies and municipalities; the story has become one of many in the past decade. In July 2010, the Court of Appeals, the state's highest court, ordered the City of Albany to release records of federally registered machine guns that were purchased through the police department and county offices.[14] In a few seconds, Lyons rattled off three more stories that include the state police, the state crime lab, and the City of Albany failing to disclose witness statements in a resident's death.[15] All are FOIL-denial cases.

In these instances, Lyons found law enforcement and the city using a claim that has long been a reliable response for denying FOIL requests. Even though no official data exist across the state, journalists are finding anecdotally that government agencies are invoking certain provisions in the state and federal laws—a trend that continues to grow with each passing year—that focus on what agencies believe is an unwarranted invasion of privacy. "Over time, that invasion-of-privacy claim is whittling away our right to records," Lyons said. "I'm seeing, in the last fifteen years, that when all else fails, they will use that to shield records or keep them from being released."[16]

Media's Strain, Media's Role

In Mark Mahoney's second-floor office at the *Schenectady Gazette*, stacks of paper fill desks of empty cubicles, a residual of staff downsizing but also an illustration of the work necessary to craft a well-articulated position that will resonate daily with tens of thousands of people.

For three decades, Mahoney, the *Gazette*'s editorial writer, has been a staunch advocate of public accountability. He recalled his publisher asking him if one of his editorials ever directly forced an elected public official to change course. Mahoney replied no but then laid out how three hundred words on a particular issue create the necessary network effect to usher in change. "What gets a public official to do something is that after I write about it, they got cornered at church, they got cornered at the supermarket, they got bitched at at the meeting—that's when they do it," Mahoney said. "The media still has a big role whether the change was made or not. You have less media now, and you also have people less educated about an issue who also have other time commitments. You have to still help people take action because government officials will do it if someone else tells them to do it."[17]

The tone and purpose of Mahoney's work have not changed since he worked as the *Glens Falls Post-Star* editorial page writer in 1999. At the *Post-Star*, he wrote 250 editorials each year. Now, at the *Gazette*, he writes more than 350. As a journalist in the predigital age, he often used FOIL to extract information deep in the recesses of government ledgers. Mahoney remembered that the process of accessing public information took longer but that the requests were usually filled in a suitable amount of time. This situation, he noted, has changed dramatically.

Before his career shifted to editorial writing, he covered government in small villages and towns in mostly rural areas of Washington and Warren Counties near the Vermont border. In the process, he developed strong working relationships within those communities. The county, city, and town public-information officers also held other positions, but Mahoney knew who to ask and knew that if information wasn't produced, something was amiss. At times, as he worked with the city of Glens Falls, his relationships with clerks even allowed him to receive additional information that he didn't ask for—the clerks simply felt it might be helpful. These relationships are critical for any journalist, but with respect to FOIL Mahoney echoed the mantra that is often relayed by Freeman and other advocates of the law: FOIL works best as the unit of government becomes smaller.

Through the 1990s and early 2000s, Mahoney began noticing a trend even with smaller municipalities, though—they weren't as forthcoming with information. Younger reporters meant less institutional knowledge, and the process of cultivating relationships that sometimes took months or years to develop had to begin all over again. Depending on the situation, Mahoney would sometimes write about public-access issues, and he found the volume of such issues increasing over time. The *Post-Star* had a tendency to attract young, aggressive reporters, and more of them used FOIL to gain access to public information.

At the beginning of the digital age for newspapers, to test the impact of online distribution in the mid-2000s, reporters created blogs, which took on a decidedly different tone than the usual reportage. Blogs were more niche, more backstory, and were written with a different purpose. Mahoney remembered pitching the idea of a *Your Right to Know* blog, which would focus on open-government matters. Among the digital staff, the idea didn't gain much traction. Mahoney suggested trying the concept in March during Sunshine Week, the annual celebration and examination of open government matters in the United States. As a result, the blog became one of the paper's most popular.

Mahoney started receiving emails from citizens asking if they could access specific information. Others didn't know they had that privilege. Some didn't know about the process. And some had no idea the government was collecting personal information that was deemed public. He continued the blog for a few years, testing ideas and sharing additional information. Mahoney said the formula was simple—educate communities on open government, then at the center of the editorial offer a solution for the community and the public officials.

During the course of 2008, Mahoney found no shortage of open-government issues in the small towns in the *Post-Star*'s coverage area. In Warrensburg, the teachers union did not allow school board members to observe classes, even after three teachers invited the members. At the time, there were discussions about poor-performing teachers.[18] Later that year Warrensburg's school board president issued a gag order on the other members of the board, basically infringing on their First Amendment rights.[19] Residents approached school board members to ask about the board's daily order of business and were met with silence.

The list of such issues continued. The Whitehall Town Board went into executive session to discuss an audit at the insistence of the state comptroller.[20] It discussed a town clerk, who would later be found to be cooking the books. The audit would eventually be made public, and the New York State Appellate Court, as Mahoney noted in his editorial, "has held that the 'entire decision-making process' of a government body is subject to public scrutiny." Then, when the Fort Edward School District and its teachers union agreed to a new contract, with raises, they didn't inform the public of their decision. The *Post-Star* filed a FOIL request at the same time that it published an editorial on the issue but five months later still had not received a copy of the contract.[21]

In the same editorial, Mahoney noted that this practice of negotiating behind closed doors, agreeing on a contract with no public comment, then announcing the outcome was common across the state. In Johnson City, the village approved a new contract with the firefighters union (a 41 percent pay increase over five years). In Utica, the school superintendent refused to publicly disclose the terms of the new teacher contract until the board of education voted (first-year raises for most teachers at 4.64 percent and lifetime health coverage for all teachers who retire after ten years on the job). And on the state level, when Governor David Paterson announced a tentative contract with the Police Benevolent Association of the New York State Troopers, his office would not disclose the agreement, stating that such an announcement would affect the final stages of the negotiations. (The agreement called for 14 percent in base-pay hikes over four years.[22]) The editorials still resonate in these areas because either reform or a change in process was the result of Mahoney's work.

His editorials gained traction, and when the newsroom began analyzing the year's work to submit annual industry awards, it marked his pieces on education, city issues, and the need for stronger legislation. Mahoney and his colleagues also found strength in the open-government editorials, at least a half-dozen of them, and Ken Tingley, the *Post-Star*'s managing editor, asked Mahoney if he had more such stories. He said he had more than twenty.

In April 2009, Mahoney was driving to an interview when he was called back to the office for an emergency meeting. He thought there would be an announcement about the budget or possibly layoffs. When he arrived, he found out he had won the Pulitzer Prize for editorial writing simply for, as the Pulitzer Board noted, "his relentless, down-to-earth editorials on the perils of local government secrecy, effectively admonishing citizens to uphold their right to know."[23]

The editorials were not part of a series written specifically for Sunshine Week. They were written during the course of 2008. The government issues they covered were not isolated, Mahoney still notes, but will forever be ongoing. "It's simple. People get ticked off when they believe they're being screwed, and I give them a reason. You have to tell them why I care. Why should I care that the report on Startup NY is three months late? What difference does it make? It's government. They take their time. Well, it's because they're funding the program for another three months; they're keeping the information secret; the legislature is coming to the end of the session; they're stringing you along, and you're paying for it. Do the math,"

Mahoney said. "You have to find a reason to be mad, and government keeping secrets is a pretty good reason."[24]

Higher Powers

Since Mahoney received the Pulitzer Prize in 2009, the disconcerting practice of government operating in alleged secrecy has continued—if not proliferated—at every level across the state. At the center of investigations of this practice remain traditional news organizations, still producing accountability journalism but with fewer resources. The draining of resources is often reflected in these organizations' product, and, perhaps intentionally or unwittingly, certain government agencies have taken notice of this trend. Under the same premise, these same agencies invoke exemptions to FOIL incorrectly or simply cite exemptions that do not exist.

On November 7, 2013, Dr. David R. Smith, who ushered in a new era of growth at SUNY Upstate Medical University in Syracuse as its president, resigned after allegations of improper compensation to him from two medical companies affiliated with Upstate: Med-Best and Pediatric Service Group LLP.[25] A week later, on November 13, *Syracuse Post-Standard* reporter John O'Brien filed a FOIL request with Upstate, the area's largest employer and public agency. The request outlined nine items, including any written contracts or agreements for compensation between Upstate and Smith, pending the investigation, which included the US Attorney's Office, the Federal Bureau of Investigation (FBI), and later the New York State Office of the Inspector General.[26]

The request was denied. Four months later, after an appeal and constant questioning, Upstate said no contract with Smith existed. The *Post-Standard* published an editorial claiming that Upstate had lied,[27] and the agency countered with a press release criticizing the news organization's use of FOIL.[28] The *Post-Standard*, supported by an advisory opinion from COOG, cited the exemption that unless the agency is creating documents for the investigation, the documents are public. In this case, COOG argued, if the contract or agreements already existed before the investigation, they should be made available for public inspection even if they were being used in the investigation.[29]

Upstate did not fulfill the request for information for months and continued to cite the investigation exemption. It was not until February 27, 2015, more than fourteen months after Smith's resignation, that SUNY chancellor Nancy Zimpher chose to publicly disclose the findings of a SUNY audit, even though the state agency, Upstate, still insisted it was not legally required to do so.[30] After this, the US district attorney and the FBI decided to drop the probe, and the audit did outline Smith's budget approval habits and compensation. It concluded that Smith had inappropriately managed a $33 million fund to benefit the medical school and that its distribution presented a number of conflicts of interest.[31] SUNY still maintained that no contract with Smith existed, but it has since changed this record-keeping practice.

From Smith's resignation to the end of the investigation and Zimpher's decision to release the documents, O'Brien and the *Post-Standard* weighed their options whether to continue to push Upstate while the FBI continued its probe. In the past, submitting documents to start the Article 78 proceedings was a natural option, but the newspaper held off, opting to publicly disclose the FOIL rift over records, a practice news organizations used to dismiss.

The fifteen-month time frame between the FOIL filing and eventual disclosure may have equaled the time it would have taken to bring forth a legal proceeding with a larger budget concern, and it's a gamble all news organizations must now consider. "Our biggest weapon in FOIL battles now are stories for noncompliance, and that exemption they gave is such a big hurdle. When you're given the choice to break the law or go against the district attorney or inspector general, they still say they have no basis to disclose, but we do [have a duty] to inform the public," O'Brien said. "They know we have no standing but to take them to court, and they push you to do so, knowing the current financial strains. We did it more frequently and always won, but now it's something we have to weigh all the time—and they know this."[32]

Policies and Potential Problems

With the advent of technology, FOIL interpretation becomes even more crucial, even down to a single word. Mahoney, like O'Brien, argued what media consider the definition of "compiled for public purposes" is and what law enforcement construes to be the practice of gathering information for investigations. These worlds often intersect.

On May 19, 2016, Schenectady mayor Gary McCarthy was accused of chasing Sarah Dingley at 1:00 a.m. in her car. She called 911 and stayed on the phone with dispatchers as she drove to the police station.[33] The *Schenectady Gazette* wanted access to footage from cameras along the street—potentially showing the mayor tailgating Dingley or harassing her—and from the camera pointing to the police station parking lot where Dingley pulled in and the mayor got out of the car. A special prosecutor was assigned to the case, but eight months later McCarthy still did not face criminal charges, even though there were concerns. The report found that "there is not sufficient information to find that (McCarthy) was impaired or intoxicated."[34] The media first watched video footage from public cameras only when the special prosecutor's report was released.

The Schenectady District Attorney Office's basic policy is that it doesn't release any footage from cameras that law enforcement controls, citing that it may be used in law enforcement or that it may reveal investigative techniques, per FOIL, or that it may reveal the location of cameras so people will be less likely to commit crimes in front of them.[35]

Mahoney agreed with this rationale, but he also argued that since the cameras are in public view, are paid for by public dollars, and record the public, shouldn't what they record be made available for public inspection? He cited the policies established in other cities—and in European countries that allow the public to access cameras through a website—based on sound and logical public-records statute interpretation.[36] "If we know where the cameras are, why can't we get access to it, and shouldn't the public be able to see what the police see? Basically, it's big brother spying on you and determining what you see, observing what you're doing, and determining what legal aspects involve you," Mahoney said.[37] He acknowledged the struggle to balance legitimate law enforcement concerns with legitimate public-interest concerns and emphasized that access to public-surveillance footage is not a black-and-white matter.

Additional internal policies, especially those involving electronic communication, have shifted through the years to keep pace with technology amid skepticism. On June 30, 2013, the Cuomo administration implemented a ninety-day email-retention policy, calling for all agencies to purge messages after this period.[38] Since emails are considered public records, the policy raised concerns, even when the administration cited server space as a primary reason for the directive. Two years later, with mixed results, the administration reversed its decision on emails that are not manually flagged for retention, which is, at best, an arbitrary practice.[39]

The practice of purging electronic records has become common among all agencies, primarily because of resources. Journalists such as Lyons at the *Times Union* understand this argument, but they also know a FOIL request is only as good as the person receiving it. This is why he makes it a practice to include another paragraph beyond his basic request—and often instructs his colleagues to do the same—in which he asks an agency's FOIL officer to preserve any record that may be responsive to the request pending the outcome, including any Article 78 proceeding, which is the next step requestors can take to bring the issue to court. "I do this so that they can't say, 'Well, you know, we got the request, we denied your FOIL, we needed room on our servers, so we deleted [the requested record],'" Lyons said. "If we appeal or sue, at least down the road we can tell the judge that we asked them to save it [the record] until we sued them, and they still deleted it anyway. It may give them pause. Now it's a preservation request."[40]

Like Freeman and the media, Lyons has noticed a change in pro-tocol under the current Cuomo administration. Media sources have claimed that all FOIL requests to any New York State agency are automatically redirected to the second floor of the state capitol—the executive branch—for review. According to some reporters, when a FOIL request is submitted, it is flagged, shared with the governor's office, and allegedly even goes into a distributed bulletin. Lyons said he believes this process is a deliberate tactic to delay disclosure even though the governor's office will respond within the required five business days that it received the request, as stated by law.

On average, Lyons said, during the current administration his wait time has been eight months to one year to receive requested records from a state agency, such as the New York State Police. Other journalists have experienced quicker results, depending on the agency and the request. This discrepancy accentuates the fact that no language in the statute exists that outlines fulfillment times, which leads journalists to question whether government exploits a loophole—depending on the size of the department or time neces-sary to navigate layers of government to compile the records—or if insufficient agency and government resources remain at the core of the delay problem.

Lyons's work on state police matters has proven to be difficult at times because of this problem. The state police, which receives requests on matters anywhere from a car accident to assault to per-sonnel records, is one of the busiest agencies in the state and now has a significant FOIL backlog. The agency has also endured budget strains over the past decade. Lyons has seen response times lengthen across all state agencies, even for requests that should be simple to fulfill. He is not alone in his assessment; other journalists and FOIL petitioners have noted the same trend—one that continues to grow.

3

Digital Media

Access and Denial

Since the mid-1980s, Jim Heaney has documented the methodical demise of Buffalo's industrial base and at the same time the fall of a number of the city's political offices and agencies. These two trajectories often collide because the western New York city on the shores of Lake Erie fits the pattern of others along the New York State Thruway and points west through America's Rust Belt. After decades of declining population and global shifts in manufacturing, Buffalo has tried rebuilding itself, only to find as many stops as starts.

Heaney is a realist and wants to see Buffalo reach its potential, but he also wants to make sure there is no government malfeasance in large-scale business deals. He did this for twenty-five years as an investigative reporter for the *Buffalo News* while covering government as well as urban and economic issues. Then Heaney retired in 2011 and started the *Investigative Post*, one of many nonprofit news organizations sprouting across the country, filling voids left by corporate media downsizing.

The *Investigative Post* boasts only three reporters, but its impact reverberates through other mediums. As a digital-only property, it does not feel the pressure of filling the twenty-four/seven online news cycle with shorter stories and updates every fifteen minutes through social media. Instead, a host of shorter stories strike a balance with deeper investigative pieces that were once staples of newspapers on Sunday mornings. Heaney, the organization's editor and executive director, also forged strong relationships with traditional broadcast-television partners, understanding that the journalism *Investigative Post* produces also has the potential to reach a much larger audience.

Through the decades, Heaney's reporting uncovered racial discrimination in the Buffalo Municipal Housing Authority. When slumlords received preferential treatment by the city's Housing Court, Heaney reported the story. State and federal charges were brought against Buffalo Common Council member Brian Davis as a result of Heaney's reporting in 2009, and *Buffalo News* readers found out about government waste at certain state agencies, including the New York State Thruway Authority, which oversees the main transportation artery across the state. His reporting has found a new means of distribution through the *Investigative Post* and other broadcast entities, but his approach remains the same. Heaney works sources and displays journalistic essentials, such as perseverance.

He has also used FOIL to unearth some of the most salient facts for these stories. "When I first started in the business, it wasn't unusual for you to call a government agency to talk to someone there who was not a flack. It was actually the guy who knew what they were talking about," Heaney said. "Now, everything has morphed through public affairs or some other misleading name that people want to describe themselves. It's an effort to really spin responses and also, along with that, slow the growing demand of FOIL requests, even to get basic documents. It's become this—government entities use FOIL as a means to delay instead of facilitate."[1]

In his State of the State Address in 2012, Governor Andrew Cuomo announced a $1 billion commitment to economic development in western New York, a six-tier plan that included the construction of a solar-panel factory that called for three-quarters of the promised state infusion of money, most of which would be paid to Elon Musk's company SolarCity to develop the plant.[2] Other projects within the plan focused on biomedical and clean-energy businesses, which, in turn, would help with urban revitalization.

The twenty-first-century manufacturing plan earned the name "Buffalo Billion," and the SUNY Research Foundation was designated as the government entity to oversee the process, along with the FSMC, established in 2009 as a private nonprofit corporation. In the Buffalo Billion project, which falls under the purview of the Empire State Development Corporation (an umbrella agency that oversees the economic plans for the state), the SUNY Research Foundation focuses on research, development, and commercialization, and FSMC oversees construction and operation.

According to the Cuomo administration, neither the Research Foundation nor FSMC must comply with FOIL or OML because each was established as a private, nonprofit entity, a "state-affiliated corporation."[3] Different entities established as nonprofit corporations are covered by various provisions of New York State law. However, as COOG has argued, because the SUNY Research Foundation conducts health and welfare research, it is referenced in the state finance law, which brings the two entities within the scope of FOIL.[4]

Less than five years after the project was established, it emerged at the center of a political corruption probe owing in large part to Heaney's initial investigation, which drew the attention of Preet Bharara, the US attorney for the Southern District of New York.[5] Bharara's office was responsible for the conviction of two longtime New York lawmakers in 2015 and 2016—Sheldon Silver, the former Speaker of the New York State Assembly, and Dean G. Skelos, the former majority leader of the New York State Senate.[6] (Both convictions were overturned in 2017, and the appeals processes were expected to continue through the courts.[7])

As plans for the Buffalo Billion were unveiled publicly, what first struck Heaney as odd in early winter 2013 were the construction projects for it and the developer qualification that required a candidate company to be in business for at least fifty years, which greatly diminished the pool of potential candidates that would be vetted by Fort Schuyler. Only one company, LPCiminelli, fit that description. Heaney reached out to the Colleges of Nanoscale Science and Engineering, which house the SUNY Research Foundation, and to Alain E. Kaloyeros, who, in addition to his role as president and CEO of SUNY Polytechnic, was FSMC's vice president. Potential applicants complained about the requirement, and Kaloyeros said that it was a clerical error and that it had been reduced to fifteen years.[8]

But once the bidding ended and contracts were awarded, Heaney was contacted by one of the unsuccessful bidders for the project. The conversation piqued Heaney's interest, and in the process, on July 30, 2014, he filed his first FOIL request to the SUNY Research Foundation for documents related to the bidding process and contracts with other businesses as part of the Buffalo Billion project.[9]

At the center of his request were two large construction firms, LPCiminelli and McGuire Development, both of which received contracts. Heaney cross-referenced the New York State political donation database and found two consistencies tied to the firms. The owner of LPCiminelli, Louis Ciminelli, and his relatives and associates had donated at least $122,500 to Governor Cuomo's campaign over the years.[10] After McGuire was awarded the contract to build a technology hub as part of the Buffalo Billion project, it donated $25,000 to the Cuomo reelection campaign.[11] The administration deflected any accusation of a connection, stating that only FSMC oversaw the bidding process.[12] After a month and a half, Heaney reached out again with an appeal for his FOIL request, and in response the SUNY Research Foundation said it needed more time. It was only when he suggested to the foundation that delay equals denial that he was given a response.[13]

The next day Heaney received heavily redacted documents. He searched through phone calls and emails to personnel at all levels of the SUNY Research Foundation, but after futile efforts up the food chain he found none. There was also another issue—not all the requested documents were provided.[14] This time Heaney filed a second FOIL request with FSMC on November 20, 2014, and not with the SUNY Research Foundation, asking specifically about the construction bidding and selection process.[15]

A week later Heaney received a response from FSMC, stating it did not have to comply with the request given its private, nonprofit status. In addition, the give-and-take became hostile between Heaney and Kaloyeros a week after the denial, with Kaloyeros responding to

Heaney's email: "I told you once and I told you a million times. We are not political operatives nor do we respond to perceived threats and terrorism."[16]

The denial sent Heaney and *Investigative Post* into discussions with WGRZ, the Buffalo-based NBC affiliate and *Post* partner, and with the Gannett Company, and on December 22, 2014, *Investigative Post* filed an appeal.[17] On March 3, 2015, COOG wrote an advisory opinion, siding with the *Investigative Post*.[18] Months later, there were still no documents, so on May 18, 2015, the group filed an Article 78 petition, asking the state Supreme Court to rule on whether FSMC is exempt from FOIL.[19] Weeks passed before a sudden turn of events.

Without notifying Heaney, FSMC posted the requested documents on its website at some point in mid-June and as a result took away grounds for the lawsuit and a precedent. The lawsuit was withdrawn. The records show that LPCiminelli's proposal was ranked highest of three to successfully win the bid.[20]

As of July 2017, there had yet been no ruling whether FSMC is exempt from FOIL. The government practice of creating public entities that are perceived to be exempt from disclosure because of their private, nonprofit status has become more common, earning these entities the title "quasi-state" entities among many public officials because they are funded by state dollars and have state employees. COOG and journalists such as Heaney believe there is no such thing—if an agency is funded by state money and run by state employees, it is a public entity.

If anything, what Heaney's work did was raise a red flag for Bharara's office and in the process force SUNY Polytechnic two years later to consolidate its two operations into one and to create new practices. Meetings are now open, and more independent board members have been appointed. On August 10, 2016, it was announced that the Fuller Road Management Corporation and FSMC, both nonprofits used to raise capital and oversee projects, would merge into one entity, with oversight provided by the Empire State Development Corporation.[21] Nevertheless, the need for transparency in state business, from Heaney's perspective, has not changed. "With state entities, a simple request may take six months or longer, and those same requests were once considered off-the-shelf reporting. I think it's intentional, but a FOIL law violation is not criminal. It's a slap on a wrist," Heaney said. "The more third parties do what government once did, it's important that transparency is involved. They're really doing the public's business."[22]

Untangling the Online and Offline Mess

For twenty years, an analyst at the New York City Department of Housing Preservation and Development raised concerns to his bosses that the agency's process of counting rent-stabilized apartments was broken and in many respects fraudulent. The negligence bothered Stephen Werner because the surveys conducted every three years were affording building owners substantial tax breaks in one of the most expensive housing markets in the country—even though a number of those same landlords did not qualify.

As state agencies continued to untangle the record-keeping labyrinth that is New York City's real estate market, *ProPublica* reporter Cezary Podkul noticed an announcement by Governor Cuomo in August 2015 that the city and state would crack down on landlords raking in substantial tax breaks even though they were not registering their apartments for rent stabilization.[23] In the New York City market, landlords were free to raise rents, making affordability even more unattainable.

After two decades of issuing warnings, the analyst, Werner, found a journalist and a news outlet willing to bring to light a misguided government program and rampant abuse by the public. As Podkul worked to obtain all records and data associated with the program, he found a number of issues after he filed FOIL requests—the government called for further vigilance on a public program that the public was exploiting, but the public information to further expose the issue was not accessible by the public. In other words, not all records of a public agency were accessible.

In October 2015, Werner met with the city's Department of Finance and the New York State Homes and Community Renewal (NYSHCR) agency, the state division responsible for all record keeping. Joining him was New York City Council member Ben Kallos, who also has a long and vested interest in open government and advocates for more disclosure at all levels through technology.[24] Data existed on the NYSHCR website, but they were not what Podkul needed. He wanted more. In the span of one week, he submitted four FOIL requests to NYSHCR, each requesting specific information or a general data set used by a state agency, including a larger data set, portions of which had already been posted publically:

Sept. 11, 2015—Please provide me copies of initial apartment registrations for the following building in Manhattan 505 W. 37th Street, New York, NY 10018

Sept. 11, 2015—Please provide me an electronic copy of the NYSHCR active registry files of rent-stabilized buildings and rent-stabilized apartment units as of the latest available registration year and four prior years.

Sept. 14, 2015—Please provide me rent histories for all apartment units listed in the NYSHCR active registry of rent-stabilized apartments as of the latest available active registration file.

Sept. 18, 2015—Please provide me an electronic copy of the underlying data used to populate the NYSHCR's "Rent Regulated Building Search" public website available at this URL: https://apps.hcr.ny.gov/BuildingSearch.[25]

All four requests were denied, and Podkul found that these denials were based on three issues. First, he had requested a specific address, one that could have been of a personal nature if an average citizen were submitting a FOIL request for the building in which he or she lives. Second, a law superseded FOIL: NYSHCR's universal denial was based on the Rent Stabilization Code and the Tenant Protection

Regulations. Finally, even though requested data had already been made public, a public-information request for the same data was denied. "This is a good example of a problem with FOIL. You can ask for stuff, and they're required to give it to you, but there are exemptions in other laws. If there is a specific exemption, an agency can't break that law. It's only as good as the laws that require disclosure," Podkul said. "We weren't surprised. We tried. I found their reasoning is OK. But the more egregious one? They disclosed some of the requested data online, and I want to ask, 'Is my building registered for rent stabilization in New York?' This is basic information. No privacy is endangered. This information will be useful. So I file a FOIL, which is crystal clear. 'Please provide this information because it's already on the state site.' They don't fulfill, then they're just being lazy."[26]

Podkul's frustration has trickled into other stories, but the findings of his reporting in a series with *ProPublica* colleague Marcelo Rochabrun showed widespread neglect in the New York City rent-stabilization system that had been happening for years. According to their research and reporting, landlords had failed to register thousands of buildings for rent regulations. The data, which was partially posted on the NYSHCR website, included almost 15,000 rental buildings that received the tax subsidies as of 2013 (two-year-old data at the time of the story). More than one-third of those buildings (5,500) weren't listed as rent stabilized, but the owners had received more than $100 million in property-tax reductions for rent stabilization.[27]

With the data Podkul requested, which were more current and perhaps more accurate to cross-reference with what the state had already posted, he believed greater discrepancies would be exposed. As more information, especially data, is being compiled and saved, jobs such as Podkul's are becoming more nuanced and specialized. Unlocking the information through a public-information request is one thing, but actually finding what information exists remains a primary concern on the city, state, and federal levels.

Podkul's path to *ProPublica* was a bit unorthodox by traditional media standards, but the pattern is becoming more common. In 2008, he left investment banking with J. P. Morgan just before the housing bubble burst and Wall Street and America began feeling the true impact of the Great Recession. Benefited by an economics degree from the Wharton School, his skills became transferrable upon his enrollment at Columbia, where he graduated in 2011 from the Stabler Center for Investigative Journalism, and continued to be in demand at *ProPublica*, where he covers finance.

Podkul's first FOIA request on the federal level was by way of an assignment at Columbia in a data-driven course, which eventually evolved into his master's thesis. The story initially focused on pet transportation projects that Congress was earmarking, a number of them focused on highway and infrastructure. Podkul initially found $2.3 billion earmarked but not much being accomplished on America's roads.

Podkul had never filed a public-records request on the federal level before, so when he approached the federal government, his initial inquiry was denied. He went to the US Department of Transportation and located its spokesperson, who then brusquely sent him away with a piece of paper giving only minor details. Little did Podkul know at the time that this piece of paper was the beginning of a story. He had to work the story in reverse and so filed public-records requests for every state, looking for all spent earmarked infrastructure money. He still didn't know what he was looking at as more requests were denied.

He then met a former Department of Transportation staffer at a conference, who was generous with his time and guidance. He described to Podkul what he should be looking for, and he reworded Podkul's requests. The primary issue with his requests was semantics—what the public may refer to by a common description, an agency may label with a different name. If a public-information officer reads the request differently, without the exact nomenclature, he or she often denies the public-records request.

With this new information, Podkul changed course. He randomly chose Pennsylvania first, knowing there were issues in Philadelphia, where he lived at the time. In just a few weeks, the state's Department of Transportation sent what Podkul described as a "very organized, very gorgeous spreadsheet" of unspent earmarked money.[28] His rationale—if Pennsylvania can do it, every state can. He sent the Pennsylvania spreadsheet, accompanied by the same language, with every subsequent submission. Podkul now spoke the same language as the public-information officers on the other end of this request.

On January 5, 2011, his master's thesis was published in *USA Today*, and a searchable database still exists to show a state-by-state analysis of discrepancies in transportation budgets—how much states spent and how much the federal government actually earmarked.[29] Other regional news organizations picked up the story, and *NBC Nightly News* broadcast an entire segment on the reporting. In the process, turning earmarked money into money spent became a major mandate for President Barack Obama during 2011. Buried in the data obtained in his FOIA request, Podkul found that almost one in three highway dollars earmarked since 1991 remained unspent. The final tally reached almost $13 billion.[30]

Podkul's experiences exemplify the disconnect that often exists between city and state agencies and, on a larger level, between state and federal agencies. Massive reproduction and duplication of efforts—or sloppy record keeping—in the current data-driven environment have led to further confusion and frustration on all public levels, in addition to fiscal waste and bureaucratic posturing.

Podkul believes exposure of these buried yet considerable oversights may lead to greater government efficiency. Or the lack of uniformity—or honesty—may create more issues because of the lack of baseline legislation. "I assume that they [FOIL requests] will be denied, or I will be stonewalled or get nothing useful. I don't plan on getting something. If I get something, I will use it," Podkul said. "That's really what I found with New York State. The request is only as good as the agency you filed with—and who is on the other end."[31]

Access Delayed, Access Denied

The response requirements are clear in the New York State law: an agency must respond to an FOI request within five business days of receipt. It then must make a determination on full or partial records and indicate within twenty days of the initial acknowledgement an approval, a denial, or a response stating an expected time of delivery if the request is deemed voluminous or there is some other factor. If more than twenty additional business days are needed, the agency must provide a reason and a "date certain" for its response, a self-imposed deadline. However, because every request is unique—from agency to agency and from records to records—there really is no absolute required deadline for an agency to fulfill. The last caveat remains the great unknown for the FOIL petitioner of public records: the "what" exists; the "when" is more problematic.

Across the *ProPublica* newsroom from Podkul sat Joaquin Sapien, one of the first journalists the news organization hired in 2008. Since then, Sapien's work on criminal justice and environmental issues has earned him a number of national awards. Much of the work *ProPublica* produces involves lengthy research, dozens of interviews, and insight into regional and national issues that expose deeper social impact. At times, this work involves wading through reams of data or combing through lengthy lawsuits. It also involves the need to obtain documents, which of late has proven to be a considerable process for Sapien and a few of his colleagues, both on the state and the federal levels.

In 2013, Sapien submitted a FOIA request to the Federal Emergency Management Agency (FEMA) for records related to Hurricane Sandy, the second-costliest storm in US history and the deadliest of the 2012 hurricane season. The storm wiped out parts of New York City and left downtown Manhattan under water for days. The cost was substantial after the hurricane first hit New York and the metropolitan area on October 29, 2012, totaling $71.4 billion in damages along the Eastern Seaboard, with more than half that total found in New York.[32] Flood insurance claims followed the storm, some of which were fraudulent, and FEMA oversaw much of the response effort on the federal level.[33] To complement the reporting *ProPublica* had already done on the storm, Sapien wanted to know the breadth of FEMA's responsibility.

Sapien waited for a response to his FOIA request—for more than three years. Even though FEMA acknowledged his request, it was never fulfilled. The agency sent him a letter in the spring of 2016, stating that because the request had been pending for several years, FEMA assumed he no longer wanted that information. From a journalistic perspective, the story had passed. From a human level, Sapien seemed conflicted. "All this time later? I'm not that interested. I kind of let it die, and I feel guilty, but I have to move on with my work," he said. "Requests like that are substantial investments in time, money, and emotion for a lot of people. I try to believe in the good of people, and I hope most people are entering the field of information law that don't have ambitions of actively withholding information, but it's really hard to know. But you get the impression sometimes that the forces that run these agencies are turning these people's moral compass—the same people who know it's the law to release information."[34]

Sapien allowed a large sigh on the other end of the phone. Waiting for fulfillment of FOIL requests has become a lengthy process. Wait times usually have a direct connection to the size of the request, but at other times there is no explanation for the delay. The frustration in Sapien's voice when discussing FEMA is also the same frustration expressed in his reporting—namely, in his *ProPublica* piece that ran on April 21, 2016, chronicling his year-long struggle with the Administration for Children's Services (ACS), a New York City child and family welfare agency.[35]

To Sapien, FEMA was different, given the scope of the destruction and the fact that FEMA is a federal agency that has faced mounting public scrutiny with each passing natural disaster. He knew the requested information would expose some trends or neglect, but he wasn't sure what. With the FOIL inquiry he submitted to ACS, however, he knew exactly what he was requesting.

When three teenage boys ran away from a group home in Brooklyn and were later arrested for the assault and rape of a thirty-three-year-old woman in Chinatown in Manhattan on June 3, 2015, Sapien began investigating these same homes that were established as an alternative for troubled teenagers from the city and state's juvenile justice system.[36] The home from which the boys escaped was placed on "heightened monitoring status" because of other issues. Sapien wanted to know how many other group homes under ACS's purview in its Close to Home program were in a similar situation.

Sapien's request was clear—he was looking for records of any other homes on "heightened monitoring status" as well as the agency's database chronicling any arrests or escapes of youngsters and any assaults or injuries suffered by staff or residents at the homes. He submitted the request on June 16, about two weeks after the arrests. On June 24, ACS's public-information contact, Janet Steadman, responded, stating the agency was in receipt of his request and that he was entitled to the documents and data. An extension on the time allowed to provide requested documents was necessary, though, so he should receive the information "on or about July 16, 2015."[37]

This date became the first of ten promised delivery dates—all of which were lengthier in wait times, with each new communication offering a new explanation, from data-retrieval issues to noncompatibility with a disc. There was also the matter of redaction because documents at local, state, and federal agencies had to be run through a legal team or an attorney before disclosure so that any information revealing identities of a minor, health information, or any other details exempt by state or federal statute could be blacked out.

Sapien was patient until after the fourth delay six months later, on December 17, 2015, when Steadman offered a new delivery date of January 8, 2016. His response: "With all due respect, Janet, this is three months later than the date you last promised. Which was made a month passed the previous delivery date. What is the hold-up?"[38]

Steadman's answer was simple and is a common one across all agencies on the local, state, and federal level—she was the only ACS employee working on FOIL responses. Four months later, on April 13, 2016—after an additional five promised delivery dates—the New York City Department of Investigation released a twenty-four-page report in response to the assault and rape and ACS's negligence in the matter.[39] Almost a week later, on April 19, Sapien contacted

Steadman and ACS spokeswoman Carol Caceres, asking for a comment about the agency's delay in fulfilling his request; *ProPublica* was going to write a story about the delay. They promised Sapien that he would receive the information he requested on April 22, which he finally did. Even though there had been ten proposed delivery dates in as many months, Caceres told Sapien that ACS would still not be providing everything requested.[40]

Sapien received documents regarding the homes under "heightened monitoring status." Data for the Brooklyn home in which the three boys escaped were not included. The agency had not yet determined if those documents were ready to be made public. "This reached a level of uncertainty that I've never experienced before. They basically just kept blowing me off," Sapien said. "Unless you are very persistent and patient and polite and know the law—and threaten to appeal if need be—or have some alternative advice from an attorney, chances are, you're not going to get anything. How many FOIL requests go on for so long, and people forgot about it? The more you let that happen, the more it's going to happen. It's illegal—and, really, dangerous."[41]

Leveling the Field

The growing support for public-records access has reached beyond traditional newsrooms and into digital communities that realize the collective power of networks. *MuckRock*, perhaps more than any other news organization, has emerged as the leader in this space, and the numbers of independent organizations is growing. Its five-person staff is deceptively small with respect to its extensive community of journalists, researchers, and activists who contribute their time and expertise to the nonprofit news organization's emerging documents and public-records library built on public-records requests. Beyond the tickers showing both requests submitted and requests filled on its website, *MuckRock* provides the public with access to more than one million released pages of documents on the local, state, federal, and even global stage, depending on the respective open-records law. And in July 2016, it launched a database of FOIA exemptions, giving users some direction regarding what public information is attainable.[42]

This was the type of news organization that attracted Jie Jenny Zou, who first discovered the impact of public-access laws as a graduate student. She earned a year-long fellowship at *MuckRock* for 2014–15, where she worked with Shawn Musgrave and editor Benjamin Lesser, both of whom were infatuated with public records. It was Lesser who tasked Musgrave and Zou with conceiving a large, investigative database project in collaboration with the *New York World*, a nonprofit, experimental news outlet at Columbia Journalism School, from which Zou had graduated.

The task was simple—file public-records request every week and see what comes back. Musgrave and Zou decided to conduct a compliance audit of eighty-six New York State and New York City agencies. In a year, along with the *New York World*, they filed 344 requests for information that ranged from basic lists of personnel to the log of all FOIL requests each particular agency had received.[43]

What began as a quest to compile an audit of agencies adherence to a law turned into an exercise in persistence. There was little consistency in which agencies across the state complied, but there were varying degrees of interpretation, from how much money an agency charged *MuckRock* to supply the information requested to how long the request would take to fill. According to Zou, the different agencies' response to a journalist from a nontraditional news organization seemed at times indifferent or indignant.[44]

Musgrave and Zou's follow-up phone calls and emails proved even stronger evidence of how public employees enforce a law. "Some wouldn't take you seriously unless you have an attorney, so I found myself threatening halfway to a lawsuit at times. Where I am now, I sit across from an attorney. He's very gung-ho about access to open records. That's rare; there are not a lot of organizations that have that person or ability," Zou said. "But after the phone calls with this project, I would just say, 'I don't understand why you're doing this. We've responded in ways we think are appropriate.' They're not inviting lawsuits, but they're implying. It's such a weird conversation to have with a public-information officer, a public servant. They're having this talk with you, and they're egging you on to sue them."[45]

The *MuckRock* and *New York World*'s methodology was sound, and they graded each agency on five simple criteria:

- How long it took to acknowledge the request
- How long it took to provide a final response
- Whether the agency provided the requested record(s)
- Whether the agency charged for record(s)
- Whether records provided were in digital format

Their findings varied according to three geographical areas: state (towns), municipalities (cities), and New York City. To fulfill a request for a list of public employees, New York City–based agencies took on average thirty-one days (municipal agencies, twenty-two days; state agencies, twenty-one days), and for the requested FOIL logs, New York City–based agencies took thirty-seven days (state agencies, twenty-eight days; municipal agencies, twenty-three).[46]

Musgrave and Zou submitted the first requests in December 2014, and by June 15, 2015, they had finished their audit, finding that compliance for similar record requests varied. State and New York City agencies were consistent in the number of requests filled, denied, and still being processed. The most significant discrepancies existed in municipalities, from Syracuse to Binghamton to Buffalo. Of the 144 FOIL requests, 87 were filled, and 32 were pending; 19 agencies showed no record of requests; and 6 did not acknowledge if the record existed.

There was also one incident that Zou did not anticipate. Once the audit was completed, *MuckRock* received a cease-and-desist letter from the City of Auburn and its corporation counsel, John C. Rossi, after Zou sent follow-up inquiries about the requests that never received answers. Rossi said that the requests were either "broad" or "denied." To this day, *MuckRock* has never received the requested documents, even though the Auburn request was identical to all others sent.[47]

Just a few years removed from Columbia and now at the Center for Public Integrity in Washington, DC, Zou has assessed the advantages of FOIL and the impact the law may have on larger communities and audiences. She has also weighed the concept of sourcing and the small likelihood that documents may be leaked to smaller, perhaps less well-known news organizations from outside a general area. She also understands how FOIL levels the playing field in the pursuit of information in the public interest and at the same time how it may invite a growing defiance from certain agencies. "That's what makes FOIL really important. It doesn't come down to sourcing. . . . I may just have to be more annoying when following up—but they're public records," Zou said. "When it's a pure denial and it's public, that's a different story. I got the impression that . . . it's easier to remedy in the courts, or there are more creative ways that people will deny the request."[48] This internal struggle is not uncommon but has fueled the growing perception that the government would prefer to remedy public-information disputes in litigation or otherwise creatively sidestep requests for that information.

Part Two

The Law and Legislation

4

Article 78

Last Resort, First Step

New York Consolidated Laws, Civil Practice Law and Rules
§ 7801 Nature of proceeding

Except where otherwise provided by law, a proceeding under this article shall not be used to challenge a determination:

1. which is not final or can be adequately reviewed by appeal to a court or to some other body or officer or where the body or officer making the determination is expressly authorized by statute to rehear the matter upon the petitioner's application unless the determination to be reviewed was made upon a rehearing, or a rehearing has been denied, or the time within which the petitioner can procure a rehearing has elapsed; or
2. which was made in a civil action or criminal matter unless it is an order summarily punishing a contempt committed in the presence of the court.

Over what may be considered a lifetime in politics, from 1995 to 2006, three men oversaw the daily business of New York State government. Beyond Governor George Pataki, New York State Senate majority leader Joseph L. Bruno and Speaker of the New York State Assembly Sheldon Silver directed legislative policy with authority and presided during one of the more contentious periods in modern New York State politics.

They also had authority in appropriating state funds and distributed dollars where they saw fit and often without having to disclose the recipient's name. Depending on perspective, the process of earmarking funds for projects is sometimes referred to as "pork-barrel spending"—the presumption of winning legislative favor or votes. From a public perspective, the concept straddles an ethical fine line, and New York's Community Projects Fund (CPF) was often called into question.

As part of the CPF, $200 million was appropriated for a pool of public funds awarded for grants, nonprofit agency contracts, school districts, and municipalities. These funds were also known as "legislative member items" or "discretionary expenditures" for projects in respective lawmakers' districts. During fiscal years 2003–4 and 2004–5, $85 million were allocated each to Bruno and Silver and $35 million to Pataki for distribution as they saw fit.[1]

As one among many individuals putting into practice the country's process of checks and balances, the senior editor for investigations for the *Albany Times Union*, Bob Port, requested certain information from the governor's office and the Senate and Assembly majority regarding the CPF, including the name of the legislator(s) who determined the allocation of each member item or discretionary expenditure. He also requested the same information from the Senate and Assembly minority, and, along with the governor, all three offices complied with the request.

However, Senate majority leader Bruno did not respond to the request; Assembly Speaker Silver produced only project titles, amount awarded, and agency. As a result, on May 10, 2006, Port filed FOIL requests for "an electronic copy of all computer data kept by the Senate/Assembly Majority staff for approved majority staff members for fiscal years 2003–04 and 2004–05, including the initiative forms for approved member items, project or grant title, location, description, funding level, name of the agency administering the program, program contact information, date and the name of the legislator(s) seeking the member item."[2]

The Assembly provided the same list again—with the addition of the names of the sponsoring legislators. The Senate at first did not respond and then provided the same materials as the Assembly—sans the name of the sponsoring members. Both the Senate and Assembly initially denied the new requests, claiming the documents were for internal use and were "not intended to be a final statement on decision making." Port and the *Times Union* appealed the decision on June 2, 2006, only to receive the same answer from both houses two weeks later.[3] Like all FOIL petitioners over the past forty years who have received a denial of both their initial request and subsequent appeal, Port was now left with a choice.

When a FOIL petitioner files for an Article 78 proceeding under the New York State Civil Practice Law and Rules, the New York State Supreme Court is the first step in the legal process and the last resort in the pursuit of public information. An Article 78 filing challenges the activities of an administrative government agency or appeals the decision of a state or local agency to the courts. As an Article 78 proceeding applies to FOIL, the burden of proof falls not on the petitioner for the information but on the government to justify the denial.

Since the law's passage in 1977, FOIL petitioners have taken the next step when they know the odds are in their favor—and if they have the time and fiscal resources—but the choice remains a gamble. Recently, there has been an uptick in FOIL-related challenges all the way to the highest court in New York State. From 2010 to 2016, ten FOIL-related cases made their way to the Court of Appeals. Even after the lower court rules, the government can still choose to present the case to a higher level—first to the Appellate Division and then to the Court of Appeals if that court chooses to hear the case.

Eve Burton watched the process of the Senate and Assembly member-item case in 2006 unfold from Hearst's corporate headquarters in New York City. As the media company's senior vice president and general counsel, she oversees a team of six attorneys, all First Amendment and public-information experts. Hearst is the only national news organization that has a staff specializing in these areas for all its properties—digital, broadcast, and print.

Burton's responsibilities extend throughout the company, but each year, given time constraints, she chooses only one case to litigate. In 2005–6, the company received eighty subpoenas across the network, including two for *San Francisco Chronicle* reporters Lance Williams and Mark Fainaru-Wada in the baseball steroids investigation.[4] But in 2006 she chose to work with the *Albany Times Union.*

They wondered whether they would receive the information Port had requested before the appeal and debated whether the Senate and Assembly were going to slow down the process. Burton knew going to court is always the last measure, so trying to secure the information through the initial appeal is desired. Then the *Times Union* and Hearst received appeal denials from Bruno and Silver's offices. "We battle all subpoenas and appeals, and one of the great things is that no one second-guesses us. There are hundreds of these cases, and most are beneficial to the public. So when people see us coming, it's not smoke and mirrors. We're going to bring an Article 78, and we knew it was happening here," Burton said. "For this, it was so clear—it [the collection of documents] was too big to give to us."[5]

After filing the Article 78, Hearst built its case for four months and received support through amicus briefs from a number of good-government advocacy groups in support of the lawsuit.[6] Even though the minority groups and the governor disclosed the requested information without FOIL, the Senate and Assembly cited two laws as reason for denial of the formal request—the Speech and Debate Clause in the New York State Constitution, which states that speech in either house of the legislature shall not be questioned in any other place, and a statute that says that neither house has to disclose to begin with, based on a statute.[7]

Hearst's legal arguments were simple. FOIL states that any internal or external audits and any statistical or factual tabulations of accessible materials are open to inspection. The legislative members' names constituted a factual tabulation. Moreover, the Speech and Debate Clause did not apply—it protects legislators from civil or criminal lawsuits, but the FOIL request was not an action against one or more legislators.[8]

On August 11, 2006, Burton and her team appeared in court to argue the case against Attorney General Eliot Spitzer's office in front of New York Supreme Court justice Robert A. Sackett. Two months later, on October 3, 2006, Justice Sackett ordered the disclosure of the names and awarded reasonable attorneys' fees to Hearst and the *Times Union*.[9] Since Burton and her team work for Hearst, they upheld the long-standing practice of redistributing the fees to the news outlet that had begun the legal process. "We were going against their [the Senate and Assembly's] fundamental argument that the bowels of state government need to be confidential to run efficiently, so if you ever had to appreciate constitutional structure, that was the day. These guys were so powerful; the concept of challenging them in court was unthinkable to most because they gave a sense of fear to everyone else," Burton said. "It was an extraordinary moment in the courtroom because you ultimately had the judiciary understanding the gruesome nature of this. It was a good day for the judiciary as a solid applier of the law."[10]

The *Times Union* ruling changed how this member-item process is reported, but the change took some time. The Assembly presented the names on November 27, 2006, after data that it had initially provided proved unreadable.[11] Bruno and the Senate would do the same in the following weeks. It was the first time the public saw how member items were distributed, and a new era of scrutiny of public officials began. The initial disclosure revealed that Silver had earmarked almost $1 million to key constituent groups in his Lower East Side District. Bruno had earmarked $5.7 million in 2005 and $6.4 million to key constituents over two years.[12]

A decade later, Burton said she was surprised not by the contempt lawmakers had for the FOIL process but by the number of projects earmarked for charitable groups across the state. She took a step back through the information Hearst had received and connected the dots, understanding that key items, she believed, were directed to groups in exchange for votes, a practice that continues to be disputed. Both lawmakers who were at the center of the FOIL noncompliance, Bruno and Silver, would be convicted of crimes in the years after this disclosure.[13]

During Burton's entire legal career, she has worked with news organizations, first with the *New York Daily News* and later with CNN, before heading to Hearst. With the journalists who worked on the stories generated from the member-item case, Burton and her team had a series of complicated conversations about political response and professional and personal attacks on colleagues and families, which continued well after the case was resolved. She still handles FOIL cases and works with many of the same *Times Union* journalists on public-access lawsuits that are now pending with the New York State Police.

The member-item case still ranks as one of Burton's most significant accomplishments—it is well revered in legal circles and paved the way for the disclosure of more fiscally related data over the next decade. "The disclosure of what is at issue is going to be embarrassing or portray the government in an adverse or negative light. So there is a very understandable human tendency to try to avoid, on the part of the government, disclosure of that information," said Michael J. Grygiel, an Albany-based attorney who has tried more than two dozen FOIL-related cases. "However, that would be precisely the type of information that should be released to the citizens of New York State. In doing so, it promotes the very accountability of the government that FOIL was originally enacted to enhance."[14]

SAFE Act, Data, and Privacy

The message on Putnam County executive MaryEllen Odell's official Facebook page on March 5, 2014, was a repurposed press release, posted just a few hours after the New York State Supreme Court ruling was passed down. Both the headline and the subhead described the actions of the legal process, encapsulating the stance that Putnam County took by not disclosing the identities of pistol-permit owners to the *Westchester Journal News* when the paper requested that information. This message was followed by a notice that the county would appeal the decision.

The time-stamped release supported the facts of the case—the Article 78 filing by attorney Mark Fowler on behalf of the *Journal News* and the decision handed down by New York Supreme Court justice Robert A. Neary in the paper's favor. What was not consistent was the opinion of what constituted public information and the interpretation of an individual's privacy as established by the State of New York.

In his brief on behalf of Gannett Satellite Information Network, Inc. (owner of the *Journal News*) on January 5, 2015, Fowler concisely laid out the issue and the central point of contention:

> The issue on this appeal is straightforward. The Legislature, heeding the call of those who deemed public disclosure of certain firearm permit holders' information to be a potential safety or privacy issue, enacted, as part of the NY SAFE Act, a law allowing holders with legitimate issues to opt out of disclosure—but otherwise determined to hold to its long-established public policy that permit holders' names and addresses shall be public records. Putnam County, in the name of the same concerns, has determined that no permit holders' information should ever be disclosed, period. The simple question for this Court is, whose determination controls?[15]

Beyond the legal documents in the case, what was not presented was any commentary noting the political and social climate that had engulfed New York State and the country, extending beyond the tragic events at Sandy Hook and even continuing into the presidential elections of 2016. At a time of heightened security and extreme sensitivity to any matters involving gun control, Governor Andrew Cuomo signed the New York SAFE Act of 2013, just weeks after twenty-year-old Adam Lanza, who suffered from mental illness, walked into Sandy Hook Elementary School in Newtown, Connecticut, and killed twenty students (five- and six-year-olds) and six teachers.[16]

The SAFE Act served as a direct response to the tragedy, and on January 15, 2013, it was passed into law. Governor Cuomo publicly praised the legislation as the toughest gun-control law in the United States.[17] The fourteen provisions included the banning of "high-capacity magazines," the requirement that ammunition dealers perform background checks, and the creation of a registry of assault weapons.[18] Deeper on the list of provisions was the following: "Limits the state records law to protect handgun owners from being identified publicly. However, existing permit holders have to opt into this provision by filing a form within 120 days of the law's enactment. There also may exist issues with respect to 'registered' owners in the new regulations vs 'permit' holders under previous law" (sec. 8 (f)).

The reaction to the legislation was divided. As other states took notice and followed New York's lead, opposition mounted from Second Amendment advocates and citizens across New York and the country. In the state legal system, at least six challenges were presented in 2013, arguing the constitutionality of the law with respect to the number of rounds in a magazine. The political response remained a considerable matter of debate, and within media circles Sandy Hook is still strongly discussed with respect to matters of ethics, coverage, and the overall welfare of the journalists who covered the events.[19]

One aspect of the tragedy's coverage focused on legal and illegal gun ownership, and with emerging multimedia tools allowing a presentation of the story in digital form, the *Journal News* used an interactive map the week following the Newtown killings. In the digital offering, the paper displayed the names and addresses of pistol-permit owners in its three-county coverage area—Westchester, Rockland, and Putnam. This display set off a larger debate, pitting the public's right to know versus the right to protect the individual gun owner's personal information. The interactive map was removed from the site, but a snapshot remained to illustrate the issue.[20]

The information given within this interactive map was based on data provided previously by all three counties in 2006. Each time the *Journal News* made a FOIL request, the county clerk of each respective county had made no objection. Given the new tenor surrounding any gun-related issue, more questions continued about mental health, ownership, and overall constitutional rights. The clock on the opt-out provision of the SAFE Act was set in motion the day Governor Cuomo signed the bill, giving pistol-permit owners 120 days to file the necessary paperwork, and just like the other news organizations covering both the tragedy at Sandy Hook and the New York legislation, the *Journal News* continued to provide stories from every angle. At the time of the interactive-map controversy, the *Journal News* publisher, Janet Hasson, said the news organization would continue to pursue public records from its coverage area, including Putnam County.[21]

On May 15, 2013, *Journal News* reporter Dwight Worley filed FOIL requests with the county clerks in Westchester, Rockland, and Putnam for the names and addresses of "all pistol-permit holders who had not qualified under the SAFE Act to exempt themselves from disclosure. The request also sought statistical information about the number of permits, number and type of disclosure exemptions, and certain demographic information."[22] The request fell on the day the 120-day moratorium expired for citizens to file exemption paperwork so that their personal information would be withheld from the public record. This provision had been included in the SAFE Act for safety reasons and covered individuals who believed their life or safety might be at risk if their names were disclosed (police officers, correctional officers, witnesses or jurors in criminal proceedings, and spouses were eligible for the exemption). Westchester provided the data. Rockland refused at first and then provided the information on a second request. Putnam County clerk Dennis Sant denied the initial request.[23]

Upon receipt of a second request on May 23, 2013, Sant denied it again and cited an unwarranted invasion of privacy and the right to withhold the requested information because disclosing it might endanger the life or safety of the persons named.[24] An appeal sent to Putnam County executive MaryEllen Odell was denied. Gannett, on behalf of the *Journal News*, filed for an Article 78 proceeding with the Westchester County Supreme Court on March 5, 2014.[25] The court ruled in favor of the news organization.

Between the two stays granted to Putnam County and the brief for petitioner, which cited thirty-two FOIL-related cases, the argument was dragged out locally and regionally. The debate over the effectiveness of the SAFE Act continues, and each legislative session includes vocal critics of the act and discussion of amendments. Also fueling the issue is the growing number of mass shootings across the country. In 2015 alone, there were 372 mass shootings (in which at least four people were killed or wounded), with 475 people killed and 1,870 injured.[26]

Even though some Putnam County legislators hailed the SAFE Act, Worley's FOIL request prompted concern regarding disclosure of pistol-permit holder information.[27] Various discussions continue on social media channels, especially through Odell's and Putnam County's social media pages and Second Amendment advocacy pages. Almost all focus on gun-rights matters, not on the public disclosure of information. After the New York Supreme Court decision in the *Journal News*'s favor, Putnam County filed an appeal. Almost two years after filing its FOIL request, the *Journal News* still had not received the requested data, and no further legal proceedings commenced until June 2016, when the Appellate Division heard oral arguments on the matter.

Even though the Supreme Court ruled in favor of the *Journal News* and its pursuit of public information, there was a small victory for Putnam County—Judge Neary did not award attorneys' fees, stating, "It cannot be said that the Respondents had no reasonable basis for denying access to the records in question."[28]

On September 16, 2016, Putnam County's appeal of the lower court's ruling in 2014 was denied by the Appellate Division. With the unanimous ruling, the *Journal News* should have access to the names and addresses of pistol-permit holders in the county. The last stop for Putnam County is the Court of Appeals, which can only grant permission to argue the case because the Appellate Division's ruling was unanimous. In response to the ruling, Odell stated that Putnam County would appeal.[29] For all parties, though, the legal proceedings were lengthy—and costly.

A Time of Transition

FOIL is a civil statute, not a criminal one, a reason why calls to and from Albany to amend the current legislation and establish penalties for neglecting or refusing a request have grown louder. Taking a FOIL-related case to court still remains a risky proposition considering the current media trend of tightening budgets, but the filing of an Article 78 proceeding offers an equally perplexing dilemma for a government agency. State agencies rely on the Attorney General's Office, meaning that a lengthy, costly legal proceeding may be worth pursuing all the way to the Court of Appeals, with few repercussions for the state budget. For cities that employ corporation counsel, litigation may mean some resource concerns with either a win or a loss in the courtroom, but enough attorneys are employed in the office to take on the extra load.

As the level of government shrinks, fewer FOIL cases are taken to Article 78 proceedings for the same reason why citizens and traditional news organizations are more hesitant now than in the past to use this vehicle. Beyond a very public legal proceeding in smaller communities—one that may result in negative publicity and stronger political repercussions—in counties, towns, and villages there is a greater chance that a case will have a significant impact on a budget. Also, a precedent may be set that could potentially affect how citizens view local government while creating a desire to gather more information.

Advocates and attorneys believe that the proposed FOIL legislation dealing with fees that continued to stall in Albany would affect all levels of government and not deter the public and news organizations from pursuing potential litigation. The awarding or denial of attorneys' fees is always a final judgment, and judges' rulings have varied on all levels. With new legislation—specifically changing the verb from "may" to "shall" in the provision regarding the awarding of attorneys' fees—decisions regarding attorneys' fees would be less subjective, and a judgment awarding these fees will be more severe than the risk of providing the requested information before litigation occurs. "Right now, it's [the withholding of requested information is] not criminal unless you find a deliberate action by a government employee destroying information. But attorneys' fees, and doubling or tripling fees like the anti-SLAPP [strategic lawsuit against public participation] law, that's where the teeth are," said Roy Gutterman, director of Syracuse University's Tully Center for Free Speech. "A public-records lawsuit isn't going to be the next O. J. trial. There isn't going to be outcry; there isn't going to be news trucks; it won't be widespread publicity, but it will impact agencies."[30]

In the past three decades, Gutterman made the transition from reporter at the *Cleveland Plain-Dealer* to clerk for a New Jersey Superior Court judge after law school to center director at Syracuse. His work examining the federal FOIA, in addition to studying and analyzing certain state's public-records laws, has uncovered a few patterns. In the future, he argued, the government can possibly make a stronger case for privacy, which is the primary focus of almost all FOIL cases that have reached the New York Supreme Court or Appellate Division in the past decade. He has also noticed trends within the judicial branch that may not necessarily disrupt FOIL—or FOIA litigation—in the next few years but may offer some guidance regarding the type of rulings to expect.

In his research, Gutterman has found that most federal judges are former federal prosecutors and that for most attorneys trying any FOIA case there is a fatalistic attitude that judges are partial to the US Justice Department. On the state level, specifically the New York Supreme Court, he found that most judges had worked for government at one time in some capacity and that most attorneys believe that agencies that are denying data and records are supported by the state Attorney General's Office and in the process may think like the government. This history of a connection to government may not appear in the final judgment regarding the information requested, Gutterman added, but it may appear in the final judgment related to fees.

Grygiel, too, sees a pattern in precedent. Of the more than two dozen FOIL-related cases he has tried since the early 1990s, he can count on one hand the number that have reached the Appellate Division. Over time, a very well-settled body of case law has developed concerning access to public information, so that fewer cases are proceeding to litigation because of recurring issues. This precedent saves time and legal fees and in most cases produces the requested documents, albeit sometimes only partially. Grygiel believes the New York Court of Appeals is interested in FOIL cases when a new issue has arisen or when it sees a different application of an exemption that it has not previously passed on, especially with the introduction of new legislation.

Grygiel speaks only anecdotally, but he has found that in cases involving local, city, state police, and other agencies, judges have taken a pragmatic approach to applying the law and explaining the decision to both the agency and the petitioner. Even though FOIL has evolved to address some societal and governmental changes in the time Grygiel has been practicing, approaches in the courtroom have remained consistent behind the bench. "I think the court is aware of its role in faithfully establishing the last word on the applicability of specifically enumerated FOIL exemptions," Grygiel said. "We are not supposed to have secrets in our government, except for extraordinary situations where there's a necessary reason to protect interests of the highest magnitude. Other than that, people are the government. Information that the government maintains in the ordinary course should be disclosed to the citizens [the government is] there to serve. I think judges have taken this approach in FOIL matters."[31]

With technological advancements, though, new precedents will be set. The legal perspective is very much in sync with that of municipalities, law enforcement, and the media. Even as more government agencies move toward digitizing older documents and setting internal and external policies to accept public information only in electronic form, there are still decades of documents and information stored in dusty rooms that exceed record-retention dates set by their respective agencies.

Archival issues are now contemporary concerns as FOIL requests—for both digital and paper documentation—are filed at all levels of New York State government. These issues lead to confusion and delays for both the guardians of data and the petitioners for those data. Most storage mechanisms are outdated in five to ten years, so policies established now must be reconsidered in less time. Agencies, especially on the lowest levels of government, still retain records on microfilm, floppy discs, and cassettes. At some point, these means of record filing must be digitized or destroyed, depending on retention policies and law.

With these logistical issues on the government side, public expectations continue to change. Just within ten years, an amendment was attached to FOIL stating that all New York State agencies that have a digital presence and have the ability to receive requests must provide public information through email. This amendment, it is believed, also helps with proactive disclosure.

The standard five-day response is not expected to change, but the information may be sent at any time after a response has been given because no provision exists concerning a timeframe for delivery. The popular perception is that with well-organized databases, compliance should be accelerated, and document sorting—even through entire databases of records—should be programmable. As for the physical redacting process, because of technology, advocates argue, disclosure should be easier and quicker.

Attorneys (especially those representing news organizations that decide to take the next step in litigation) say that, among other issues—antiquated digital systems, competing agency policies, and a technological learning curve for some public-information officers—swifter disclosure is not necessarily being resolved. Given his experience, Grygiel sees a willingness in today's environment for many state agencies to push the time envelope in not disclosing information to requestors immediately. There are no data available, but, anecdotally, he believes this happens more at a state than a local level. If an agency does not respond to the initial inquiry, there is no immediate legal recourse except to file an appeal. Any citizen in New York State can then reach out to COOG, and if there is resistance on the part of the agency—through denial or unresponsiveness—the next step is to file for legal proceedings.

Attorneys wonder whether citizens and media organizations are more cautious now than they were in the past about taking a case to court. How many citizens have the resources—or gumption—to take that next step? "You need someone pretty sophisticated and determined, and most often you need an attorney to do it. FOIL is a tool. It's a powerful tool. It would make it more powerful if there is a reasonable likelihood that an agency receives a genuine penalty for delay or failure to comply," said Fowler, who tried the SAFE Act case for the *Journal News* and was a legislative adviser for the anti-SLAPP law amendment, which sought to reign in frivolous libel lawsuits filed only to censor and silence critics.[32] He, like other attorneys, also understands the budgetary impact on a local public agency if a judge awards attorneys' fees in a FOIL case when that agency fails to disclose the public records. Larger government agencies, Fowler feels, with ample resources and sometimes out of public view, often wait to see whether an Article 78 is filed and only then turn over records to settle a case.

5

Exemption, Ethics,
and the Joint Commission
on Public Ethics

When Karl J. Sleight was appointed executive director of the New York State Ethics Commission in 2001, something struck him as odd on the legislative side of government. Sleight was the first former prosecutor to head the Ethics Commission, and he thought he brought a very different perspective. He knew the commission had a legislative agenda, but it never proposed any laws to weed out corruption in Albany and across the state. When Sleight took the position, he also assumed that everyone in Albany wanted to improve the ethics law—but he quickly found out that was not true.

Now, a decade since he left the public sector, Sleight remembered that some of the laws seemed, at least on paper, so basic that he questioned how reasonable minds could disagree on some aspects of potential ethics reform. The investigations were a commission function that ended up on the front page of the newspaper, but the confidentiality of an ethical situation was paramount to Sleight. The matters the public believed are shrouded in secrecy at the highest level of New York government would materialize, but at the core of the commission's mission was its ability to serve as a confidential setting for the 150,000 state government employees to disclose a situation and receive advice. "At the end of the day, you can talk about changing the ethics laws—and trying to improve them—and that's going to stop corruption. But the reality of it is, if simply making something illegal was going to end the conduct, murder would have went out of style with the Ten Commandments," Sleight said. "It's critical in ethics that the vast people in government have a place to go and get an opinion they can rely on—and if they follow the opinion, it's a safe harbor from any prosecution. You want to foster that environment, and that environment has changed significantly in New York since I left [the State Ethics Commission]."[1]

Because open records serve as such a powerful curb on corruption, FOIL functions as an ethics law, but, as many in legal and governmental circles have noted, it is not *the* ethics law. The coexistence of such laws leads to greater discussion about how they relate to corruption and whether strengthening either would serve as a deterrent. The argument for each remains strong, but over the past four decades enough high-profile cases have emerged to accentuate each statute's complexities and the moral and legal obligations of task forces or agencies established to curb such improprieties. With FOIL, the government has most often decided that ethics equals exemption.

Even though the State Ethics Commission was not explicitly written as statute, it and its cases were exempt from FOIL in process but not necessarily in final product. The now defunct State Investigation Commission was exempt, and the Commission on Judicial Conduct is not fully exempt, but there is a section in the judiciary law stating that any information it receives is confidential unless there is a finding of guilt or misconduct.

There are also agencies that operate under statutes that make some of their records exempt from disclosure, most notably law enforcement. There are four exemption clauses within FOIL related to criminal investigations. In addition, law enforcement officials often cite New York Civil Rights Law section 50-a, which shields police officers, firefighters, and correction officers from the disclosure of their personnel records. During the 2017 legislative session, COOG called for reform of this statute because more law enforcement agencies continue to exercise this exemption in legal matters involving officers.

The mental health agencies operate under the premise that records specific to recipients of assistance are exempt, but the agencies' administrative records are covered by FOIL. New York City's Conflicts of Interest Board (COIB), which operates in the same capacity as state ethics bodies, exempts certain documents from disclosure by virtue of the New York City Charter. The board was created before FOIL and was added by the Charter Revision Commission established by the state legislature in 1975. However, at the beginning of 2017, only one state agency's records and investigations, written in statute, were completely exempt from FOIL—the controversial and oft-scrutinized Joint Commission on Public Ethics (JCOPE).

From a legal perspective, Sleight explained, two approaches are taken to ethical investigations: such investigations are treated similar to grand jury testimony, and advisory opinions regarding ethics are treated with the same confidentiality that anyone would find in attorney–client privileges. Ethics investigations are patterned after grand jury investigations: there's a notice to the target or subject; the subject has an opportunity to be heard; and that conversation is confidential in nature. Not until the commission agrees that there has been a violation of an ethical standard—or probable cause to believe a violation has occurred—do the findings get reported and become public information. Because of this standard, Sleight said, a commission must balance a public employee's or elected official's personal reputation and integrity against the public's right to know.

The same applies with ethics opinions. If a state government employee is in business and considering bankruptcy, or if they're having marital problems that may present a conflict of interest and they want to weigh their options legally, the identity of the person seeking advice given by the commission must stay confidential. Sleight argued if the employee or official is conducting their personal business legally, it should not be the public's right to know.

Halfway through his tenure as executive director of the State Ethics Commission, Sleight and his office had to weigh this balance. There had never been an investigation of a statewide elected official—the governor, lieutenant governor, attorney general, or state comptroller—for an ethics violation, but Alan G. Hevesi changed this record. He served in the New York State Assembly from 1971 to 1993 and then won the New York City comptroller's race and oversaw the financial welfare of the city from 1994 to 2001. In 2002, he ran again for the position of state comptroller and won, and in July 2003 he reached out to the State Ethics Commission for confidential advice.[2]

Hevesi asked Sleight and the commission if he was entitled to security, paid by the state by virtue of his job position, because of alleged threats against him and his family based on positions he took on pension funds and investments in places such as Israel and Ireland. Also, his wife was ailing, and the request would cover health-related travel. Sleight and the agency offered a confidential advisory opinion that if a state police security review demonstrated need, then state-funded security wouldn't be a violation of the ethics law.[3] Hevesi left the room, and neither Sleight nor his staff ever heard from him again.

Then, as Hevesi once again ran for state comptroller in 2006, an allegation surfaced in September that his wife had a state driver serving as a chauffeur. Sleight recalled that he had written the opinion and that when the state police did perform the requested review of Hevesi's situation, they found that he did not need security. The story escalated.[4]

The allegation turned into a confidential investigation by the State Ethics Commission, but the commission was faced with a lose–lose proposition given the timing, just months before the election. If the commission did anything before the election, what it did would be seen as political; if it did anything after the election, that would also be considered political. The commission worked for more than two weeks on the investigation, with no overtime pay, and interviewed sixteen people, including Hevesi, over a period of four hours. When Hevesi left the interview, there was concern that some of the statements he made under oath may have implicated him in felonious activities. Ultimately, the commission decided that he had violated the ethics law. The commission produced a notice of reasonable cause—which is best described as an administrative indictment or a charge instrument—three weeks before the election.

Under the law, once the commission has made such a decision— which it had never done before this point—it must offer the findings to the president of the Senate and Speaker of the Assembly, and in the process the report will become public record. However, the law doesn't state what happens next. Instead, the State Ethics Commission gave the Hevesi case to the Albany district attorney.

The ethics violations became a point of contention in all debates, and the time it would take for the district attorney to compile a case also allowed Hevesi to defend himself. On the first Tuesday in November, Hevesi, a Democrat, won the election for state comptroller by sixteen points.[5] Just a month later, on December 22, 2006, he resigned from office, and in February 2007 he was levied a $5,000 fine and permanently banned from holding elective office again. There would be no jail time, but four years later, on April 15, 2011, he pleaded guilty to charges of corruption in a pension-fund scheme and was sentenced to one to four years.[6]

Five years after Hevesi was convicted, Sleight replayed the timeline in his head and balanced his ethical compass. He argued that the commission had to be exempt from FOIL in this case so it could conduct that investigation without being subjected to examination publicly. In the context of an election, it would have diminished the credibility of the Ethics Commission and be counterproductive to the investigation if the commission had to respond to a FOIL request at the same time. The example illustrates the role of an ethics body in a case that connects politics and potential criminal activity, but, depending on the case, the commission also must work in concert with the attorney general, district attorneys, legislative bodies, and, especially within the past two decades in New York, the US Attorney General's Office.

Ultimately, the full, unredacted materials of the State Ethics Commission investigation of Hevesi were sent to the state archives. The commission's entire body of work that led to Hevesi's downfall is there in full public view. Only one person has looked at these documents, raising questions about public interest once a news and election cycle has passed. "There's that aspect of FOIL that comes into play, and that principle is true in any investigation. The way they [the investigations] are set up is that they should be confidential for a reason because you don't want the investigation to appear on page 1, and you don't want a situation that someone didn't violate the law because then you can't get anyone to write about it," Sleight said. "But the entire investigation was produced—produced for public review—but not in real time because you have to weigh the balance. What's more important—a dispassionate, accurate, thoughtful investigation or the public's right to know in real time?"[7]

Four Uncertain Years

Guided by this philosophy, Sleight ran the Ethics Commission until he resigned on February 27, 2007, to enter the private sector. Colleagues and others in the legal and political communities often tell him he left at the right time, before allegations and convictions in both the legal courts and the court of public opinion. He left before widespread leaks to the FBI and media and a decade of heightened political maneuvering. The timing of his departure coincided with a series of events that government officials claim has led to stronger ethics reform but that the public and the media claim has led to a decade of corruption.

On March 26, 2007, the Public Employee Ethics Reform Act (PEERA) of 2007 became law in New York State. At the time, good-government groups such as the Brennan Center for Justice at New York University, believed it was the most comprehensive modification to the state's lobbying and ethics laws in more than twenty years. The act combined the staffs, jurisdictions, powers, duties, and functions of the New York Temporary State Commission on Lobbying and the State Ethics Commission into the New York State Commission on Public Integrity. The combined commission became operational on September 24, 2007, during Governor Eliot Spitzer's first year in office.[8]

Only months later, Spitzer's involvement in a prostitution ring became public knowledge and led to his resignation. Under the old structure, this case would have crossed Sleight's desk. So would have the eventual charges against Senator Joseph L. Bruno. And in the years the Commission on Public Integrity existed, it handled a mounting level of perceived corruption, only to give way to a new administration with the election of Governor Andrew Cuomo and the creation of JCOPE.

JCOPE was established by the Public Integrity Reform Act of 2011 (PIRA) to oversee and regulate ethics and lobbying in New York State and began operation on December 14, 2011.[9] The commission has broad regulatory authority and oversight over officers and employees at state agencies and departments, including commissions, boards, state public-benefit corporations, public authorities, SUNY, City University of New York, and the statutory closely affiliated corporations. It also oversees the ethical function of the four statewide elected officials (governor, lieutenant government, comptroller, and attorney general), members of the legislature (and candidates for legislative offices), legislative employees, certain political party chairpersons, and registered lobbyists and their clients.

What has caused concern for legislators, good-governments groups, and ethics watchdogs is the composition of the fourteen-member commission—three are appointed by the president of the Senate, three appointed by the Speaker of the Assembly, one appointed by the minority leader of the Senate, one appointed by the minority leader of the Assembly, and six appointed by the governor and the lieutenant governor. JCOPE's chairperson is selected by the governor.[10] Through 2017, in the commission's seven-year existence it has had five executive directors.

Exemption

The statute that established JCOPE doesn't say that FOIL doesn't apply to it, but the Executive Law does say that. "The law pertaining to JCOPE specifies that FOIL does not apply to its records [of ethics cases]—instead, it says, only these records specific to JCOPE are public," explained Bob Freeman, the executive director of COOG. "I don't know of another agency that is treated in exactly that fashion. That, to my mind, is unique."[11]

Commissions that are created by an executive mandate or the dozen that have been created under the Moreland Act of 1907, which was designed to weed out corruption, fall under a statutory exemption from disclosure—meaning that its records are exempt as provisions of the Executive Law. The FOIL exemption can change only by an executive order or if the language establishing an agency specifically states a provision can be changed by vote. Some agencies created specifically to focus on ethics, especially since 1987, have a complicated history with FOIL. Governor Andrew Cuomo's Commission to Investigate Public Corruption, created under the Moreland Act in July 2013, is one such agency. It was shuttered less than a year later, in March 2014, allegedly compromised by political intervention.[12] The records created by this short-lived commission, it was decided upon its creation, would be exempt from FOIL. This was not the first time an administration did not work with COOG on FOIL matters.

According to Freeman, when the Spitzer administration discussed the creation of the Commission on Public Integrity in 2007, it asked COOG for a letter of support or opposition. Freeman wrote a letter of reconsideration instead, explaining that the plan to establish a committee on government integrity that is not covered by FOIL or the OML was unfathomable. The governor's counsel asked Freeman to take back the letter, wanting unanimous support for the commission, but Freeman and COOG never reissued an opinion. When Governor Andrew Cuomo's administration created JCOPE, according to Freeman, it never asked COOG for the same courtesy. The law has not changed much in thirty years, but in the forty years since it was enacted, people and its implementation have and so has the culture in Albany.

In 1976, a year before FOIL was enacted after appeal, Governor Hugh Carey by executive order mandated the direct filing of financial statements by certain officers and employees within the executive department.[13] The law stated that all state employees with a salary of more than $30,000 must report their financial holdings. A lawsuit was subsequently brought against the government by a union that said it couldn't mandate financial disclosure—or, it could do so only by statute—and the Court of Appeals agreed: the government could make appointees disclose their finances, but not everyone else. In addition, more was asked in disclosure than of the current legislation. Then, seven years later, on January 18, 1983, this changed. Governor Mario Cuomo signed into law 4.3 Executive Order No. 3, which established the Board of Public Disclosure, which required government employees—elected or appointed—to file a financial disclosure statement with the board.[14]

Financial disclosure was only part of the ethics equation, however. The other piece was not adopted until 1987, when Governor Mario Cuomo established the seven-member Commission on Government Integrity, also known as the Feerick Commission, to investigate the causes of government corruption.[15] Chairman John Feerick, dean of Fordham Law School and a labor lawyer and scholar, appointed Peter Bienstock as the commission's executive director from 1987 to 1990.

Twenty-five years after Bienstock served in this position, he couldn't recall a FOIL request ever being submitted or there being a specific staff member to handle the inquiry if one did arrive. In that time, during the debates over two dozen pieces of litigation, there was never a public request for the materials uncovered during an investigation, all of which are now bound in a book detailing the commission's work. Even though these records did not fall under the FOIL exemption, Bienstock said FOIL was never invoked. He also argued that this period was a much different time in New York politics.[16]

An advocate of full government transparency, Bienstock cited many of the same reasons Sleight gave as to why an ethics investigation should be confidential—an individual may potentially be innocent or blameless or potentially a target of the investigative agency who would later be exonerated. For example, Bienstock still receives media calls asking if the commission ever investigated Donald Trump. There is a public-hearing transcript in which Trump testified in response to the campaign-finance system, but Bienstock said this testimony is completely inconsequential compared to other things for which Trump might be investigated. "On the other side of [the] confidential versus public [issue], one would argue, and I would agree, that an exonerated target should not have their file exposed, probably ever," Bienstock said. "I haven't thought about after death. That's unclear."[17]

In many ways, the Feerick Commission found corruption, which was well known in New York government during the period in which the commission operated, from 1987 to 1990, and now some of the same problems exist. In his *Fordham Urban Law Journal* article "Reflections on Chairing the New York State Commission on Government Integrity" (1991), Feerick called the time on the commission "the most difficult, challenging, frustrating, and rewarding" of his life.[18] The article offered reflections of the forty-month life of the commission, which was granted subpoena power by Governor Mario Cuomo's mandate under the Moreland Act. The article was also prophetic. Although written more than a quarter-century ago, its words ring true today.

The commission was not widely accepted, and its creation was borne out of tension between the governor and the legislature. However, the legislature agreed to provide funding for the commission in the amount of $5 million, specifying that none of the fund could be used for the investigation of the legislature's management or affairs.[19] There were other concerns. Many members of the commission wanted it to operate like a "prosecutorial or inquisitorial body," but this approach was not sanctioned by the executive order or by the US Attorney General's Office. As Feerick also noted in his article, "There were few legal restraints except those the commission chose to impose on itself." He also noted the more large-scale concern that still resonates today: "A government committed to ethics reform is more open, more competitive, and less subject to corrupting influences, and it gains the confidence of the public it serves."[20]

The commission's investigations and recommendations focused squarely on ethics and lobbying. Some suggestions led to repeal of legislation, and the political culture began to change, but even as the governor's office changed hands, corruption still persisted. The Feerick Commission raised the level of concern for an open government, and two main issues were addressed by the creation of subsequent ethics and fiscal accountability agencies. Both agencies operated with the same intent as FOIL. Both battled outside and ethical interests, and both met a similar fate.

Integrity

JCOPE's predecessor, the Commission on Public Integrity, was created to join two agencies, the Temporary State Commission on Lobbying and the State Ethics Commission. There is some dispute as to how and why this happened, but during the course of 2007, from Governor Spitzer's executive order to the Commission on Public Integrity's first day, the transition was not easy.

Just like the Feerick Commission's recommendation and the current climate of lobbying and campaign finance in 2017, money influencing politics remains a contentious issue. For twelve years, save for an eight-month spell in 1998, the Temporary State Commission on Lobbying was led by David Grandeau, who took a decidedly different approach to public information than the State Ethics Commission, which was run by Karl Sleight. The Lobbying Commission's name implied a quick solution to lobbying efforts, but for more than a decade the commission took on the combative personality of Grandeau, whose career in government began as city manager of Troy and ended in controversial fashion when the Lobbying Commission was made obsolete with the creation the Commission on Public Integrity in 2007.

During his time as executive director of the Lobbying Commission, Grandeau approached investigations very publicly (lobbying records are by law public). He took entertainment mogul Russell Simmons to task in 2003 for lobbying legislators to soften Rockefeller-era drug laws without first registering as a lobbyist.[21] Then he questioned Assembly Speaker Sheldon Silver on whether Silver received a discounted stay in Las Vegas courtesy of Caesars Entertainment.[22]

Grandeau's list of enemies grew longer, so long that in the final days of the Lobbying Commission in 2007 Governor Spitzer did not publicly comment on Grandeau's position, nor did Senate majority leader Joe Bruno.[23] Over the years, as attorney general Spitzer had to defend the Lobbying Commission, he and Grandeau were often at odds. Bruno had given Grandeau his start as an attorney in his communications firm and helped him ascend to city manager of Troy in his home district, but their relationship soured because of Grandeau's aggressive investigative practices against associates. Also, Feerick, whom Spitzer tapped to chair the Commission on Public Integrity, did not comment as to why Grandeau was not even considered for the executive position of the new agency.[24]

When it came to public information, Grandeau took the stance, and still does, that no government business should be kept private. As the lobbying commissioner, he spoke with the media all the time—perhaps a little too much for some. He said his office never denied a FOIL request and never needed to; he always made information available. Grandeau's entire time as commissioner is documented in files now secured by JCOPE, but even though he said he operated an open commission, the Lobbying Commission had the same limitation as other ethics agencies established by executive order—it was exempt from some aspects of FOIL.

Grandeau is quick to point out that he never was fired from his job as executive director but rather that the job was phased out. He now operates a law firm specializing in guiding companies through the lobbying disclosure process. For many in Albany, his switch to representing the people and companies that he once regulated raises questions about his credibility. According to Grandeau, he now uses his practice to exploit loopholes and damage the credibility of an agency he once was passed over to run.[25]

Grandeau's approach always rankled some. At the agency, the means by which Grandeau filtered information to the public infuriated some of the commissioners. He said he wasn't leaking stories—he was telling them. As soon as the commissioners discussed this approach with him, Grandeau would turn around and implore the media to ask him a certain question, or he would encourage reporters to send a specific FOIL request so his office could officially respond. What constitutes public information has always remained a prisoner's dilemma for Grandeau. The concept analyzes why two individuals might not cooperate on the same matter, and the debate at hand concerned open communication and information.

This is where, Grandeau believes, FOIL doesn't act as a disclosure device but rather like a shield for any agency that uses exemptions. "The legislature and the governor know that the person they put in to run an agency like JCOPE—whether it comes from the governor's office or not—is not going to provide information unless the commissioners allow it, and the commissioners aren't going to allow it as long as they are appointed by the people who don't want to let it [the information] out," Grandeau said. "So what they'll tell you is this—they won't tell you that they're not subject to FOIL; they'll tell you that they're prohibited. That's the excuse they use—they're prohibited under statute."[26]

Grandeau remains perhaps JCOPE's most vocal critic, but he is not alone. The agency's 2015 annual report paints a complex picture of the current state of money in politics and the investigations the commission has undertaken. During the lobbying year ending December 31, 2015, 6,119 individual lobbyists were reported on 5,231 lobbyist registrations filed with the commission, representing 4,064 clients. During the same period, 86 public corporations retained lobbyists and filed as clients of these lobbyists. In 2015, more than 43,000 filings and lobbying contracts were reviewed and processed.[27]

According to the client and lobbyist reports filed, the year 2015 saw record-level spending across multiple categories. A record total $243.1 million in lobbyist spending was reported for the year, representing an increase of $17.1 million—approximately 8 percent—from 2014. JCOPE's investigations and enforcement actions in 2015 resulted in penalties totaling approximately $189,300. JCOPE entered into settlement agreements to resolve twenty-six matters: twenty involving violations of the Public Officers Law by executive-branch employees and six involving violations of the Lobbying Act by registered lobbyists or their clients.[28] The records of these investigations, even after settlement, remain confidential. If an issue is resolved by a hearing, exhibits connected to the agreements may be available for public review. Overall, though, the records of the full investigations are subject to subpoena; nothing is barred from a judicial subpoena.

The data reflect the potential for JCOPE's growing influence, but the structure in which JCOPE operates leaves questions concerning what is underneath the data on the granular level. The commissioners remain appointees, as does the executive director. The indictment and conviction of two top lawmakers, Dean Skelos and Sheldon Silver, caused some former executive directors and critics to question JCOPE's role in those actions, given the fact that the cases were not referred to the US attorney general or to the FBI or the district attorney, as would have been done by other ethics agencies in the past. Also in question were JCOPE's handling of other legislative cases that drew considerable public scrutiny.[29]

In March 2016, Seth H. Agata was named as JCOPE's fifth executive director after a nine-month search, a period in which the agency was left without top leadership for more than half of 2015 after the departure of Letizia Tagliafierro in July.[30] Agata, a former counsel to the governor, was elected by an eight-to-four vote, the closest margin of the fourteen-member panel. But perhaps it was commissioner Joe Covello's letter after Tagliafierro's departure (along with three other commissioners) that precipitated the business-as-usual perception at JCOPE. The resigning commissioners strongly suggested that the next executive director come from outside state government. In Agata's first year at JCOPE, commissioner turnover continued.

Two commissioners resigned in April 2016, including Covello, when the annual report for 2015 was released. David Arroyo, one of Governor Andrew Cuomo's six appointees with the lieutenant governor, resigned with time remaining in his term, which led to more changes.[31] Mary Lou Rath, a former Republican state senator from western New York, stepped down on November 21, 2016.[32] Days later the resignation of Daniel J. Horwitz, JCOPE's chair since 2013, left four open seats on the commission.[33] At the start of the 2017 legislative session, these four seats remained open, and JCOPE remained exempt from FOIL.

The Most Uncomfortable Job in Albany

Before Agata discussed perception, he offered some context concerning ethical behavior in New York. Since JCOPE was created in the wake of the Hevesi case, the Spitzer case, and to some degree even the case of Spitzer's short-term successor as governor, David Paterson, the regulatory agency already was challenged to meet a high political and public level of expectations. These high expectations were only exacerbated by a litany of indictments and convictions through the legislature over the first five years of JCOPE's existence that continued to fuel a political divide between the branch responsible for crafting policy and an office squarely focused on ethics reform.

This scrutiny of JCOPE also spilled into the appointment of Agata, some of which he took personally. Even though the vote was the closest allowable by the agency's policy, he had the support of both political parties and both chambers of the legislature, in addition to that of the governor. And even though he had served in the government for more than thirty years of his legal career, Governor Andrew Cuomo's administration did not contact Agata. He was chosen from two hundred applicants by means of his credentials and the process. His client is now JCOPE.

Agata helped in the writing and negotiating of PIRA in 2011, which called for the creation of JCOPE. He found the popular perception to be that if you create a new ethics commission, you should be able to solve large-scale corruption issues and more serious government crime. But JCOPE, he said, is not the US attorney or even a district attorney.[34] It is the first commission that has a combined function in a regulatory role for lobbying and ethics, and from the outset there were concerns that by bringing the legislature into the oversight system, there was the possibility that politically motivated creation of records would be leaked, precipitating an even greater mistrust between the different layers of government.

The investigative function that JCOPE fulfills is not completely open, and Agata pointed to a New York City Bar Association opinion in 2011 that suggests that JCOPE is merely a glorified agency that deals with conflicts—ethical and lobbying—which is the stance Agata takes in his new position. He continues to point to enforcement of laws and the levying of fines and punishments. If a case is criminal in nature, JCOPE, much like its predecessors, will pass it on to the appropriate authorities, whether the FBI, the district attorney, or the US attorney general. This procedure was not necessarily enforced in the past.

Upon his appointment as JCOPE's executive director in March 2016, Agata wanted to see further changes, especially on the digital side. He graded JCOPE's digital presence as "terrible." A few weeks after he took the position, the commission released its annual report on lobbying, with a full picture of activity in the state, which it only publicly released then and not in real time. The public can examine activity on unwieldy spreadsheets with little data-cutting functionality, and lobbyists can provide their information every two months through an antiquated portal. Since 2011 via the passage of new amendments, however, lobbyists have been asked to disclose more, leading to less redaction and more transparency.

In his first five months at JCOPE, Agata created a new organizational depth chart and divided the commission between ethics and lobbying as he attempted to facilitate the full digital transition to a searchable, user-friendly online presence. Since the lobbying data are not disclosed in real time—that is, are posted only after review—calls for more transparency have only grown. A new website was scheduled to launch during the spring of 2017, in the middle of the legislative session, but remained months behind its expected launch date.

Agata said he's a gradualist, not a revolutionist, but he's not happy about the slow proactive disclosure of some public records. Since JCOPE's creation in 2011, more money continued to pump into lobbying, and more lawmakers were sent to prison. When the law was written, Agata said it was an executive and legislative decision not to contact COOG about it, but he couldn't recall whether it was an explicit decision not to reach out to the agency. He said it certainly was a conscious decision to have the law read the way it does to cover the full exemption from FOIL, but he questions whether the language is still necessary. "My views may be different than others. I'm not afraid to say it. I'm not troubled. I think the current FOIL law would adequately protect JCOPE's investigatory powers and other aspects of JCOPE," Agata said. "I personally would not be troubled by that all—and I think it may be a good idea. That's a personal opinion. I'm not sure if it's shared by the commissioners or staff, but I've expressed it before that it [JCOPE] should be covered by FOIL."[35]

Ultimately, Agata explained, such a decision to allow the application of FOIL to JCOPE would allay transparency concerns. He offered the caveat that this idea is balanced against raised political concerns regarding the potential that open records might be used to embarrass someone—a political enemy, an opponent. He also echoed earlier calls from executive directors of state ethics agencies who still believe JCOPE should protect its investigatory files in the same way police exemptions are written under FOIL or treated like grand jury proceedings. This can happen only with a change in the law, however. Agata noted that the most recent ethics reform proposal from Governor Andrew Cuomo included this language, which would mean JCOPE would be covered by FOIL, supported by an opinion from Agata. In past years, given the political climate, Agata said, this would never have happened, and he recognized the current dilemma presented in any democratic process.

For JCOPE, the most pressing challenge is to create an integrated role between regulating ethics in the executive branch and regulating ethics in the legislature, given the separation of powers—and Agata recognized the obstacles. "I'm not the legislature, and I'm not the governor," he said, "but I think open government solves a lot of problems."[36]

In March 2017, his office attempted to do just that. By examining past decisions and weighing the sometimes volatile relationship between the executive and legislative branches of government, Agata and JCOPE released staff-created legislative proposals that emphasize financial disclosure and investigations. Before the commission issued these proposals, it decided not to take a vote on them and instead posted the proposals online for public comment while reaching out to counsel in the legislature. The proposed reforms focus on amending the Executive Law to allow for greater disclosure of information for public inspection and clearly making JCOPE subject to FOIL and the OML.

For instance, Reform A would give JCOPE more discretion to decide whether confidential information obtained during the course of an investigation should not be disclosed, except as authorized by the commission or in response to a court order or a subpoena lawfully issued by a federal, state, or local prosecutor. In Reform H, the provisions include more discretion on matters of disclosure of alleged wrongdoing, procedural history of the complaint, the findings and determinations made by the commission, and any sanction imposed, including any settlement or compromise of a complaint or referral that includes a fine, penalty, or other remedy. As the 2017 session ended in Albany in June, neither proposal had been taken up by the legislature.

6

The Legislature

Two FOIL Bills, One Veto

As the clock rolled into the early morning hours of Saturday, June 18, 2016, the halls of the state capitol in Albany were comparatively quieter than in past years. The last day of the New York legislative session came to a close with the passage of bills through the Senate and Assembly that had immediate social impact. Of note, new requirements for school water testing, stronger antiheroin laws, and the approval of daily fantasy sports websites capped the six-month session.[1]

A host of ethics reform laws passed, but none focused on high-level legislative malfeasance in the wake of corruption charges for two legislative leaders, Dean Skelos and Sheldon Silver. The measures focused on the reporting requirements for political action committees (PACs) and independent expenditure groups, a positive step lauded by lawmakers, including Governor Andrew Cuomo, but no proposed law included the stronger penalties needed to address the legal or ethical issues that had plagued almost forty New York lawmakers since 2000, a running count courtesy of Gannett News Services.[2] What also didn't gain traction during the session were measures concerning ride-share expansion by companies such as Uber and Lyft outside of New York City, new laws on medicinal marijuana access, and eleven FOIL-related bills from the Senate and Assembly.[3] For advocates of open public records, the closing of this legislative session would end a perplexing stretch that had begun six months earlier.

As Albany was closing business on 2015, two FOIL bills that many advocates argued would strengthen the law in terms of government compliance crossed Governor Cuomo's desk on December 11.[4] In one message, he vetoed both measures, citing a number of political and practical concerns. One proposed measure granted a FOIL petitioner attorneys' fees if a court were to rule against the government. This provision would change the judiciary discretion of "may" to the undeniable "shall" with respect to the awarding of such costs. The other bill called for a shortening of a government agency's time to file an appeal of a court decision, from nine months to sixty days.

Both bills had gained widespread and unanimous approval from the Senate and Assembly. The governor vetoed both, but there was a twist—one gained some support in a subsequent executive order. For all lawmakers involved, the vetoes meant returning to Albany in January for the start of the 2016 session with work to do: address the concerns in Governor Cuomo's veto message.[5] Then, as the 2016 session drew to a close in June, one bill stalled, and pieces of the other moved ahead.

For Assemblywoman Amy Paulin, a Democrat from the 88th Assembly District in Scarsdale just outside of New York City, this was the first time in her fifteen years in Albany that she experienced such ineffectiveness regarding a bill that could affect the entire state. The issue at hand wasn't between parties or between the two houses— both the Senate and Assembly gave full support to attorneys' fees bill in 2015. Instead, major constituencies that trumpeted the measure could not agree on the rewording of the bill. "What was shocking was their inability to do so, and much more not communicate with me, who is a friendly sponsor for them. If there was agreement, we would have had a law instead of nothing," Paulin said. "They [the concerned constituencies] objected to it [the wording] the last week of the session, and we didn't have time to address the problem. I've never seen those same good-government groups kill something that they were so determined about."[6]

The good-government groups included Reinvent Albany, Common Cause, and the New York Civil Liberties Union, and along with the New York News Publishers Association, these groups helped draft the language in bills A09506 and S06949C. The Assembly bill was sponsored by Paulin and cosponsored by twelve of her colleagues across party lines. The Senate bill was sponsored by Senator Patrick M. Gallivan, a Republican from the 59th Senate District, which extends from Rochester to Buffalo. The bill would amend chapter 492 of the *Laws of 2006*, which a decade earlier had strengthened the cause of FOIL petitioners who were once reluctant to take the government to court. This amendment, which won unanimous approval from two key Assembly committees—Government Operations (in a 14–0 vote) and Codes (in a 21–0 vote) as late as June 6, almost two weeks before the end of the session—would give more power to the petitioner. The proposed language would read:

> The court in such proceeding shall assess, against such agency involved, reasonable attorneys' fees and other litigation costs reasonably incurred by such person, in any case under the provisions of this section in which such person has substantially prevailed unless the court finds that the position of such agency was substantially justified or that special circumstances make such assessment unjust; or the agency failed to respond to a request or appeal within the statutory time, unless the court finds that the agency provided substantive evidence of inability to comply.

With the replacement of "may" with "shall" at the beginning of the provision—"the court in such a proceeding may assess"—the judgment whether to assess attorneys' fees would be taken out of the court's hands. If the FOIL petitioner prevails over the government in an Article 78 proceeding, then attorneys' fees "shall" be assessed and awarded to the petitioner.[7] The concern now was a different matter—the changing of "reasonable attorneys' fees" to "all attorneys' fees" if an agency does not meet a deadline.

By multiple accounts, the good-government groups met with Paulin leading up to the final hours of the 2016 legislative session. The new language, after the veto message, included the FOIL petitioner's right to regain attorneys' fees if an agency misses any deadline. Diane Kennedy, from the New York News Publishers Association, wanted to include language that would allow an agency, in the event it did miss any deadline, to provide substantial documentation as to why. The good-government groups, however, opposed any language dealing with extenuating circumstances. According to all parties, the governor's office was adamant that the section be taken out completely even though a New York judge has never awarded attorneys' fees to a FOIL petitioner simply because an agency missed a deadline.

Generally, Paulin explained, if a bill is trying to solve a local problem but will affect the state, it is not difficult to pass the bill through both chambers. She has either sponsored or cosponsored other FOIL-related legislation in the past, including laws concerning the act of proactive disclosure by an agency and the videotaping of local meetings. Bills with widespread impact, Paulin explained, are difficult for any governor to veto. For a FOIL-related bill, Paulin said, this was the first time she ever had such conflict with three forces in play—news organizations, who took FOIL denials to court more frequently; a legislative body at odds with the governor; and good-government groups that all but wrote the amendment that they would later object to before the end of a session.

Paulin said her bill would have been more sensitive to the needs of news organizations, which found open-access obstacles to both Governor Cuomo's administration on the state level and New York City mayor Bill de Blasio's office at the city level. Media members said they had met either denial of FOIL requests or stall tactics since Cuomo and de Blasio took office. What also struck Paulin and other legislators as odd was the language in the veto message, in which Governor Cuomo called attention to the legislature not being subject to the same rules regarding denial of FOIL requests.

Different accounts show Paulin pushing for the bill on the floor and both the New York News Publishers Association and good-government groups lobbying a number of offices either to advocate or to kill the bill in the waning hours of the 2016 session. Ultimately, the business of the Senate and Assembly pressed on, and all parties agreed to shelve the measure—the bill was dead. "I think we got all tangled up with solving a problem along with a new conflict, with the governor saying that the legislature should be subject to FOIL, which I don't disagree with it. But it is a rule that the administration was also in violation of," Paulin said. "Maybe this was going to become the norm all around, but it wasn't the norm before."[8]

The governor's second veto focused on bill A00114, introduced by Assemblyman David Buchwald, also a Democrat from the 93rd Assembly District in Mount Kisco, just north of Paulin's district. Like the attorneys' fee bill, this bill was linked with a Senate bill (S01531) and was also sponsored by a Republican colleague, Michael Ranzenhofer, from the 61st Senate District in Buffalo. It would limit the time state agencies have to appeal an Article 78 Supreme Court judgment against them for FOIL violations.

Prior to the introduction of the bill, the law was that even if a judge rules in favor of the FOIL petitioner, a state agency has up to nine months to perfect an appeal. During this time, it has no obligation to provide the requested records, meaning the information that may be timely may no longer be relevant by the time the records are received or events in that timeframe may alter the records. Bill A00114 would require all government agencies who appeal judges' FOIL decisions to submit the appeal within thirty days and to finalize the appeal paperwork after no more than sixty additional days.

The administration had concerns about this bill, as it did about the attorneys' fee bill. Just hours after sending the veto message, primarily citing that both bills needed to include the legislature, Governor Cuomo issued an executive order on December 12. The executive branch would be subject to a sixty-day appeal process, but more FOIL reform, the message stated, was necessary to cover all agencies and branches of the government.[9] This executive order was a small victory, but it didn't feel like one.

Buchwald reworked some sections of the appeals-timeline bill during the 2016 session, and it received widespread support in both the Senate and Assembly, never facing the same concerns as the attorneys' fee bills. He, along with FOIL advocates, would now wait for months until the bill crossed Governor Cuomo's desk before the end of the year. "Part of the reason why we had some success after the governor vetoed the bill [and] then implemented some of the bill for state agencies was because of the backlash. The night of the veto, you feel the loss, but I wasn't to bear it in solitude. There were a lot of folks who worked to fill a temporary setback," Buchwald said after the 2016 session ended. "We offered revisions to a productive bill, basically updated the bill as a response to message, and sent it to the governor. He now has a chance now to improve with promised reform—but I'm not really assuming success yet."[10]

Behind the Bills

Each lawmaker invites challenges from his or her respective constituencies, and sometimes lawmakers' backgrounds offer a compelling mosaic of reasons why FOIL-related bills would serve their local districts at a time when noncompliance by statewide agencies continues to remain a pressing concern. Most bills are sponsored by different senators or assemblymembers, but many names appear on multiple FOIL-related measures. The names cut across parties, geography, and chambers. The widespread approval of legislation offers a signal that reform is necessary in the wake of FOIL denials or abuses, while sponsorship also serves as an indication that there is disconnect between the government and the constituencies it serves. A sampling of other proposed FOIL bills on hold until the next session implied a need but all address contemporary issues:

- Prohibits certain agencies from charging for the process of a FOIL request made by state and local agencies or the state legislature.
- Relates to information available pertaining to rental histories of rent-stabilized units through FOIL applications.
- Requires entities that submit records to state agencies that are excepted from disclosure under FOIL to periodically re-apply for the exception.

• Provides that each state agency that maintains a website shall ensure that its website provides for online submission of requests for records subject to FOIL.[11]

Like the previous FOIL amendments, most bills often go through a two-year or longer process to gain favor. Usually a bill is proposed and adopted as a response to an event of high importance beyond any governmental control, such as the Sandy Hook tragedy. Few bills submitted under such circumstances offer solutions in addressing systemic failures. A bill is often presented only when the specific event in question affects the lawmaker or any of his or her constituents. These bills were different.

The veto message on December 11, 2015, also presented an opportunity for reflection among sponsors of the bills. Some harbor emotional attachment, cultivated after years of experiencing the impact of FOIL on their respective professions or constituencies. Others recognize the importance of transparency at a time when the public believes the word carries a hollow meaning. With FOIL, designed to create full government transparency, the actions and subsequent response crossed all these thresholds while also continuing to highlight the political disconnect between the state's chief executive and the legislature.

Senator Patrick M. Gallivan—
Sponsor of S06949C (Attorneys' Fees)

Given his law enforcement background, Gallivan's primary concern with the attorneys' fees amendment (S06949C), at least on the surface, had little to do with privacy or law enforcement exemptions. It had more to do with what he heard in his district, a sprawling area in western New York that links rural with suburban between two industrial cities.

In the Senate, Gallivan chairs the Committee on Crime Victims, Crime, and Correction. Wyoming County, which is in his district, is home to two state corrections facilities—Attica and Wyoming. He began his career in law enforcement as a state trooper for fifteen years before serving as Erie County sheriff from 1998 to 2005. As a rank-and-file state trooper, he would not have received or dealt with FOIL requests, but his tenure as a trooper straddled major changes to the law because of technological advancements and reporting policies. He became more conscious of what he reported and the materials he kept track of in the event that a request might be made. The same concern law enforcement now has about body cameras Gallivan experienced with dashboard cams. He pointed to his district, where each level of law enforcement raised an issue after the district attorney purchased body cameras with property-seizure money.[12] In the end, the wearing of these cameras has become the norm.

Gallivan's district is not atypical in upstate New York, with a mixture of small towns and urban sprawl. He has seen FOIL work best on local levels, a point he has reiterated in the same fashion as public-access advocates. He is also quick to note his position in the state Senate and how open-records laws apply to his work in government, mostly with expenditure reporting to the secretary of the Senate, who handles FOIL requests in this house.

A few years ago Gallivan began to notice a trend in constituents complaining about denied or unfulfilled FOIL requests and the inability to secure basic information they thought was public. At the same time, Paulin was proposing legislation to improve FOIL compliance in the Assembly, which piqued Gallivan's interest in the Senate. As Gallivan began to discuss the issue more with lawmakers, they found a trend forming not on the local level but in state agencies, largely those within the executive branch, such as the Department of Motor Vehicles and the Department of Environmental Conservation or any agency dealing with retirement issues.

He wondered what would push for more compliance, so Paulin's focus became his beginning in 2014, but after Governor Cuomo's veto of the attorneys' fees bill a year later, Gallivan and his colleagues began dissecting the bill's language. There was consensus that the administration had raised a valid point. Gallivan, along with his colleagues, also believed there was more in the veto message. "I didn't think that the complete discussion was on what applies to legislative compared to executive in both bills. He [Governor Cuomo] hid behind that. It was a distraction, a diversion, or whatever you want to call it. I thought it was a little disingenuous," Gallivan said. "The point that he makes is this, that there could be legitimate reasons for delay. That was a fair objection on his part. But let's really look at the big picture, though. If agencies just complied with this, we probably won't be talking about it."[13]

Gallivan still believed that changing the language from "may" to "shall" regarding courts' determination of the payment of attorneys' fees would change the entire dynamic of FOIL and how citizens can access public information in the current political climate. But he also pointed to additional language, based on circumstance. A judge will be allowed to issue an award of legal fees if the standard is substantially justified, Gallivan rationalized, but he posed an extreme hypothetical that in reality has affected New York State residents: if a state agency promised a window of time to deliver requested information, but a large-scale event such as Hurricane Sandy did not allow the agency to comply with the FOIL request in the reasonable time, then that explanation is reasonable and acceptable.

It is this example that lawmakers must consider in drafting language, but Gallivan punctuated his thought by saying he was also trying to find a "common sense" clause along with an "honesty exemption." In the case of the FOIL-related attorneys' fees and legislation, he saw the same obstacles in crafting an amendment that would please all groups. "If government was more open or more transparent, things would be easier," Gallivan said. "But with this bill, it should have been an example of not letting perfect be the enemy of good."[14]

Assemblymember Amy Paulin—
Sponsor of A09506 (Attorneys' Fees)

Among the leaders in FOIL-related legislation are a group of Democrats, mostly assemblywomen, from the lower Hudson Valley into the Manhattan. Over the past quarter century, they have carved a niche in this area, working closely with COOG and other advocacy groups. From that group emerged Paulin, and her desire to amend FOIL stemmed from the lower levels of advocating for government reform.

In 1990, Paulin was working for the League of Women Voters in Westchester County, attending community and county legislature meetings. She began receiving packets of information at village and school board meetings, but she also noticed other elected officials at the table had more information than she did. Two years later she became president of the Westchester County League of Women Voters. During one county legislature meeting, Paulin became more aware of the discrepancy in the time before proactive disclosure of public meetings and technological advancements. Sandy Galef, a schoolteacher turned county legislator from Ossining, noticed Paulin and the lighter version of the documents. She turned to Paulin and assured her that in future she would get a full packet because as a member of the public she was entitled to them. It was then that Paulin realized that the same information lawmakers possessed should be available for all public inspection.

Now, more than twenty-five years later, Galef and Paulin work together as assemblymembers in Albany. Paulin sponsored A09506, the Assembly version of the attorneys' fees bill. Galef was one of the cosponsors. "At committee meetings," Paulin remembered, "it really depended who was chair, and if they would feel like giving me all the documents, then they would give it to me. The unfriendly chairs wouldn't give me documents, so I couldn't follow the meetings, and the only members of the public in those open meetings were me and the newspaper. They purposely decided to not give me the piece of paper, and I realized without that piece of paper I was useless. I was not looking to be confrontational in any way. I thought I had input. That's what I wanted."[15]

From there, she began exploring FOIL and OML and took that approach to governance when she was elected to the Scarsdale Village Board. In 1995, the seven-member board began filming its meetings on public-access television because of Paulin. During the first budget meeting, as a matter of tradition, they adjourned to go into executive session, but Paulin objected that doing so was illegal. She did not mean the objection as a slight to her colleagues, but they did not know. It was how they always conducted business related to the budget. They looked up the law and found Paulin was correct. To this day, budget matters in Scarsdale are discussed in public.

It was also around this time that Paulin began understanding the dynamic between lawmakers and constituents and the process of solving problems from the lowest levels up to the top. She remembered one of the most significant reservations voiced by the Scarsdale Village Board members when they began filming meetings. Some elected officials felt exposed, knowing their command of an issue was not what it should be and that in the process this ignorance would hurt their chances in the next election or create a negative public perception of them.

Paulin thought the opposite. She realized she lived in Scarsdale, thirty minutes from Manhattan, in a community of professionals who she knew had more expertise than she did on a number of matters. Her approach—there was no issue that it couldn't benefit the residents living in the area to know about, and if they were interested, she wanted to give them as much information as possible. This approach is an anomaly in a time of career politicians, but by multiple accounts Paulin has remained the same. "I know that fundamental feeling of exposing what I don't know—and that's not a bad thing. It's not the same approach by everyone in Albany, but I feel the electorate genuinely has expertise. We don't, and why should we shy away from that?" Paulin asked. "It doesn't always work that way in Albany. We see it now—the legislature has deteriorated in people's eyes."[16]

Few legislators, let alone New York State citizens, can understand FOIL from three angles: filing a FOIL request, crafting FOIL legislation, and being on the receiving end of a FOIL inquiry. Paulin can, and in some ways her experience illustrates the uneasiness of some lawmakers in Albany. Paulin talked about when her office received a FOIL request for her email correspondence. She explained that most times when a FOIL request comes across her desk, it is because she may not have a friendly relationship with the person who "FOILs" her. But, she rationalized, because of her experience with FOIL, people do ask for information, and because she knows that information is FOILable, she doesn't think about it and just honors the request.

For some lawmakers, she said, if a FOIL request comes out of the blue, and they know it can do harm to their work or reputation, they become suspicious. In the case of receiving a FOIL request for her emails, she said, her office knew she wasn't the target of the inquiry, but since there was an exchange of emails with another public official, those records were open.[17]

She asked aloud if she believed the request for her emails was frivolous and what would happen if she did not comply in a timely way. Concerning the larger picture of the use of FOIL in general, Paulin tries to take the perspective of some her colleagues, asking whether the legislation she's sponsoring will affect her office and government negatively. "Overall, I think the governor's office is nervous about awarding attorneys' fees if it's a frivolous case. Then the easy answer, to counter this, is just comply," Paulin said. "People feel vulnerable when giving any information, and government trust is at a complete low. It just makes you think."[18]

Assemblyman David Buchwald—
Sponsor of A00114 (Appeal Time)

There is no seminal FOIL moment for Buchwald. First elected to the Assembly in 2012, he arrived in Albany from local government as a member of the White Plains Common Council after earning his juris doctor from Harvard Law School and a master's degree in public policy from the John F. Kennedy School of Government at Harvard. He doesn't have the same exposure to FOIL as some of his colleagues who have longer political or law enforcement careers, but Assembly bill A00114 resonated with him differently because he understood the widespread implication of a shortened FOIL appeal process for New York citizens.

Buchwald could not ask for much more backing. The bill received support from sixteen good-government groups, including Reinvent Albany, Common Cause, the League of Women Voters of New York State, the New York News Publishers Association, the New York Civil Liberties Union, and the New York Public Interest Research Group. On the national level, the Sunlight Foundation and the National Freedom of Information Coalition also voiced strong approval. The bill passed 62–0 in the Senate and 147–0 in the Assembly.

Then Buchwald received a phone call from the Office of Counsel to the Governor on December 11, 2015. From Buchwald's perspective, the appeals timeframe allowed a government agency to slow down the process of responding to the public. He viewed the literal function of the law, not the practical implication, as problematic. The veto message recognized the concern but found issue with the measure, specifically its focus on the executive and judicial branches and the possibility that it "would radically transform the litigation process" in addition to serving "to perpetuate a fractured system of transparency and data production by intentionally excluding other branches of government."[19]

The response echoed beyond Buchwald. By grouping both the attorneys' fees bill and the appeals-timeline bill in one veto message, the administration called for expansion of their scope to include the legislature, accentuating the continuing power struggle between branches that often accompanies a large portion of proposed measures in New York State. That night, Buchwald and others in various advocacy groups both publicly and privately had conversations with members of the administration. Even though both FOIL-related bills carried substantial weight in continuing and expediting the process, they were different measures with different implications for FOIL petitioners and the government.

On December 12, Executive Order No. 149 came down. The order outlined the governor's issues with both bills but called for further action on the appeals measure, which it felt created an imbalance between the state agencies and the FOIL petitioner because only the state agency, not the petitioner, would fall under the sixty-day provision. In addition, the order questioned whether the state's four appellate divisions were allowed to set their own rules regarding the perfection of an appeal. The order "expedites the FOIL appeals process, but does so without incentivizing irresponsible litigation by ensuring state agencies are not forced to pay attorney fees regardless of a case's outcome." It went into effect immediately, promising further action on more comprehensive reform.[20]

After comparing the two bills, Buchwald weighed the possibility of how the proposed language would affect the government fiscally, perhaps a reason for partial implementation. Ultimately, the decision was a Pyrrhic victory, a signal to all parties that more work was needed for practical and perhaps political reasons. "Of course, I think both bills should have gone through, and I understand why some with the executive-branch mentality are entitled to having a different perspective on things, but I also think the governor is attuned to what New Yorkers are saying," Buchwald said. "At some point between now and the end of the year, it's not our decision to make; it's up to the governor. I like to think it's a good chance, but I shouldn't put my life savings on it."[21]

Buchwald noted that the governor's administration is fond of arguing that FOIL doesn't seem to apply to the legislature, but he believes this assessment is incorrect—that the amendment to the appeals timeframe took into consideration all parties and how each Appellate Division, which would receive the appeal after a Supreme Court decision is handed down, would handle the next steps. Once a legislative session ends, bills that pass the Senate and Assembly are sent to the governor in batches, and once they are sent, the governor has ten days to sign them. His decision could be announced Labor Day or New Year's Eve, and Buchwald, who has sponsored other

FOIL-related bills, was not sure when—or if—he would receive a call telling him the bill has been signed. Buchwald said he would be sure only when the ink is dry—and that happened five months after the legislative session ended, when his bill was sent in a batch to the second floor of the capitol. On November 28, 2016, Governor Cuomo signed the appeals bill.[22]

Part Three

Local

7

Policy

Police Cameras and the Public

In the months after the death of Eric Garner, an unarmed, black Staten Island man who was being arrested by New York City police officers for allegedly selling "loosies" (single, untaxed cigarettes), the public outcry for justice became a daily staple through social and traditional media and set off anger and discussion across the country. The New York Police Department (NYPD) prohibits the use of chokeholds, which, along with chest compression and poor health, contributed to Garner's death, according to the New York City Office of Chief Medical Examiner. What fueled the tension, however, was the video that captured the arrest and subsequent death—video not taken by any of the arresting officers.[1]

As protests unfolded across New York City and the country during the summer of 2014, the legal system and the NYPD began wading through the process of untangling the case from the law enforcement and public-relations angles. Even though no officer has been charged criminally, the Garner family received a $5.9 million settlement from the city.[2] Video, though, has served as compelling evidence for the public and law enforcement in cases that once relied solely on witness testimony and officer documentation. Police forces across the country have used dashboard cameras for decades, but not body cameras on all officers. The policies on the use of this equipment are quickly changing.

Combined with the ubiquity of cameras, more incidents are being captured on video, leaving law enforcement, the legal system, and

107

the general public questioning the constitutionality of some arrests and of privacy and safety issues during what could potentially escalate into a highly volatile situation. The Garner case is not unique: other arrests and law-enforcement-related deaths have been captured on camera across the country since that incident. In New York State, for law enforcement officers wearing body cameras, the footage they capture is now considered a public record subject to FOIL. To what extent FOIL applies is a matter of debate, one that is becoming a defining issue in the first half of the twenty-first century in a society increasingly more reliant on video.

In December 2014, the NYPD began a pilot program to equip officers with body cameras. Over the next fifteen months, more than two thousand hours of footage were captured, with some of that footage used as evidence in criminal cases, and other footage was used to investigate allegations against officers.[3] This dual purpose has the potential to close cases earlier while also improving the relationship between law enforcement and the public. At the time, the Garner case served as the most public example of video capturing an arrest and death, but a program for the NYPD was already in the works by July 17, 2014, the day of the incident. A year earlier, US District judge Shira Scheindlin had decided that NYPD's stop-and-frisk practice violated the rights of minorities and that filming such interactions could reduce issues. As a response, the New York City Police Foundation used $60,000 to support the program.[4] Garner's death made the program a priority.

From a policy perspective, the case has also forced police departments and municipalities to work collaboratively to find solutions. A move in the direction of adopting such policies also creates not only a budget concern because of the personnel possibly needed but also technology issues, such as where and how to store such video and how long a record should be retained. Both are a strain on resources. In June 2016, the NYPD planned to expand its pilot program from fifty-four to one thousand body cameras in a step to reach its eventual goal of twenty-three thousand, but the program took a step back due to legal and labor issues. Less than a year later, in February

2017, there were zero cameras on the street, and the plan was being reassessed.[5] Still, the Garner case had become the seminal moment in the police body-camera movement across the country, equipping advocacy groups and the legal community with enough evidence to strongly argue for the full deployment of cameras.

Municipalities have only one opportunity to get this right, City of Rochester corporation counsel Brian Curran believes, so quite a bit needs to be considered to draft sound policy for and seamless deployment of body cameras. At the center of these discussions between his office, city leadership, and the police department has been the Freedom of Information Law. "There's no doubt that the rise of high-level incidents around the country has had an impact on elected officials, and a move like this is heavily influenced with community relations in mind. We want a good relationship with the citizens as much as possible, and we want to be as open as possible," Curran said. "For us, this wasn't a decision made in the abstract; it was community based. There are groups that are concerned about civil and community rights. This was not brought on by an incident here in Rochester, but just for concern."[6]

Curran said this weeks before the start of Rochester's Body Worn Camera (BWC) Project. The target deployment date, July 1, 2016, was set a year after the request-for-proposal (RFP) process began for a vendor. This was also months after a press conference by Rochester mayor Lovely Warren and the police department on December 18, 2014, announcing an agreement to launch a body-camera program for the city's patrol officers.[7] The program was a sizeable initiative for officers who serve the 210,000 city residents and the largest current rollout for any city in New York State, including New York City. No precedent existed. Six hundred active body cameras were the desired goal. The decision to take one full year before a multistage deployment of the BWC program was the correct one from all three perspectives—legal, city, and police. This view was corroborated by a public-opinion poll issued to all Rochester residents between April and June 2015. Almost 3,000 residents offered opinions, with 87.7 percent believing a camera initiative was necessary.[8]

As a result, on September 22, 2015, the city received a $600,000 federal grant from the US Department of Justice to fund the program, allaying any initial resource concern.[9] Across the country, 284 law enforcement agencies applied for such grants, with 72 receiving them. Rochester's application was substantial, totaling 222 pages, compared to the applications submitted by other New York cities, such as Syracuse, which filed a 14-page proposal to equip a force half the size of Rochester's.[10] Ultimately, the initiative became a commitment as Warren decided to make police body-worn cameras and FOIL one of her top priorities in an effort to create safer and more vibrant city neighborhoods. The mayor also wanted to increase the level of trust and transparency between the community and the police, and she believed a program like this one would achieve some of her goals. At the time, she noted, Rochester would be the largest municipality in New York State to roll out this many cameras. She sided with Curran, her corporation counsel, on matters of due diligence and the program's unique position in having no precedent to follow in establishing this program.[11] The response from multiple stakeholders pointed to adoption, but the public response was potentially exacerbated by an earlier incident.

Before the grant application was submitted, the public-opinion survey was released at a time of escalating tension in the city. On the morning of May 31, 2015, Richard Davis crashed his red pickup truck into another car. According to testimony, after first responders arrived, Davis, a fifty-year-old black man and military veteran, returned to the scene on foot, jumped into his truck and drove off, and crashed into a residential property, knocking over a gas meter. He allegedly locked himself in his truck and after five minutes of officers shouting that he raise his hands, Davis left the truck and charged at the officers. He was Tased, and after he was handcuffed, an officer saw he wasn't breathing. He was uncuffed and given CPR but was later pronounced dead at the hospital.[12] On March 31, 2016, Monroe County medical examiner Caroline R. Dignan ruled Davis's death a homicide—a medical, not legal, determination. Beyond testimony by Rochester residents and first responders, parts of the event were captured in video, and this footage was later used in grand jury testimony. Ultimately, the jury ruled the officer's use of the Taser was justified.[13]

Rochester police chief Michael Ciminelli said what helped in justifying the use of the Taser—and in communicating with the public—was the video. The ability to capture the entire incident via police cameras, which the police force did not have at the time, would have helped to validate the use of the Taser and to expedite the legal process, he said. "The bystander video, some portion of it, was helpful, including the audio, to lay the situation out for the community," Ciminelli said. "Ultimately, our objective is to improve trust. If someone believes an officer is wrong, the video is there; if there was an arrest on video, it's there. But the first big lines we have to draw are determining whether there is a difference between police activity in a public place and private home and in the process how does that impact public records?"[14]

The first step in the policy-creation process was to bring in the information technology department. The City of Rochester then issued an RFP as state and national shifts in legislation spurred a new consumer market devoted solely to the creation of technology-based law enforcement systems, from data collection and predictive analytics to video. Companies such as VIEVU LLC and Taser International Inc. cornered the market, and new players also helped drive down the cost of cameras to an average of less than $400 each. The City of Rochester now faced the same issue that all police departments are encountering: the primary concern is not the camera, but rather the data-recording and record-maintenance parts of the system. Curran rationalized that companies can produce good cameras, but the city was more focused on the system because of the predicted size of the necessary video-storage facility. The city received four bids before issuing the contract to MES Lawmen, a multistate subsidiary of Municipal Emergency Services, Inc., which supplies equipment to law enforcement and first responders.

Next, the city began to develop a set of guidelines for camera use by officers. This step in the process addressed the overlap between the police and legal departments, with the police department leadership producing guidelines to follow, such as when to activate the cameras, how to report and log footage, and the steps necessary to document an arrest situation. This decision was a policy-driven and an organization-driven approach, both Curran and Ciminelli said. The overall policy focused on simplicity and clarity so that the new initiative could be understood by the public.

Then FOIL became a primary concern for the city's legal department. At the time, Curran oversaw a department of fourteen attorneys and assorted support staff. Over the span of a year, one attorney, Meghan McKenna, spent more than a quarter of her time working on the BWC initiative. As the legal department staff examined FOIL and its impact, especially the law enforcement amendments and provisions that focused on privacy matters, they started with the understanding that a video recording is a record that is just as disclosable as a piece of paper. Then, in order to create an overall policy focused on receiving a video-related FOIL request, they looked at the law and how it interacts with the guidelines the police department had established.

Consistent with other municipalities, Rochester has its own FOIL process policy, steeped in interpretation and practicality. The Rochester policy has remained the same for decades, with the communications department responsible for the intake, the appropriate department dealing specifically with the forwarded request, and the corporation counsel handling the appeal process, if necessary. An attorney in Curran's office is also designated as the chief FOIL attorney, mainly because of the high activity in the area. Curran estimated that law enforcement inquiries always compose more than 50 percent of all FOIL requests each year, but they are primarily requests for paper records. With the proliferation of video, he anticipates that requests for video records will become the most pressing legal issue.

Curran said it's difficult to estimate how much video should be saved. Storing it is costly, so records retention needs an expiration date, and there must be an accurate filing system buoyed by naming conventions. The first step Curran's staff took was to look at the retention requirement. They then decided four months was ample time, given storage considerations and the likelihood that police video that old would be requested for legal purposes. Most often, such a request would be filed immediately after an incident. The larger questions focus on the written framing of a request for a video public record versus the framing of a request for a document. For a public-information officer who receives a FOIL, the request includes the petitioner's description of the file requested. Fulfillment or denial of a request sometimes relies on semantics. Also, the City of Rochester debated how the officer would review the video and what he or she would be searching for to comply with the request. This debate was capped by a longer discussion about privacy—an individual's identity can be withheld in a paper document simply by redacting the document. The process is not as simple with video, and a cautionary tale can be heard from across the country.

In November 2014, a hacker from Seattle's robust technology sector filed thirty requests under the State of Washington's Public Records Act, asking for all video, "every 911 dispatch on which officers were sent; all the written reports they produce; and details of each computer search generated by officers when they run a person's name, or check a license plate or address." The *Seattle Times* detailed the pursuit, and coverage of the story raised a number of questions, including the identity of the man who filed the requests under the name "policevideorequests" and from the email address policevideorequests@gmail.com. When the news organization tracked down the petitioner, he said he "wanted to call attention to what he believes are significant flaws in deploying body cameras without enough thought to privacy."[15]

The city said fulfilling the request was impossible. In five years, the Seattle Police Department had collected more than 1.5 million videos, accounting for 364 terabytes of space.[16] The review process and the number of personnel needed from both the information technology and legal departments would overwhelm the largest city in the Northwest. In addition, privacy laws and the legality of releasing such footage would require a team of attorneys to review every second of footage. The petitioner thus exposed a number of privacy and process flaws in the policy.

The city took the unusual step of inviting the petitioner to the Seattle Police Department to see if he would agree to help find a solution to protecting privacy and to withdraw the public-records request. Ultimately, Timothy A. Clemans, a twenty-four-year-old computer programmer who agreed to use his real name and drop the request, helped the city take its first steps in finding a better method of searching videos, with privacy remaining the guiding issue.[17] In the comments section of the *Seattle Times* story, he suggested that "the plan is to remove the audio and use YouTube's automatic face blur tool. For cases with a nondisclosure flag for an individual like a victim every frame will be pixelated. While removing audio is not ideal it is a dramatic step in the right direction. Both can be done automatically. Stripping audio would be done on [the Seattle Police Department's] computers using a free open source tool called ffmpeg that runs on Windows. The face blur tool would be used by running an iMacros script that automates clicking buttons."[18] In addition, a hackathon was scheduled as Seattle tapped its most precious commodity, its tech community, to offer other solutions. The Seattle Police Department also hired Clemans, who said he created a computer program that helps 911 dispatchers do their jobs more efficiently by highlighting the most serious calls.[19] Ultimately, in the heightened age of surveillance and privacy concerns, there is no universal—or ideal—solution, but other departments, including Rochester's, use the Seattle Police Department case when drafting policy.

Curran said that when diving deeper into policy creation, he and his staff began looking at defining categories of video, which is information based and sometimes prohibited from being released because of state and federal law. For example, there are privacy protections driven by statutes, such as never disclosing the identity of a person with HIV or AIDS or of an individual who has been the victim of a sexual assault. Internally, Curran said, there was little discussion on these issues because his attorneys were confident that 95 percent of the total video footage would not include cases where these exceptions would apply, consistent with more than a decade of case-classification data from the City of Rochester.

Over the year in which the Rochester BWC was discussed and planned, the corporation counsel viewed the most pressing FOIL consideration as the most contentious—the law enforcement provisions. "There is a tendency for people who don't have a complete grasp of the law to view this [issue] as cut and dried and [to] create the perception that law enforcement is hiding something," Curran said. "There is a list of items under the FOIL statute that you can deny, but [they] are discretionary, not obligated. The primary amount of legal work has to be defining issues, and some of the areas are judgment and interpretation. The most difficult to administer are exceptions of unwarranted personal invasion of privacy. Easy to say, not easy to practice. All of this is in context, and we consistently try to interpret FOIL based toward disclosing unless there is a reason not to."[20]

Like most municipalities and police departments, the City of Rochester and its police department are trying to anticipate certain circumstances, although they know a great deal of uncertainty exists. From a resource perspective, operating without precedent is risky, but Curran said they will adjust. There will be a staff of three people receiving frontline FOIL requests, and this dedicated staff will have a checklist of guidelines to reduce the level of ambiguity while labeling and categorizing images that fall within a certain pattern. This staff will interpret the video and judge whether FOIL requires disclosure, further clarifying any issues or making the search process less cumbersome. In the Rochester corporation counsel's FOIL process, video is considered no different from other types of public records. Curran and his staff realize that reviewing every second of video teeters close to the impossible, so summary guidelines will be established to send potentially more contentious matters to a higher level of legal experts in his office.

Much like other departments, including the NYPD, the Rochester Police Department has deployed the BWC in phases, with patrols being the first to employ body cameras. The city has also relied on proactive disclosure through the entire process, posting all matters involving the BWC initiative online, including a timeline, links to proposals, and other documentation detailing the steps needed to launch the program. It will also post all the guidelines established by the city, its corporation counsel, and the police department to decide if a video is exempt from FOIL.

Corporation counsel will also rely on human judgment to anticipate FOIL-related actions, especially in any case that can be deemed high profile by either a staff of attorneys or the media, such as the Davis case in 2015. If a captured video involves a public figure or an action of deadly force or a citizen in any potentially life-threatening situation, a forty-eight-hour moratorium will exist before Curran's office will release the video to the public. Such events, Curran explained, usually prompt six different FOIL requests from news sources—all print, broadcast, radio, and digital outlets. Curran remained pragmatic in his approach, knowing that an attorney, city, or law enforcement agency cannot anticipate every situation. He said that the most practical approach is usually the best, but gray areas will exist. What he, like most attorneys and municipalities, does know is that video and its role in law enforcement have emerged as a contentious issue—an issue that perhaps will grow even more prevalent in the coming decades.

8

Public-Information Officers

Boards and the Bored

On the wall in Mikale Billard's tenth-story office hangs a framed organizational tree of every municipal unit that operates within the 1,248 square miles of Oneida County. From his office window, he can also see beyond the Utica city limits into three or four of the twenty-six towns within the county, but the others—including two additional cities, seventeen villages, thirteen hamlets, and three census-designated places within the county—are easier to find on a map.

In an interview, he made a point to underscore the complexity of the system—some of his colleagues would have trouble pinpointing every unit and municipality within Oneida County. Billard wondered how, even with technological advancement, the average citizen begins to approach the task of finding the right outlet for any questions beyond the basics, especially matters regarding public information.[1] This is not a slight criticism of the public or his peers, but the reality facing government employees and citizens across the state.

By New York State standards, Oneida is a smaller, midsize county composed of three elements similar to areas found outside New York City and its immediate radius: urban centers, a handful of suburbs, and a heavy concentration of rural areas. The governments of such New York counties often find themselves caught between the state legislature and the governments of the smaller towns and villages they work with or serve. With the inclusion of services deemed essential to living, such as water, snow removal, road maintenance, power, law enforcement, and health and social services, the legislative labyrinth that is New York State government becomes even more complex.

As clerk of the Oneida County Board of Legislators, Billard's job is often to direct traffic for the twenty-nine elected county officials he serves. He often consulted the state's OML, and even though he was not the county's public-information officer, his office was usually the last step before a FOIL was filed or redirected, which was more often the case. He also knew he might be an exception in extending the courtesy of pointing the public in the right direction. "Overall, I think, there is a lack of understanding of what FOIL is on all levels, and then the public doesn't know who to go to. You take that idea, and now we go back to the public and how they perceive government," Billard said. "They want information, but no one is really making it easy. That's what you try to avoid. It's really just good business practice to guide the public; that's all it is."[2]

By 2016, Billard had been with the county for sixteen years, six of them as legislative clerk, but he was not the county clerk. That position was held by Sandra DePerno, and she was an elected official, which often created additional confusion outside government. But within the government, the delineation was clear. The county's approach to FOIL requests has changed over the years. Billard understood the push–pull of accessing public information, but he said what helped him and the county in terms of efficiency is the concept of proactive disclosure.

In 2010, when Billard was three months into his current position, a county legislator asked him for a copy of a contract, but only two of the required five sheets were in Billard's possession. In the scramble to find the remaining pages of the contract, Billard realized that he did not have them. Heading into the next meeting, Billard proposed as a solution to this problem that all the same documents that the county legislators were reviewing be posted online in advance of the meeting. There hasn't been a problem since.

The policies in place in Oneida County are basic for government officials, and all have an underlying yet direct edict—treat every document that comes into government offices as an item the public can access. Businesses that would like to work with the county are directed not to submit any documents that may give a competitor an advantage. They are also notified that their bids from an RFP can be viewed by the public. County employees who are requesting a transfer are told that there is no need to provide personal information about health status because sometimes HIPAA provisions come into play. Also, county employees are directed not to conduct official business on their personal email accounts. If a county email redirects to a personal account, that email is open for public inspection.

These practices aren't just sound ones for Oneida County but are universal across thousands of government agencies across the state. All these records are considered public, and yet state employees—hired and elected—still disregard this fact and these policies every day. What these actions also do, Billard said, is prompt questions many clerks and public-information officers from any agency face: How much information is too much, and whose job is it to decide? Most clerks and public-information officers on the lower level of government must interpret the law either from decades of experience or simply according to logistics and resources. They often do not have the luxury of a corporation counsel, as cities do. Some villages and towns do not have a full-time attorney. If clerks and public-information officers in such villages and towns need an opinion, they call Albany and COOG. Billard said proactive disclosure has helped to reduce the number of requests for smaller units of government. There are redundant requests for public records, so efficiency is more attainable if clerks and public-information officers disclose the documents and data that are most often requested.

For instance, after his second month as clerk for Oneida County, Billard began posting two sets of documents online—an abridged communication packet highlighting everything the county board is considering, including a summary of proposals and contracts. If the public or a legislator wants to see contracts in detail or the updated procurement policy, they would consult the full document, which runs hundreds of pages each month. There was no resistance from any legislative body when Billard implemented this policy in 2010.

The only concern was expressed by the county's information technology department, which issued a small complaint about the bulky file sizes.

This was six years ago, and technological advancement, which often outpaces the law as a response rather than a proactive measure, now allows smaller, searchable pdf files, so that information is easier to find for the general public. The move has also reduced the time devoted to meetings in Oneida County. If citizens were to attend any open meeting, they might believe the county legislature simply rubber-stamps every measure, but it doesn't: all the research and analysis are conducted ahead of time because all pertinent documents are posted online.

There are two reactions to requests for basic disclosure, Billard explained. One is rational, following input from a number of stakeholders over time; the other is an immediate reaction by one individual who may be unfamiliar with the legalities of the request and in the process prompts suspicion within government and the public. "I think that's where a lot of municipalities get in trouble. I think people just get nervous when you're asking for information. I can't tell you how many times I call for another municipality's budget, and it's like asking for nuclear secrets. It's amazing. You're just another municipality asking for that info, and people get scared," Billard said. "Well, we want it. It's a public document. It's available, and it should be readily available. And they ask, 'Why do you want it? What do you need it for?' The psychology is interesting, and this is just government asking government for information. Basically, it comes down to this—the more open you are, the less likely you're going to get a FOIL."[3]

The most substantial concerns are communication and knowledge of the law on the county level. In May 2016, Billard's fellow clerks from across the state gathered for the New York State Association of Clerks of County Legislative Boards annual conference. As they discussed the issues surrounding FOIL in the Kingfisher Tower Room at the Otesaga Resort in Cooperstown, three issues continued to surface—privacy, interpretation of the law, and open communication. For

Billard and Oneida County, this trifecta had aligned when complex societal problems collided with the interpretation of a law's principles.

On April 24, 2013, the *Utica Observer-Dispatch* published a story reporting that the Oneida County Department of Social Services placed eight homeless level 2 and level 3 sex offenders in motels in the city over a two-week span.[4] According to Billard, highway departments, health departments, and social services receive the most FOIL requests of all county agencies. In New York State, counties are required to find housing for anyone needing assistance. In Utica in February, those numbers increase.

The *Observer-Dispatch* filed a FOIL request during the spring of 2013, asking for a list of all homeless citizens who requested assistance from the county in order to cross-reference certain public databases to see which motels were housing homeless sex offenders. One problem, however, was that the list would also include citizens who were not in the sex offender registry and were just looking for a warm place to sleep. Then the original request went to the wrong department, causing further delays and frustrations, followed by the county's denial of the request, citing privacy laws.

In response, the *Observer-Dispatch* filed an Article 78, and in February 2014 the court decided in the newspaper's favor.[5] The records requested showed a county correction because it rarely paid for motel stays after the end of 2013.

As the media held government accountable, Oneida County Social Services searched for a better system. County offices also examined and revised their FOIL request processing system. In the past, each agency would receive specific FOIL requests and then consult the county attorneys. Now, all FOIL requests go to the county attorneys before they are distributed to the appropriate agency. Even though this new policy may create more work for the county attorneys during the initial five-day response period allowed by law, it streamlines the process, holds each agency accountable, and creates a system to track requests. "The approach I take—I work for that legislature, and that legislature will not hire me in two years if the public complains, so you should be responsive. Not only does it make me look bad, it makes them look bad. That's not the goal of government," Billard said. "I don't take this approach to keep my job, but the last thing you need is someone calling the media and telling them they asked for information instead of working with them. If there's an issue, let's fix it."[6]

Frequent Flyers

In 1986, Harold Konigsberg, a former mob hitman serving twenty years to life, wrote to the New York State Department of Correctional Services and asked for all documents in his case file.[7] The department denied his FOIL request, so Konigsberg took his case to court, eventually winning in the Court of Appeals, the highest level of the state's judiciary. Chief Judge Sol Wachtler ruled with FOIL, arguing that the agency in question could locate these records, so the request for a copy of the 2,300 pages in Konigsberg file should be fulfilled.[8] Just a few years earlier, the now defunct *Knickerbocker News* submitted a FOIL request for all documents produced while longtime Albany mayor Erastus Corning 2nd was in office. He served from 1942 until he passed away in 1983. The City of Albany initially denied access to nine hundred thousand documents. The court decided against the city. If the city could locate the documents, it ruled, the request was proper.[9]

The New York State Department of Corrections and Community Supervision (formerly the Department of Corrections) and the City of Albany employ legal teams to see to these requests, but during the annual New York State Association of Clerks of County Legislative Boards conference in Cooperstown, more than half of the individuals in the room oversaw a county office consisting of only one or two people. One of those clerks was Christa Schafer from Delaware County, located in a rural part of the state south of Oneonta and with a population of forty-eight thousand.

There is an assistant clerk, but Schafer wears a number of hats and has done so since 1992 as the clerk of the Delaware County Board of Supervisors. For FOIL requests, she is the judge, jury, and executioner, and at least once a year she will receive a request that is not as voluminous as ones submitted by the *Knickerbocker News* and Konigsberg but extensive enough to pull her away from her other duties for the equivalent of a week, all on the taxpayer's dollar. "When I receive a FOIL [request], the first question I ask myself is, 'What purpose is this information going to provide?' I'm all for transparency, but you do get people who are using it for the wrong reasons. I can't ask that, though," Schafer said. "If the record is there and it doesn't fall under an exemption, it's yours."[10]

When FOIL was created, the framers established that anybody can request anything from the government and who you are is irrelevant. Schafer cannot ask about intent; however, she can deny a request based on exemptions. This is how she approaches FOIL, and even with the increase in proactive disclosure her office watched the number of requests rise over three years, from thirty-nine in 2014 to forty-nine in 2015. In 2016, the number reached seventy-four. Her office is also similar to others on every level of government—some have one foot in the past and the other in the digital age. Some paper files are tucked away in backrooms collecting dust and take longer to retrieve. Others are digitized, so the search is easier. Still, the documents must be reviewed to comply with FOIL.

Schafer lives and works in an area where most people know each other, making the requests even more unique or highly questionable, adding another difficult interpersonal dynamic. In 2016, she received a request regarding the new county addition to the K-9 unit. The FOIL petitioner wanted to know if the dog was certified as well as a copy of its recent vaccination history and birth certificate. The individual also wanted to inspect any and all veterinary bills. It was a case where Schafer needed further consultation. She offered a hypothetical—What if the dog has an allergy to red meat and a criminal knows this and so entices the dog with a steak? She was able to honor only half the FOIL request.

Schafer also began keeping track of the number of requests in 2013, when she began posting more information online. She said the issue is not the number of FOIL requests, which has grown, but the depth of the questions. In 2016, she received a request for fifteen points of information on more than five hundred county employees. The FOIL petitioner asked for all personnel records, dates of hire, civil service test results, rate of pay when they started and at the current moment—among other items. Some material would need to be redacted because of FOIL exemptions, and an employee needed to retrieve and review the records from more than twenty county agencies. That employee would be Schafer. The petitioner also requested the files electronically, adding another layer of work that would also fall to Schafer.

Some agencies, especially for digital retrieval of emails, will charge the hourly rate of one of their information technology staff, which is usually considered a specialized position. This fee assessment can potentially lead to large costs—to the FOIL petitioner. With this request, Schafer would need to consult all the county's agencies, wait for the response, review and potentially redact the records, and then provide the records. Yet she could not provide an estimate of the time it would take to do so and could only offer the FOIL petitioner a potential delivery date. "I think people have stretched it [the law]. They take advantage of it. There may be only one or two people, and they generally misunderstand the law. That's how it works with everything. The same person will write you once every few months, and you provide the same response because they don't actually read the law," Schafer said. "Everyone wants to be informed, which is good, and if it's for the betterment of society, I'm all for it. But get a better understanding. If you have time to write the request, you have time to read the law. You want this information for a reason."[11]

Smaller World

The requests for information made of local government vary, but some are memorable. There was the activist who continually submitted FOIL requests for information on every aspect of animal control in the county. There was the local vendor who did not win a bid and wanted all documents related to the RFP process. Then there are the inmates who submit FOIL requests for information on their cases to Cheryl Ketchum, the clerk for the Wyoming County Board of Supervisors, even though they shouldn't go to her. They should go to the district attorney, and she politely redirects the inmates to the appropriate agency. This happens often in a county of forty-three thousand people, four thousand of whom, according to the US Census, reside in Attica or Wyoming Correctional Facilities.

Ketchum is practical in her approach to FOIL requests, and she has found, through conferences and conversations, that most public-information officers are the same. There are exceptions, she explained, especially in cases when someone who holds higher rank within government issues a directive. But, like Schafer, Ketchum is the only clerk for the Wyoming County board, and only if a serious FOIL request arises does she consult the county attorney. "We're willing to provide anything, but people get impatient. Most people have the reaction to pull out the big guns right away, and that's not going to help. This is the same everywhere from New York City to here," Ketchum said. "Ask first. It's your right, and you've made a request. But also remember that life happens. We will reply in the time the law states, but we're doing other work. Also, be human. Now that you've called me, I'll see if I can move it up the pile."[12]

Ketchum isn't exploiting the law. She abides by it all the time, especially the provisions that are time sensitive—the "five days or less" allowance is etched on her mind. If she needs more time, she acknowledges the receipt of the request in writing and indicates an approximate date by which she will respond to the request, which is usually not more than twenty additional business days. However, beyond this period, the fulfillment of a request is predicated on the size of the inquiry and the difficulty of the subsequent retrieval and review—and if Ketchum must fulfill other obligations at the same time. She is just one of the thousands of public-information officers across New York. "You know when information is going in the right hands. If we feel there is some maliciousness involved, there will be denial based on an exemption, and if it's a longer request, it's going to take some time," Ketchum said. "Just tell me what you're trying to accomplish. If it's huge, come in and search the documents. If they're asking for a list of things, if you ask nicely, we probably have it. By and large, the keepers of information, like us, are willing to work with you. But we're also realistic. You hear and read the stories all the time about citizens and government alike—someone has an agenda. I'm just not going to be a party to that."[13]

The Committee on Open Government offers an often used maxim that FOIL works best as the unit of government shrinks. Public-information officers such as Ketchum are on the other end of requests, but at higher levels of government unjointed systems often leave the public guessing about simple delivery—and in some cases even about who reviews the inquiry. On the local level, there is little ambiguity. On the state level, internal systems have improved over time, but public perception remains unclear about who makes the final decision regarding a FOIL request.

9

The Business of FOIL

The mailing address of JMS Recovery Services, LLC, is an office park along Towercreek Parkway in Atlanta, and its customer-service number includes a New Mexico exchange. As part of its business process, it sent an email to the Town of Colonie in New York from a nondescript address, jmsfoia@gmail.com, on Wednesday, July 15, 2015. The company, exercising its legal right, requested a copy of the town's accounting of all uncashed checks that had been outstanding for 180 days or more, including the payee name, check number, amount, issue date, and last-known address. JMS Recovery Services, LLC, was also prepared to pay up to $50 for the request, made under FOIL.

The practice is widely used, and out-of-state companies with little semblance to a traditional enterprise are becoming more common, which leaves public employees working in tax-related agencies often frustrated and sometimes curious about the nature of FOIL requests from such companies. Still, they are required by law to abide. This instance was just one of thousands of inquiries handled each day by similar government employees across the country.

JMS incorporated with the State of Georgia on May 25, 2015, and in just a few weeks began sending public-records requests to all regions, including towns across New York State. The company is in the asset-claims business, so for a percentage of the successful claim it will help you recover any outstanding property in your name. JMS is not the registered agent, though. That agent is the United States Corporation Agents, Inc., which helps business owners incorporate in all fifty states and other territories. In Florida alone, it has helped file the necessary paperwork for hundreds of businesses. Even though JMS is a registered business, it can still be a FOIL petitioner. The Town of Colonie and its receiver of taxes and assessments, Michele Zilgme, were left with a choice—comply or deny. "I'm old enough to feel that it's predatory. I understand that people do that. I just think you can go about it different ways without targeting groups who will benefit," Zilgme said. "As a public servant, I hate to see someone taken advantage of. That information about unclaimed property should go to the citizen, not a third party. Perhaps if it were a nonprofit saying, 'This is what we do; we're funded by other sources,' then I will change my mind."[1]

There is a FOIL exemption that pertains to a commercial entity in order to protect the company but not the public information. In section 87, "access to agency records, Part 2 (d)," the law states that "[e]ach agency shall, in accordance with its published rules, make available for public inspection and copying all records, except that such agency may deny access to records or portions thereof that: are trade secrets or are submitted to an agency by a commercial enterprise or derived from information obtained from a commercial enterprise and which if disclosed would cause substantial injury to the competitive position of the subject enterprise" (see appendix A).

Some companies in the private sector use FOIL to collect data for business purposes, which serve as the information backbone of their financial models. FOIL requests are sent to tax offices, municipal agencies that deal with utilities (mainly water and energy), and even entities that oversee garbage pickup. Depending on the municipality's FOIL request process, heads of each agency—or the village, town, or city attorney—handle these requests. Unless a FOIL exemption is found, they must provide the public records requested. Trade secrets or intellectual-property matters that may become an issue in the competitive bidding process remain a gray area, but vendors who enter the RFP process for government business will provide documentation that is considered an open record.

Otherwise, most tax information, save for personal income tax, is for public consumption. During the 2015–16 New York legislative session alone, 1,987 tax-related bills were raised in the Senate and

Assembly. It is up to individual tax receivers to stay current on the passage of any laws, especially exemptions that focus on the School Tax Relief (STAR), which provides a partial exemption from school taxes for most owner-occupied, primary residences. The twenty-year-old law has two exemptions—a Basic STAR exemption available to almost all New Yorkers who own their home, condominium, or apartment; and the Enhanced STAR exemption available to residents sixty-five or older with an income limit, which is increased annually according to a cost-of-living adjustment. In the same legislative session, 35 STAR-related bills were proposed by the Senate and Assembly, everything from raising the income cap for senior citizens applying for the Enhanced STAR property-tax exemption to providing the STAR exemption to small businesses with one hundred or fewer employees. The exemption affects all New Yorkers in some way, and the law changes constantly to adapt to societal shifts. For the STAR exemption, which is based on age and income, residents are required by law to provide their personal income tax.

Also hanging on a bulletin board in Zilgme's Colonie office are lists documenting what certain individuals have requested on a constant basis, including those searching for land or vacant properties. Some residents drive around the town, which is one of the most expansive and geographically diverse in the Capital District, covering 11 percent of Albany County just north of the city limits. They find properties that look vacant—maybe the grass looks as if it hasn't been mowed for a few weeks; perhaps the house is in a bit of disrepair. They call her office and ask who owns the home and which bank has the mortgage or deed. They are legally allowed to do so. Their primary objective is to flip properties. All of this requested information, Zilgme reminds them, is public and online somewhere. With nineteen suburbs, villages, and hamlets, four public-school districts, Siena College, and Albany International Airport, the tax codes have changed as quickly as the area, which continues to develop.

A lifelong Colonie resident, Zilgme began working for the town in the appraiser's office in 1986 and became the receiver in 1996. A

FOIL request on a town referendum in the late 1980s introduced her to the public's insatiable desire for information. The FOIL petitioner requested names and addresses to cross-reference another list to see if the listed people actually lived in the town. A few people in the office were required to compile the list by hand, its items numbering in the hundreds. In turn, they provided the list to the petitioner.

Since then, most of the FOIL requests to the Town of Colonie are redirected to the town attorney, which receives more than 1,500 annually, including a large portion for law enforcement. But over the years these requests have concerned tax information for class-action lawsuits, title searches, real estate, water usage, and tax rolls. The request for the latter, Zilgme noted, does the requestor no good because an exemption is going to alter the figure given in the assessor's information provided. Again, she reminds the requestor that the tax rolls are available online through Albany County and proactive disclosure. The tax rolls are complicated, but, Zilgme said, if the citizen is spending the time to put in the request, he or she should spend the time to understand the information.

Overall, the idea of using government agencies, such as the tax assessor or receiver, as back offices is not a new idea, but the response to this approach is a mixture of contempt and confusion—and the feeling is widespread across New York State. At the annual meeting of the New York State Association of Tax Receivers and Collectors in June 2016 in Lake Placid, as ambiguous company names were mentioned, dozens of heads began to nod when asked if any of these companies had contacted their offices through a FOIL request. Each name elicited a different response, but the vocal responses grew louder by the minute. Almost all the listed companies dealt with utilities—water, property, and energy being the most popular.

With the concept of proactive disclosure comes the proliferation of data and analytics. These spreadsheets filled with government data are vital to the intelligence of a company such as JMS, and the juxtaposition that exists between personal and governmental public information offers a challenge to offices such as Zilgme's. In the end, such companies want information mostly regarding taxes.

The list continues for the Town of Colonie. Across the room from the "most frequent callers" list is a packet of information for Home-Serve USA, which specializes in insurance for plumbing, electrical, heating, and air conditioning. Within the past decade, more calls have also come in asking for information on veterans who receive exemptions for various reasons. Then, the most significant target is the sixty-five-and-older demographic, whose information is important for solicitors. Zilgme's office also receives public-information requests for lists from fire districts to cross-reference people who live within a zone. She complies with these requests, but the law states that such a list can be withheld if requested for solicitation or fund-raising.

Water-meter information, namely usage, is also public information. Every address varies in its usage, even neighbors who may have the same size house down the street. From the tap to the waterline, HomeServe USA insures the line that connects the municipal water line to private homes. A water break or pipe rupture is a problem, Zilgme estimated, that happens only once every forty years, but companies continue to search for exemptions to see which category particular residents fall into. "If someone comes in, you have to give it [the information] to them, though, if they don't fall under an exemption. Sure, I have to comply, but sometimes I make it harder for them to get the information," Zilgme said. "We're still all protective of certain things."[2]

In reviewing JMS Recovery Services' request for a list of all uncashed checks for the Town of Colonie, Zilgme ultimately found an exemption—an unwarranted invasion of personal privacy when requested information is used for solicitation or fund-raising. She did not provide the list.

Turning Public Records on Their Heads

Jeff Rubenstein served as an auxiliary police officer with the Delray Beach Police Department, but the anecdotal stories he shared can be heard in every municipal public-service building in the country. The police department was preparing to buy defibrillators from one distributor, and by chance the city fire department across the street had just bought the same product from a different distributor at a lower price—same municipality, same product, different prices—and the taxpayer was on the hook for both.

For most entrepreneurs, their company's mission often centers on solving a problem, and for Rubenstein the concern was government-procurement waste. The business of government stretches beyond town, state, and country borders and remains a complex and fragile web that includes vendors, elected officials, and taxpayers. As recently as 2014 in the United States, the government-procurement industry, which includes goods, services, and construction, reached $9.5 trillion.[3]

In general terms, according to the Office of the United States Trade Representative (USTR), government procurement accounts for 10 to 15 percent of the country's gross domestic product (GDP), ranging from individual contracts to goods such as toilet paper to services such as large-scale construction projects.[4] For Rubenstein, a seminal moment involved the defibrillators. More than five years after finding the overlap, he is now the CEO of SmartProcure, a company that provides government-purchasing data to vendors and municipalities in an effort to cultivate more efficient fiscal practices. The leadership team is a mix of executives from the technology, government, and legal sectors. Rubenstein has a background in all three and counts former Florida US congressman Ron Klein and Florida House of Representatives member Bill Hager on his staff. As Rubenstein explained, some members of his team bought F-18s for the US Navy, and others sold software to the same agency.

Once bidding is complete, a local vendor's RFP is public information. The data compiled by all municipalities for procurement purposes are often used internally for budgetary reasons and are public information. SmartProcure wants all the data, which it then compiles for contractors and municipalities. Rubenstein's staff navigates its way through the more than ninety thousand government agencies in the United States, asking for their procurement data. It has reached out to the Town of Colonie and other agencies through the state and New York City. Most of the time, Rubenstein said, agencies are unsure whether SmartProcure is trying to sell them a product. His employees explain they are not, which leads to further confusion. They tell agencies they are trying to help them, which then leads to silence on the other end of the phone.[5]

Whereas a company such as JMS Recovery is requesting a list with the main goal of selling a product to citizens, SmartProcure is requesting data to help government save money and in the process to save those same citizens dollars. All SmartProcure wants is the data, and 99 percent of the time its employees are told to go through the proper channels and submit a public-records request. The company uses the data for procurement reform, asking government agencies to make all of their data open. "We know the requests that [these agencies] get are disproportionately large. They get thousands, and they have to do [the research and provide the information] for free. It's an enormous responsibility, but we're trying to minimize waste all around," Rubenstein said. "We're not a watchdog group that's getting your data. We're actually now known to have a reputation that is government friendly because we're simply cutting wasteful government spending."[6]

Through 2016, the company collected data from fifteen thousand agencies across all fifty states and boasted fifty-five employees. For these agencies, SmartProcure has every purchase order and its associated data from the past five years. SmartProcure is not alone in using public-records request for government contracts. Deltek, a Virginia-based software company, processes FOI requests for government contracts as part of an effort to help its clients win more government work with its contracts database of more than 1.7 million entries.[7]

At first, SmartProcure began appearing on a number of business watchdog forums. In the effort to maximize efficiency and minimize government waste, the push for public information has both its skeptics and advocates, including SmartProcure clients such as the City of Los Angeles, Citrix, AT&T, Hewlett-Packard, and the University at Buffalo. Then, the stories about SmartProcure began appearing in the *Washington Post*, *Bloomberg Business*, and *Forbes*, and it began to gain some credibility.

The data secured through public-records requests is repurposed into licensing packages that allow municipalities and vendors to assess analytical performance through data-cutting tools. Once SmartProcure receives an agency's data, it gives the same agency access to all information at no charge. On the vendor side, a more competitive government-procurement marketplace is born as companies evaluate competition and take note of pricing. In addition to its exposure through media, SmartProcure has forged relationships with key technology players, such as Code for America, which takes on mostly social benefit projects. Rubenstein said SmartProcure falls into this category, perhaps unconventionally, and a survey administered by Code for America in 2013 supports the initiative. Among the survey's major findings, which drew the attention of municipalities ranging in population from 13,881 to 2.7 million people, 75 percent of respondents reported that improving information technology procurement was a medium or high priority for their local government.[8]

The infrastructure and its products are driven by Code for America, but the data are essential. Rubenstein isn't shy about sharing his philosophy and inverse approach to using the federal FOIA. He authored a chapter entitled "Hacking FOIA: Using FOIA Requests to Drive Government Innovation" for a book on transparency edited by Brett Goldstein, the former chief data officer for the City of Chicago.[9] In the chapter, Rubenstein offers the argument that the FOIA gives citizens an advantage and exercised best as a tool that government agencies can use to help themselves. He also believes the FOIA offers a blueprint for innovation and efficiency, which serves as the engine for SmartProcure's business model. "We're in a strange position. If we went around and submitted a FOI request to every agency, people are not happy, and I truly feel their pain," Rubenstein said. "Even though government agencies don't think like this—to have a business run off of their data or if they think it's not healthy or the request is work for the agency and may be annoying—it still comes down to transparency."[10]

Rubenstein knows time and convincing are still needed, especially with government agencies. He now has time and a growing database courtesy of public records to strengthen his argument.

Part Four

More Information

Citizens, Advocacy, and Data

10

The Citizen

George and Helen of Troy

The Rensselaer County chapter of the League of Women Voters holds its annual meeting every year in May to discuss official business while also extending an invitation to a guest speaker. On this night, Bob Freeman broke bread and shared chicken marsala with a group that consisted of thirty people, mostly women nearing or at retirement age. (The league modified its charter in 1973 to include men.) Established in 1920 by suffragist Carrie Chapman Catt six months before women were given the right to vote via the Nineteenth Amendment, the league still exerts its nonpartisan power in what can be considered discreet ways by current political advocacy group standards.[1] In addition to the league's national offices in New York City, it boasts fifty-one chapters across the state, mobilizing to register new voters and push an ethics-reform agenda. On its modest website, tucked between information about voter registration, are direct links to SeeThroughNY, My Open Government, and the Freedom of Information Law.

After Freeman navigated his way through an overview detailing a bit of FOIL's history and the law's current challenges, he opened the floor to questions. During his seventy-eighty speaking engagements across the state each year, Freeman fields questions that pertain to both FOIL and the OML. The questions range from current newsworthy events, with that night's focused on the public–private dynamic of the SUNY Research Foundation, to the sometimes erudite and obscure. A question is posed about what constitutes a political caucus during an open public meeting of elected officials, considering that each level of government varies in size. In an era of more distinct party lines, this question is becoming more common. Toward the end of the session, a spry, silver-haired woman stood up, neatly folded her napkin, and placed it on her chair. Helen Bayly took a few steps toward Freeman, draped her arm around him, and began to share the story about the importance of FOIL and how it had affected her twelve years earlier.

When the original FOIL legislation was enacted, it was designed to serve all citizens of New York and not just journalists, advocates, and legislators. Anyone can submit a FOIL request in any state, and everyone has an agenda in the pursuit of information. Some citizens request on a hunch, not knowing if the public record exists. Others know exactly where the information is located. Some requests are for political purposes; others for financial. And some FOIL requests are for all of the above as citizens exercise their legal rights out of anger and love. Ultimately, petitioners just want to know.

Bayly is now an octogenarian, a longtime member of the League of Women Voters who is sometimes affectionately known as "Helen of Troy," bearing the name of the city where she has lived with her husband, M. Brian Bayly, a professor emeritus of structural geology at Rensselaer Polytechnic Institute (RPI), since the 1960s. She grew up in pre- and post–World War II Sydney, Australia, running barefoot amid the business of the city's whaling industry. She eventually became enamored with the ballet and graduated from the Royal Academy of Dance in 1951.[2] Her husband's job brought her to the United States in the 1960s, first to Chicago and then to Troy.

Bayly emerged as a vocal advocate for women's rights and through the next four decades wrote for area publications and hosted her own public-access show. When she first arrived in Troy in the early 1960s, she was approached by Olivia Folsom, the wife of the president of RPI, Richard G. Folsom, who had helped usher in the first class at the college to admit women in 1960.[3] At the same time, New York governor Nelson A. Rockefeller began to gain support for what would become the Saratoga Performing Arts Center (SPAC), with the

New York City Ballet (NYCB) serving as the centerpiece of his vision of a summer series at Saratoga Spa State Park.[4] His administration mobilized support, including Olivia Folsom, and Folsom, knowing Bayly's background in dance and the arts, asked her to help fundraise for the state venture. Bayly liked the idea of a regional ballet presence for upstate New York, one that could potentially reverberate down the Hudson Valley, up to Canada, and west to Buffalo, so she agreed to help.[5] She was also an admirer of George Balanchine, who cofounded and led the NYCB, considered to be the top company in the world.[6]

With the help of the New York State legislature, the SPAC amphitheater was constructed on state land, thanks to the private Rockefeller Brothers Fund and a steering committee comprising Saratoga and Capital Region families. The legislature and Rockefeller Fund contributed $2 million each to foot the $4 million construction cost for the 5,100-seat amphitheater. On opening night, July 8, 1966, Balanchine and the New York City Ballet performed *A Midsummer Night's Dream* on a stage built to match the ballet's home at Lincoln Center.[7] "There was a lot of trust between members of SPAC—the people of New York and the people running the organization. We felt for thirty years this belonged to us, and we knew the New York City Ballet and SPAC made excellent contracts, along with a couple of the state's and nation's theater and orchestra directors," Bayly said. "There seemed to be that care."[8]

The relationship between the state and SPAC is unique and serves as perhaps a template for modern-day, public–private relationships. SPAC has nonprofit status—501(c)(3)—and is a tax-exempt organization. Its mission, detailed in its federal Form 990 tax documents, is clear, with an emphasis on the performing arts and educating the public. Also, according to public documents, the title was transferred to the state in exchange for exclusive use of the amphitheater from June through September each year. SPAC does not pay any rent for the use of the state park facilities, nor is it responsible for the capital improvements to its physical plant (which includes the amphitheater, grounds and parking lots, the Hall of Springs, and the Spa Little

Theater).[9] SPAC is essentially a private organization that operates on public land with a very favorable agreement.

For the better part of four decades, Bayly believed SPAC's mission and the relationship between the organization and the state was sound. Attendance fluctuated with each season, and over time a more diverse schedule brought in other acts such as Bruce Springsteen, the Grateful Dead, and Phish to generate new audiences. Ticket prices increased a bit, consistent with the prices charged at other regional and national venues, but membership remained steady. It wasn't until 2001, when signs of discontent began to emerge privately and publicly.

In August 2001, Marylou Whitney, the philanthropist whose name is synonymous with Saratoga and a cofounder of SPAC, abruptly resigned from the board of directors.[10] She did not discuss her criticism publicly, but media accounts cited sources who said poor fiscal management by SPAC president Herb Chesbrough was at the core of her decision. SPAC ended the 2000–2001 fiscal year with a $460,000 deficit, according to tax documents, as Chesbrough drew a $263,000 salary. Also, SPAC no longer booked its own concerts. The board had transferred responsibility to SFX, at the time the world's largest concert promoter, which now operates as Live Nation Entertainment.[11]

Over the next two years, numbers that measure an organization's fiscal health began raising more questions about SPAC. Ticket prices for the ballet increased, but SPAC revenue declined overall. Documents show that the NYCB performance fees dropped from $2 million in 2002 to $1.8 million in 2003. In 2002, attendance at the ballet dropped to 51,548, only a decade after 84,613 attended in 1991. Also, attendance for the Philadelphia Orchestra, originally booked in 1966 to balance the ballet's cultural impact, dropped almost 25 percent in the same decade. In 2003, Chesbrough said SPAC lost $990,000 in revenue in hosting the NYCB's normal three-week residency.[12] Over a three-year span, revenue dropped from $5.7 million in 2001 to $5.1 million in 2004 as expenses increased from $6.7 million to $7.8 million. This drop occurred even after a state infusion of $3.9 million for capital improvements and a $300,000 matching grant promised for 2004. The financial trouble was documented and public knowledge—to a point.[13] Just like any nonprofit, SPAC is required to file Form 990 annually with the Internal Revenue Service and New York State Form 497, its annual financial report.

SPAC also had an annual external audit commissioned every year by UHY Advisors of Albany. According to its fifty-year lease, which runs through 2019, SPAC is required to provide New York State with a copy of its certified annual financial statement. (Repairs, maintenance, grounds, and security costs are also subsidized by the state.) Beyond these filings, though, SPAC was under no legal obligation to report publicly.[14] Then, in February 2004 Chesbrough and SPAC announced that because of mounting financial difficulty and the loss associated with the ballet, it was dropping the ballet's annual three-week residency after thirty-nine years.[15]

For Bayly, a longtime SPAC member, three years of uncertainty raised further concern, but she was not alone. The New York State Office of Parks, Recreation, and Historic Preservation, the agency that oversees the state's relationship with SPAC, launched an audit on February 28, 2004.[16] Longtime SPAC members, who numbered more than two hundred, began to grow suspicious. There were some informal discussions, and after an initial outcry in response to the decision to drop the ballet, the SPAC board decided on March 31, 2004, to bring the ballet back, but for only a two-week residency.[17] Cutting the original premier staple of the summer at Saratoga Spa State Park would alienate the base, but the initial decision had already prompted skepticism.

On the first night of the 2004 season, longtime members and ballet enthusiasts brought signs to show support for retaining the ballet and began congregating on the lawn beyond the amphitheater, a community mainstay at the venue as much as the ballet. Isolated groups discussed next steps, but they did not know where to go or how to proceed. Over the years, informal bonds had been made over the ballet, with members often seeing each other in the same place. Bayly knew George Neary, who had begun attending rock concerts at SPAC in the 1980s and eventually was drawn to the ballet by his young daughter. Like Bayly, he was agitated by the SPAC board's decision and wanted to know more.[18]

As a state employee, Neary had spent time in three state offices in Albany, the last being the Office of Real Property Services as a computer programmer, after stints in the Department of Labor and the Department of Audit and Control. Just a few years from retirement, he began spending more time at Saratoga during the summer and watched how his habits and SPAC's habits changed over the years. He went from watching rock concerts in the pit to taking his daughter and her friends to the ballet matinee with a decidedly more mature audience. In 1991, tickets to the matinee cost $12 for adults and $4 for children. For the 2004 season, tickets cost $24.75 for adults and $19.50 for children. As ticket prices increased, attendance dropped.[19]

Beyond the casual observations, Neary, like Bayly, wanted to know even more. "Everything we heard, everything we read, it was from the people who knew the inside of SPAC. As lifelong members, we were informed on some things, but we had questions, and I knew there had to be more," Neary said. "We wanted the contracts—what was included, what wasn't included. We wanted [board meeting] minutes. I think as the season went on, we just became more agitated. We just wanted information."[20]

Along with others, Bayly and Neary began asking Chesbrough and other board members for more information, and repeatedly they were told the board couldn't provide that information. After all, it was under no written or legal obligation to do so. As a state employee, Neary knew of the complex nature of private–public entities, but he also knew of COOG. Beyond what was already public, he was unsure of what other information SPAC supporters could legally obtain. Bayly and Neary then remembered that Parks, Recreation, and Historic Preservation commissioner Bernadette Castro and her office had launched the internal investigation and audit of SPAC.

They were an unlikely pair—Bayly, a mother of five grown children, an advocate of women's rights, and an extrovert; Neary, a lifelong government employee only a few years from receiving his pension, with a programming background and an understanding of documents and data. He had traded in his rock concert T-shirts for a straw fedora and perfectly pressed pants. They reached out to COOG and waited. "We knew we may have been in the minority, so close to it, but we also know the relationship the ballet had, that we had, with state land," Bayly said. "Answers. That's all we asked for."[21]

On November 22, 2004, Charles E. Mather III, the chairman of SPAC, received a preliminary audit from the Office of Parks, Recreation, and Historic Preservation's chief counsel, Paul L. Laudato. A day later the findings were made public.[22] "The audit findings are profoundly troubling, and we recommend that immediate action be taken by SPAC to overhaul the existing management system and restore the organization to sound financial footing," Castro said at the time.[23]

The audit found a number of discrepancies, including Chesbrough's claim that the loss from NYCB performances was the most substantial for SPAC, even though audited documents also showed that the Philadelphia Orchestra lost almost just as much ($732,149 compared to the $754,375 at NYCB). The loss occurred despite the fact that, according to attendance figures, the average ballet attendance at SPAC was higher than the average attendance at the ballet's home at Lincoln Center. Overall, SPAC had lost an average of $1 million each year from 1999 to 2003.[24] In addition, there was no evidence of SPAC attempting to heal itself as it hemorrhaged money. A long-range business plan did not exist, and compared to figures in 1997, when the organization's net assets were $10.6 million, the audit figures in 2004 showed a significant loss, with assets of only $4 million.[25]

Much of the ire was directed at Chesbrough, who had served as SPAC's executive director since 1978, and before the audit press conference he announced he would retire at the end of 2004 season with two years remaining on his contract. (Chesbrough passed away in 2014.) He negotiated a severance agreement for almost $400,000, and his final salary almost doubled the average of similar organizational heads across the country. His wife also served as chief fund-raiser for SPAC.[26] Later in 2005, the board appointed Marcia White, who had served as a staff aide to former Senate Republican majority leader Joseph L. Bruno, to lead SPAC.[27] Chesbrough stayed on as president, even as the Office of Parks, Recreation, and Historic Preservation called for his resignation through March 2005, months after the audit was released.[28]

The audit also noted two items that resonated with Neary and Bayly the most: "The decision to end the ballet was based on 'inaccurate and incomplete' information," and the "Board of Directors should be expanded and made more 'transparent to the public.'"[29] In response, longtime members examined the bylaws. Even with the complex nature of SPAC's private–public partnership, Neary and Bayly felt more steps could be taken to add public input to the non-profit's decision making. The board of directors had consisted of a collection of local residents of considerable means and always two members of state government. As much as Chesbrough was to blame for what they believed to be the fiscal decay of a proud organization, Neary and Bayly felt the board should also shoulder the burden of blame and make appropriate changes for the future.

The audit report served its purpose, but Neary and Bayly wanted to find more information on the essentials of the organization, and their wait was over. The audit had created boxes of what were now considered public records, so two weeks after Castro's office set the changes to SPAC in motion, on December 7, 2004, Neary filed a FOIL request to the Office of Parks, Recreation, and Historic Preservation's Office of Legal Counsel to inspect "documents or materials that have been received or accumulated as a result of the management audit from your agency of the Saratoga Performing Arts Center (SPAC)."[30] After the preliminary audit was made public on November 22, 2004, months passed before it was finalized, so the FOIL request needed to be amended, and Bayly filed another on April 17, 2005. She also requested to inspect all of SPAC's tax returns from 1993 to 2003. Both requests were granted, and during the early summer months Bayly and Neary found themselves in a windowless library in the Office of Parks, Recreation, and Historic Preservation examining more than one thousand pages of documents related to the SPAC audit.

Using the audit as a guide, the two worked backward to find more details about compensation and how board meeting documents outlined some of the financial troubles the organization faced. As the audit had found, receipts were missing for trips and expense reports, and meeting minutes were sparse at best. Neary and Bayly also closely examined minutes from the meetings in which the NYCB was canceled and Chesbrough's eight-year contract was approved. SPAC's fiscal mismanagement was largely corroborated and supported by other documents. Neary and Bayly photocopied more than six hundred pages of documents, each at twenty-five cents, per FOIL, and paid the bill. They made three copies—one for themselves, the other for the media, and the other for the records room at Saratoga Springs Public Library, where it sits to this day.

Neary and Bayly wanted to ensure that the events of the previous few years would not be repeated, which meant that stronger oversight was needed. As a result, they also wanted to run for seats on SPAC's board of directors. They believed a public representative would add a voice to a public–private relationship. Equipped with the audit and further documentation from the FOIL request that put equal responsibility on Chesbrough and the board, they went to the annual meeting on May 25, 2005, at which almost two hundred voting members (each of whom paid $275 for an annual membership, with voting privileges) unanimously approved a new seventeen-member board of directors. It was the largest member gathering in SPAC history. During comment, Neary said he had obtained 160 proxy votes to nominate a SPAC member to the board. SPAC vice chairman E. Stewart Jones, however, said that SPAC's bylaws didn't allow board members to be added by a floor motion, but such an action would be considered in the future.[31] Through 2017, it never has been.

For ten years after the changes, SPAC finished in the black, according to Form 990 documents, and White retired as president and executive director after the 2016 season, the organization's fiftieth anniversary.[32] The traditional mix of contemporary music offerings continued to complement classical music and the NYCB. In 2012, citing declining attendance and other scheduling conflicts, SPAC reduced the ballet's residency to one week. The ballet then found firmer footing, with a two-week residency through the 2016 summer season.

Both Bayly and Neary also remained SPAC members, and for fifteen years they continued to question the inner workings of a private organization operating on what they believe is the crown jewel of New York State's public-park system. Like many in the Capital Region, Neary has spent many summer nights at Saratoga Spa State Park over the past four decades. Like many summer-concert attendees, he also moved to Saratoga in retirement. However, he is still unsure of what disappoints him more—his failed bid to join the board with proxy votes or, from his perspective, not much change between the public and SPAC. "I know it's just the blue-hairs, me, and a classroom at a ballet matinee, but we lost two generations of potential arts enthusiasts because one person let an organization go. Or was it a group of people? Who do you blame?" Neary asked. "With the documents, I think they just verified what I was thinking all along, but sometimes you just want to know—and after reading the documents I left disappointed again—and mostly in people."[33]

The choice to pursue the documents through a FOIL request, he said, remains the correct one because it was his legal right and because the venue sits on public land. He has met opposition for his actions with respect to SPAC, but he still believes that the year 2004 was life changing for him because the documents provided answers that he didn't necessarily just want but also needed.

11

Watchdogs

Transparency and Civil Liberties

When Tim Hoefer first arrived at the Empire Center for Public Policy in Albany in March 2008, he began to notice a national push to make more public records available online. With a fiscally conservative public-policy think tank such as the Empire Center, he believed a void could be filled that was consistent with the nonprofit's mission. In addition to making basic state payroll and pension data available through easy-to-use online tools, he and his colleagues believed an ancillary public resource could be valuable to balance their position papers on state spending and taxes. The concept of a companion website, built specifically to drive the public to the center's work, appealed to the group. Hoefer also wanted the public records to drive something else—the conversation.[1]

At the same time, the Office of the New York State Comptroller began compiling information for Open Book New York, an online public resource for residents to track basic facets of state spending. Following the comptroller's lead, the New York State Office of the Attorney General set in motion the first steps of what is now NY OpenGovernment, which tracks campaign contributions and contracts. As a nonpartisan, private organization, the Empire Center did not coordinate its efforts with the state offices, but the timing worked. With just four staffers and two interns during the spring and summer of 2008, the Empire Center set out to collect the surface-level payroll and pension data simply because the group was hearing more anecdotally about how much state salaries have grown and about changes in the state pension system. The organization also realized a learning curve existed when people discussed the costs associated with the defined pension-benefits systems and the reasons behind salary increases.

A challenge also existed—the center could do more in collecting these data than what any government agency could do with a simple directive. Few Empire Center staffers had any experience with the Freedom of Information Law, but the statute became their driver in acquiring the records. The data-gathering process during 2008 became an educational experience for the Empire Center, and as Hoefer and his staff quickly found, the exercise also became a crash course for government agencies that had never heard of this think tank but would quickly realize it wasn't going away anytime soon.

Before filing a FOIL request, the Empire Center established an approach that would work over the next eight months with varying degrees of success. The staff began to call offices to figure out how they could get information. As Hoefer put it, they approached these offices and agencies from a "let's be friends" perspective: "I assume you want to give me this information. I'm looking for payroll information. I'm looking for names and titles. So what's the best way for me to ask for it?"[2]

The Empire Center took this approach with hundreds of entities—the comptroller, school districts, villages, towns, and counties—and most of these entities asked for a FOIL submission, but the process took time and resources, especially human capital. In 2008, the Empire Center submitted more than 1,500 FOIL requests. It FOILed every school district in the state and dozens of municipalities. At this time, Hoefer and his staff realized that "FOIL" served as a noun, verb, and adjective ("FOILable"). The mass effort began showing results, but the process also systematically uncovered other things. Once his staff began submitting FOIL requests, Hoefer said he began to see problems.

When school districts did not comply with the requests or simply did not respond, the Empire Center remained persistent and appealed. It found that another set of the more than 690 New York

State school districts didn't even know what the Empire Center was requesting or that the public could obtain these basic records. Some districts did not know they needed a FOIL officer, nor did they have an appeals point of contact. Basically, they had never before been pushed on the process.

With legal direction, the Empire Center reached out to those noncompliant districts, which were spread out across the state. There was no geographical or socioeconomic trend. There was just noncompliance, and the think tank threatened each with a lawsuit. Eventually over eight months, all but fifteen districts in that first year complied without the threat of lawsuit, providing payroll and pension data along with contracts such as superintendent and teachers unions agreements.

In the process, SeeThroughNY, a database of all New York State employees' salaries and pension benefits—among a growing list of other data sets—was born. "Internally, we felt like there had never been enough emphasis put on this. The whole basic premise behind SeeThrough was to get people access to their data, which is, really, the whole premise behind FOIL," Hoefer said. "I mean, it's your data, it's your tax dollars. You should know where they go and how they're spent. So the fact that this had been so largely ignored, it caused a real shift in our focus here. We had to work really hard just to get a school contract, so we started wondering, 'How do we fix FOIL—this legislative and practicality standard of moving forward?' The goal wasn't to become experts in FOIL; it was just to make data available. And then we realized along the way there were a lot of problems interpreting and following FOIL. So that led to a whole secondary avenue of things we did."[3]

On July 31, 2008, SeeThroughNY went live online, and within three hours traffic crashed the website.[4] Hoefer heard that the comptroller had to put a block on the site through its internal server because so many people were using it. Later, when the organization looked at the analytics, it noticed an overwhelming number of state web addresses. Through the rest of the year, dozens of media stories covered not so much the launch of the SeeThroughNY website but what the site revealed about state employees of interest, whether in local or state leadership positions.[5] Once the voyeuristic surge of the first few days waned, Hoefer said the public reaction was mixed.

He and staffers at the Empire Center spent hours of their day explaining to people why the ease of accessibility to public information, especially salary and pension data, was important to New York residents. Some state employees, paid by state tax dollars, were upset that their salaries were listed online. There was also a positive reaction from other state employees and members of the public. Beyond providing general knowledge, the data were used for everything from voting to crafting policy in the years to come. Some people didn't know they had access to these data. Others wanted to know how the Empire Center had compiled all the data. Hoefer simply told them time, perseverance, and FOIL.

The Empire Center immediately began analyzing what people were searching for when they accessed SeeThroughNY—payrolls, pensions, keywords, time they spent on certain pages. It found that, aside from curious users looking up their neighbor's salary, visitors to the site were also performing real analysis from the database. Since 2008, the process has been repeated every year, with SeeThroughNY introducing new tools so the public can access the basic data—contracts, pensions, and payrolls. The audience has also been consistent. Hoefer said the website has generated more than one million unique visitors and between seven and ten million page views annually since its launch. The focus, he added, is not on simple growth but on consistency in usage, which, he believes, is a true gauge of the public's appetite for information.

Hoefer and his staff aim for easily accessible data, knowing the government resource issue that may exist on the other end. The site has operated for almost a decade, fueled by a constant stream of updated data. Still, beyond the hundreds of mentions a year in news stories, SeeThroughNY is secondary to the nonprofit Empire Center. "As we saw the different types of people were using it a lot of different ways, we were getting both positive and negative reaction[s], but it [SeeThroughNY] was driving the conversation, and that's the whole point," Hoefer said. "If you want to have a conversation about spending or if you want to have a conversation about numbers, or if you want to have a conversation about the terms of a contract, to have that information, here it is, let us give it to you. Be informed."[6]

Even though traffic to the site serves as a telling barometer of success, access to the necessary data and certain agencies' noncompliance with requests remain problems for the Empire Center and other advocacy groups that use FOIL to support their work.

Gaps in the Process

The Empire Center remains focused on conservative fiscal policies, but the initial experience of submitting FOIL requests during the summer of 2008 allowed it to analyze systemic issues within another realm of government, issues that may have led to government inefficiencies not only in process but also in spending. The nonprofit took another approach—one that was beyond its original mission and resource capability—and devised a twofold process to ensure its FOIL requests would be filled in a timely manner every year by the same districts and municipalities across the state. The strategy was simple and, Hoefer believed, rational to generate compliance. It also served as a litmus test to see what information should be readily available. The same information easily provided by one district became a cause of consternation by another.

In the first year of the SeeThroughNY project, the Empire Center notified sixteen noncompliant districts and agencies that it had drawn up Article 78s—eight complied immediately, but the other eight did not, so the lawsuits were officially filed. First, the center filed the lawsuits to make a splash, sending a signal to agencies that the organization was serious about taking the next step. Second, Hoefer wanted to figure out what exactly the consequences were for a noncompliant agency because FOIL, he said, is ambivalent on next steps in the process. Various lawyers advised the center that there was no reason to keep going in the legal process after it received the information it requested without having to go to court. No precedent aligned with specific Empire Center cases, so the center never took the additional step of appealing for attorneys' fees.

In an organized fashion, the Empire Center keeps track of every FOIL request it submits. Once the request is in, the center counts five business days before it files an appeal if there is no compliance. The nonprofit notifies the agency or district in an appeal that it is prepared to file an Article 78 and take the entity to court. If there is still no compliance, Hoefer even calls the agency to let it know that the center will file an Article 78. He has never received a clear answer as to why the agency has not fulfilled the request, even if it is because of an exemption, or he doesn't know if agencies finally fill the request only because of the threat of a lawsuit. He estimates that in the past eight years the Empire Center has submitted only nine Article 78s. "We've never got a clear consensus whether it's malicious on their end—malicious from the standpoint of 'Are you purposely pushing me off, or do you just don't know the process of going through FOIL? Or is there just incompetence in your office that you can't hit the timelines?'" Hoefer said. "We don't know if it's the culture—or if it comes from the top—or that you push things off until you can't just push off anymore."[7]

In the first year of having to threaten school districts with lawsuits, Hoefer said the most glaring conclusion the Empire Center came to is that agencies fall into two categories: some are acclimated to the practice of ignoring FOIL requests until an Article 78 is filed, and they respond then only because noncompliance still hasn't cost them anything; and others are simply not well versed in following the law.

Because the Empire Center is a small nonprofit with an annual budget that peaked at $1.03 million (2015 reporting), Hoefer has to make choices, with the help of the board of directors and staff, to see how far the center is willing to push a FOIL-related lawsuit, knowing it may run into the same issues as anyone else—it may receive the records by judgment, but it may not be reimbursed for legal fees, and the data may no longer be timely. Since all school districts, certain agencies, and the comptroller know they will receive a FOIL request annually from the Empire Center, however, the prospect of litigation has been minimized over the past eight years.

On May 6, 2014, though, one of the center's legal battles progressed to the next step. The case set a precedent and gave the Empire Center more credibility, but it was one of many legal battles it still faces. In a 6–0 decision, the New York State Court of Appeals ruled in favor of the Empire Center and decided that the names of state and local government retirees receiving pensions are subject to public disclosure under FOIL.[8] In this decision, the court overruled the state Supreme Court Appellate Division's ruling that the New York State Teachers' Retirement System (NYSTRS) and Teachers' Retirement System of the City of New York (TRS) did not have to disclose the names of pension recipients. As a result of the Court of Appeals ruling, the data, including names and payment, were provided to the Empire Center along with attorneys' fees. Almost a year later, on April 2, 2015, a state Supreme Court in Brooklyn ordered the New York City Fire Department (NYFD) Pension Fund to release the names of its retirees and the amounts they received after the fund claimed that disclosing this information was an unwarranted invasion of privacy.[9]

Even two years later, these decisions justified the Empire Center's work, but Hoefer said that sometimes the center's work feels like nonstop litigation with various agencies, including the NYPD and the NYFD, refusing to disclose data on their pension funds. He went down the list, highlighting the compliant agencies and even applauding their diligence, and then naming the noncompliant entities that have posed a challenge for almost ten years.

The list has grown. The Empire Center filed a lawsuit against the Metropolitan Transportation Authority (MTA), which had habitually not complied in a timely manner with the nonprofit's request for the authority's payroll data. There are seven MTA entities, and Hoefer said two or three are late every year in supplying the requested information. The Empire Center filed Article 78s against those branches, New York City Transit Authority. The proceedings made it to appeals, and on the eve of oral arguments, because the Empire Center's case was strong, the sides reached terms of agreement. On August 6, 2015, the MTA wrote a check for legal fees and costs, and the action remains in public records with the courts.[10]

Other good-government organizations trying to accomplish the same feats as the Empire Center have noted these legal victories, but Hoefer remained conflicted on two fronts. He questioned why a request for public payroll records has to become a legal struggle. He also questioned variance in government transparency and fiscal responsibility from agency to agency. Hoefer explained that one of the founding principles of the SeeThroughNY project is to show government that it can on its own easily disclose the same information that the Empire Center is requesting. In 2008, no entity was posting data online. Now, with the data portal, more information is being provided by proactive disclosure. Even collective-bargaining contracts, which are not exempt by FOIL, are being made readily available by districts and unions.

Hoefer also tries to balance time and resources, given the fact that SeeThroughNY continues at considerable expense—for site maintenance, fees for FOIL requests, and technological upgrades. In the project's lifetime, the website has been updated three times to remain current and responsive in design. Hoefer said if another organization were providing the same information in a more aesthetically and complete manner than the Empire Center, he would gladly defer responsibility to that group. Overall, his goal isn't to have the comptroller, attorney general, or governor build a website that sorts and moves data the way SeeThroughNY does. Hoefer sees the project as an organizational investment. He acknowledges the high cost for government to undertake the same project. "I don't think it's the job of government to do that, to duplicate data efforts," Hoefer said. "It's the government's job to make it [the information] available."[11]

Systems and Flaws

Beyond political and geographical divisions, New York City and New York State are irreversibly linked but seem to perpetually proceed at two speeds. The same may be said of the state's open-data efforts and attempts to make the FOIL and government processes more transparent. John Kaehny is aware of the paradoxes that exist between city hall in Manhattan and the state capitol in Albany. Both continue to push open-data initiatives. Both have governing bodies that want to improve the FOIL process and preach the virtues of open government. Both have championed proposed legislation but are often stymied by process. Each also has seminal moments when leadership has advocated for FOIL improvement, but actions suggest otherwise.

Bill de Blasio ran for mayor of New York City after serving as public advocate and implemented the city's Open Data for All initiative in 2015 on the heels of his predecessor, Michael Bloomberg, signing a law in 2012 requiring all city agencies to post their public data on a central city portal by 2018.[12] In the process, the move would cut down FOIL request volume by proactive disclosure and automate the other public-record inquiries. Yet de Blasio then claimed that email exchanges from his office to outside contractors are exempt from FOIL.[13] Likewise, although New York governor Andrew Cuomo publicly pushed for more FOIL and ethics reform in Albany, he vetoed two FOIL bills in December 2015.[14]

After working as an environmental and transportation advocate for decades, Kaehny is familiar with political maneuvering in legislation. His work as executive director for the advocacy group Transportation Alternatives and later with the national group Alliance for Bicycling & Walking, allowed him to study governance and the associated complexities of systems. When he cofounded Reinvent Albany in 2010 as a good-government advocacy organization, its mission was strictly transparency, but he quickly realized that FOIL reform could be the first and strongest step in fulfilling that mission.

He also found the same systemic failures as the Empire Center and soon realized that technological advancement might prove to be a quicker and more effective solution to system-wide concerns. Soon enough, he found the central issue of these problems. "How do you make this work? That was our biggest question. One, when you look at FOIL, its glaring between policy and practice. We think that agencies are noncompliant, but by taking them to court, [we make them] lose a lot, and they spend a lot, so their behavior improves," Kaehny said. "So the carrot here is the technology in automating the practice. One of the things that happened in the last decade, the government has automated the FOIL process and made the barrier to [the] public cheaper and cheaper. The problem? It's very easy to file but not respond [to a request]."[15]

Through its transparency initiatives, Reinvent Albany has experienced varying levels of success. Its research focuses on assessment tools that have been successful in other parts of the country, and in the process its advocacy work highlights where solutions can be found first in New York City and then across the entire state. The efforts by Kaehny and a small staff, which included attorney Dominic Mauro, who helped draft the proposed New York City Open Data Law and the NYC OpenFOIL Law, also focus on parts of a transparency system that begins with public-official accountability and ends with processes that the public can understand and implement. As an advocacy group, Reinvent Albany continues to build consensus that may be best exemplified by a letter sent on behalf of seven advocacy groups in April 2015 asking New York City corporation counsel Zachary Carter to provide guidance to agencies in making FOIL responses.[16]

Kaehny also included as supporting information for Reinvent Albany's FOIL-reform initiative his testimony to the New York City Council Technology and Government Operations Committees on June 9, 2014, in support of two measures that would mandate the posting of city laws on websites in searchable form and require the City Record to be posted. These measures were not end solutions, Kaehny explained in his testimony, but early steps in showing government how difficult and in many respects how antiquated FOIL systems are in New York City. His testimony also referenced Mayor de Blasio's work when he served as the public advocate for FOIL compliance.[17] The report *Breaking Through Bureaucracy* (2013) found that 10 percent of FOIL requests to the city agencies were "lost or forgotten" and that agencies such as the NYPD had 577 outstanding requests in late 2011.[18] In a response to the report, the NYPD cited the volume of requests, which the three-month analysis highlighted in 2013: in that span, the NYPD received 1,833 requests.[19] The policies gained traction, but even four years after de Blasio changed roles from public advocate to mayor, Kaehny found himself once again returning to the concept of systems and the disconnect between theory and practice.

Even as the push for more open data tips stronger in New York City's favor, the concept of proactive disclosure resonates more with statewide agencies than with city agencies. The de Blasio administration implemented a voluntary open-records initiative, but Kaehny said voluntary compliance is still not working four years later to counter other systemic issues—the high volume of requests, archaic processes, and no order in how or when requests are filled.

All advocacy groups sing a similar refrain, but the past few years have yielded some results to complement the call for more automation to the FOIL process and tracking systems to see what is being requested of New York City agencies and the length of time between filing and fulfillment. The precursor to what is now the city's Open-RECORDS portal was created in 2013 by Code for America fellows and the City of Oakland after complaints claimed the public didn't know where their requests stood. The tracking system also serves as a submission portal—all in public view. If a request itself doesn't violate any privacy laws, the city will post it.

The OpenRECORDS website launched on March 11, 2016, almost two years after the NYC Transparency Working Group, a coalition led by Kaehny and Reinvent Albany, supported the Open-FOIL bill. Although the bill did not become law, the OpenRECORDS portal, the de Blasio administration said, was the first step in establishing proof of concept.[20] The working group wanted full transparency as in FOIA Online on the federal level, which includes the name of the requestors, the request, and the response. OpenRECORDS serves as more of a tracking tool, even noting when agencies need more time to fulfill FOIL requests.

In total, only 25 percent of the recommendations offered in the OpenFOIL bill promoted by the NYC Transparency Working Group were adopted by way of the launch of the OpenRECORDS portal. "That issue of fairness is what we want to get at," Kaehny said. "Where technology can help, human process has to change, not technology. So, really, this goes back to the politicization of the system and mainly structural issues."[21]

Understanding processes, Kaehny knows that convincing city hall is easier than convincing the state legislature, and the steps that work in the five boroughs, he hopes, may resonate across the state. To complement position papers, deeper examination of FOIL inefficiencies are highlighted in analysis of larger data sets. The approach is very much like the Empire Center's—Reinvent Albany wants to see what is available and then see what the data offer.

In its publication *Listening to FOIL: Using FOIL Logs to Guide the Publication of Open Data* (July 23, 2014), Reinvent Albany examined the New York State Department of Environmental Conservation's (DEC) FOIL log for 2013, which included 3,977 requests. It found that 80 percent of the requests were business related and that only a small portion (3 percent) was from journalists. Twelve requestors accounted for 20 percent of all requests, and about 55 percent of requests were related to spills.[22]

The most telling caveat came in the form of the disclosure that the DEC kept accurate and detailed FOIL logs. With the launch of both New York City and New York State data portals and guidance from the staffs that oversee such initiatives, more credence is given to data sets as a whole to aid in proactive disclosure and to remove inefficiencies, but the double standard—and exploitation of the law—were noted at the time. "The DEC gets these requests seeking data from three data sets—air, water, and soil contaminants. That's a huge deal when you're financing any land purchase, and that's something the people doing the financing want to know. They hire investigators to look into this and use the DEC as [a] back office, so we didn't know FOIL was such a big business tool," Kaehny said. "Like people with New York City buildings, seeking info for permits, FOIL is used for procurement. There's a lot of insight in that data and proof; there's two sides to the open-government coin."[23]

High Profile, High Stakes

The letter sent to NYPD commissioner Raymond Kelly on July 25, 2007, served as a FOIL request, but it did not read like a standard public-information inquiry for stop-and-frisk data. Instead, it read like a narrative, outlining the power struggle between the New York City Council and the NYPD, while also detailing a consistent history of noncompliance.

The request came from Chris Dunn, a longtime attorney and associate legal director for the New York Civil Liberties Union (NYCLU), eight months after the fatal shooting of Sean Bell, a Queens native who, along with three other men, was shot at fifty times by NYPD plainclothes and undercover officers the night of his bachelor party.[24] Conflicting reports from eyewitnesses and police during the trial of three detectives led to their acquittal.[25] The shooting happened on November 25, 2006. Five days later Dunn and the NYCLU wrote a letter to Kelly questioning the NYPD's failure to release several years of stop-and-frisk reports.

The heavily analyzed findings have been a point of contention for more than fifteen years since the NYPD's fatal shooting of Amadou Diallo, a twenty-three-year-old immigrant from Guinea, in 1999.[26] The NYPD eventually produced the stop-and-frisk data for the New York City Council, but only for a portion of 2006, not for all of the years requested, stating in explanation that it had hired an outside organization, the RAND Corporation, to perform an independent audit.[27]

Dunn's next FOIL request asked for more data and gave the NYPD a month to produce them. The NYPD did not, prompting another appeal letter. The NYPD did not release the data until February 2007, at the same time the independent audit was completed. The findings set off a renewed interest in racial profiling and resulted in new policies on releasing data, but the change took some time, and additional

FOIL requests from the NYCLU to the NYPD asking for race-specific data were subsequently denied until the department supplied the data when a judge ordered it to do so.[28] As a result of these struggles, the department now makes this information public via proactive disclosure, and within the past fifteen years the number of stop-and-frisks has dwindled, from a high of 658,724 in 2011 to 22,565 in 2015.[29]

The NYCLU's use of FOIL is not prolific. Dunn estimated that if the NYCLU files 12 requests a year to the NYPD, which usually receives between 10,000 and 12,000 such requests annually, that would be excessive.[30] An obstacle also exists. Even though the provision that all agencies must receive FOIL requests via email became part of the law in 2006, for more than a decade the NYPD offered only two options for filing a request—mail or fax, no electronic communication. Only a lawsuit settlement on June 29, 2017, changed this practice, and so the NYPD now accepts FOIL requests via email.[31] Besides the stop-and-frisk disclosures, the NYCLU has also filed requests for firearm-discharge data, which has resulted in a similar reluctance by the NYPD to disclose, prompting the organization to follow the same steps.[32] "Law enforcement agencies are far and away the least cooperative when it comes to FOIL—across the board," Dunn said. "It's not the number of exemptions [that are causing the problem]. Overall, I think it's the agency's approach."[33]

The law enforcement exemptions in FOIL are often interpreted differently depending on who is doing the interpretation, but public-record advocates continue to raise an issue with police agencies' use of these exemptions. Records are exempt if they

(e) are compiled for law enforcement purposes and which, if disclosed, would:

i. interfere with law enforcement investigations or judicial proceedings;

ii. deprive a person of a right to a fair trial or impartial adjudication;

iii. identify a confidential source or disclose confidential information relating to a criminal investigation; or

iv. reveal criminal investigative techniques or procedures, except routine techniques and procedures. (FOIL, sec. 87.2; see appendix A)

Not included in the FOIL exemption is a statute referred to as section 50-a, the New York Civil Rights Law, which shields the personnel records of police officers, firefighters, and corrections officers that are used to evaluate performance toward continued employment or promotion. Dunn said the NYPD invokes section 50-a regularly in denial of FOIL requests, even when the request does not include a direct reference to a personnel record. He is quick to note that section 50-a is not an exemption in FOIL but an exemption in reference, adding that the NYPD has taken a broad interpretive view of anything that relates to police action. From 2014 to 2017, COOG's annual report to the governor and the legislature has called for closer examination or full repeal of section 50-a, requesting the same level of accountability for law enforcement officials as for all other public employees.

In Dunn's time at the NYCLU, which has spanned more than twenty years through three mayoral administrations, he has not experienced appreciable differences in how leadership views FOIL. He believes that in order to achieve widespread reform and compliance, government agencies have to embrace openness. A government can have very well-written statutory schemes, he argues, but if the philosophy is one of secrecy, transparency will always be an issue. He also argues whether the issue is more administrative or societal. Ultimately, Dunn has found the same issue as other FOIL petitioners—it is as difficult to obtain public records now in the current political landscape in New York City as it was twenty years ago.

12

Data

Numbers In, Some Numbers Out

Executive Order No. 95: Using Technology to Promote Transparency, Improve Government Performance and Enhance Citizen Engagement

March 11, 2013

WHEREAS, the State possesses vast amounts of valuable information and reports on all aspects of life in New York State, including health, business, public safety, and labor data as well as information on transportation, parks, and recreation; and

WHEREAS, new information technology has dramatically changed the way people search for and expect to find information, and such technology can aggregate ever larger quantities of data and allow government to provide information to the public with increasing efficiency; and

WHEREAS, the State can use these powerful tools to enhance public access to government data and make government in New York State more transparent in order to promote public trust; and

WHEREAS, ensuring the quality and consistency of such data is essential to maintaining its value and utility.

Coulter Jones counted off the possible reasons why some of his initial public-information requests for data were not fulfilled when he began as a reporter for WNYC, the public-radio station in New York City. He then guessed it was all of the above—his lack of experience, the city's sprawling nature, and a simple lack of disclosure on the part of agencies. He arrived at this answer in 2010, and it remains the same today.

The records request that gave Jones the most trouble was for teacher-related data. He wanted to see the location and zip code of every New York City educator. Jones didn't want to know the names—just addresses—to see how salaries shift in boroughs, how commutes compare to wages, and other stories that data can tell when you have tens of thousands of rows of numbers on a spreadsheet. If the reason for a partial FOIL denial was privacy, and an agency opted to redact or not include names, Jones was fine with this. He was interested in addresses, the key to a number of data-related stories.

Jones also knew that sending a public-information request is usually a last resort. A simple phone conversation usually yields the best results in acquiring public information. An overwhelming number of journalists, attorneys, and advocates agree. If the request is denied over a conversation, the denial usually means one of two things—it is internal agency policy that a FOIL request be officially submitted in order to track the exchange of information, or there are red flags surrounding the requested information. Jones found both in his quest for teacher-related data. "I had a terrible time with every department I called with that preconversation and mixed levels of success. With the ones that both didn't require a request and did, there were delays in getting me the information. I just thought I was new on the beat, so I started questioning myself—then I didn't," said Jones, now a part of the data investigation team at the *Wall Street Journal*. "Instead of an agency saying, 'I can't answer your question until I see the request,' there was just flat denial—and for innocuous data. This, as I have found since, is standard."[1]

Since 2013, a significant push for open data has been felt on every level of government from the village to the federal level. What constitutes "open" remains debatable. As tabulation software grows in popularity to track numerical-based information, so do the number of records and the amount of information that can be found on a basic Excel spreadsheet. In terms of FOIL in New York State, most data records already exist, meaning the language in the law that states an agency does not have to create a new record is moot. With public knowledge that these data exist in electronic form, the requests can be more focused, and at the same time proactive disclosure is exercised more often—either by an agency's own accord or by legal mandate.

Perhaps 2013 can be marked as the most important year for open data in New York State. On March 11, Governor Andrew Cuomo signed Executive Order No. 95, which established a mandate for all New York government agencies to treat data and information like documents and in the process to allow public inspection through new digital tools.[2] Two months later, on May 9, President Barack Obama signed an executive order that made open and machine-readable data the new default for government information.[3] These mandates generated newfound optimism but were also met with a healthy degree of skepticism. The usual FOIL exemptions still apply in proactive disclosure—through public posting online or through a request—and, of course, not all agency data will be disclosed. For many agencies, the publicly disclosed data on their websites or through other portals are just a small portion of the data they maintain. As in the case for documents, the questions regarding digital records are: Which data are known to exist, and which data are desired but the public is unsure of their existence?

For *Politico New York* reporter Bill Mahoney, questioning what information is made readily and publicly available by a state agency and what remains in the system is a daily occurrence. He has worked in Albany in a number of capacities spanning four administrations (Pataki, Spitzer, Paterson, and Cuomo). He estimates that with the latest push for more online data, the number of records posted online by the Cuomo administration is greater than that of all his predecessors combined. Conversely, with respect to FOIL and receiving timely requests for data and records that he knows are out there, Mahoney said it seems as if the FOIL process is slower now than in past years. "The things that they choose to make public are fine; we've seen vast improvements in that with this administration," Mahoney said, "but if you wanted to FOIL Eliot Spitzer's emails, I'm sure you would have gotten something more back."[4]

The story of public access and data in New York is best told from three perspectives that are often intertwined—political posturing between the State of New York and New York City, a constant push by human and technological advancements, and the general desire for more information. The geographical division is also responsible for separate efforts to create more searchable databases, and with these initiatives come more demand and even more scrutiny. As technology continues to outpace the law, reactionary measures have outnumbered proactive steps aimed to correct or improve antiquated public policy. There are also debates related to implementing widespread system-wide initiatives instead of isolated efforts by individual agencies. Such isolated efforts lead to incomplete or outdated data, which by the time they are received by a requester are sometimes useless to him or her. This also leads to agencies taking it upon themselves to release or respond at will—and through different formats.

The New York State Department of Corrections and Community Supervision follows the same policy that the NYPD had in place until June 2017, allowing only those FOIL requests sent via FAX machine or mail. Some state agencies have internal policies to wait three months before releasing the previous quarter's data, arguing that they need time to evaluate the results. Some pdf files are just scans of scans and are not machine readable, so search functions are useless. And a database, such as campuscrime.ny.gov, is only as strong as the data from other databases that it pulls information from using an application programming interface. The campus-crime database pulls from data.gov, which culls information from federal agencies such as the US Department of Education. For example, in early 2016 the database provided only a five-year snapshot of on-campus criminal offenses, from 2009 to 2013. The incoming freshman class of 2014 may have used those data in making their decisions on which college to attend, but the data were not updated by the time that class graduated, so classes behind them did not have the same luxury of being able to examine new data. In the past, such data could be accessed only through a public-information request or an FOIA or FOIL submission. Improvements have been made in the system; however, games continue in the struggle between public acquisition and government release.

In 2006, Mahoney arrived in Albany to work for the New York Public Interest Research Group (NYPIRG), a good-government advocacy organization. His introduction to FOIL began when the group submitted requests to various state agencies to check if they were complying with two state laws—the eFOIL requirement that allowed petitioners to submit requests via email and the requirement that if an agency possesses records in electronic form, it must disclose those records and send a digital copy to a requester. (The release date was set for March 11, 2008, but on March 10 the *New York Times* broke the Spitzer prostitution story,[5] so the announcement and findings of NYPIRG's FOIL efforts were postponed and then released later.)

What appealed to Mahoney more was the state's campaign-finance system. He started to create his own databases via programs such as Access and Excel and began diving into one of the most complex— but perhaps most telling—regulatory systems in the state. Mahoney wanted to tell the stories that he found in the data, knowing that just conversations at a fund-raiser were not enough to explain the interconnected system that includes campaign finance, lobbying, and legislators. He would walk into the Alfred E. Smith Building in Albany and spend days combing through financial-disclosure statements for a project he was working on with Ben Kallos, an open-government advocate at the time (Kallos is now a New York City councilman). Mahoney sifted through 213 financial-disclosure statements, one for each member of the New York State legislature. Before this, a citizen would have needed to submit 213 different FOIL requests to gain access to each member's statement. This requirement changed in 2011 with the creation of PIRA and the establishment of JCOPE. All campaign-finance records are now in JCOPE's possession, and a FOIL request should be unnecessary.

When Mahoney began at *Politico* in November 2014, his focus remained on campaign finance. The story of money in politics only accelerated in 2010 after the US Supreme Court's Citizens United decision, which opened the fund-raising valve and allowed money to flow into state and federal coffers at an unprecedented rate.[6] As a matter of form, JCOPE posts lobbying disclosure data twice a year. Also, as a matter of form, the media and, by extension, the people of New York are notified of which companies are paying lobbyists. Mahoney also knows JCOPE keeps the data in electronic form, but the release of these data is not in real time.

JCOPE also releases a lobbying report in April, so Mahoney submits a FOIL request a few weeks after the filing deadline for companies and lobbyists. On March 11, 2016, he submitted his request for that year. On April 7, he received the data at 11:15 a.m. Three hours later JCOPE released its 327-page annual report, based entirely on the agency's analysis of the data Mahoney had requested.[7] "Clearly they had the database in a form good enough to write this report, but did they manage to write that entire report in the fifteen minutes between [when] they finalized and sent it to me, and had the commission voted to release the findings?" Mahoney asked. "Often, it's a losing battle. If it's something that I really want or if it's intentionally being denied to me, we can mount a legal challenge or write a story if this agency is blocking this particular egregious example that people may find interesting. Smaller examples like this are just laid out. It may have saved me three or four hours over a course of a month if I had this data earlier. Would that have been worth many more hours in court or force them to release? Probably not."[8]

In 2016, Mahoney was not denied the data, and JCOPE complied with state law. More media outlets and legislators are finding that delays have accelerated. In addition, the "first-in, first-out" or "order of receipt" formula is not followed for FOIL requests, especially those for large amounts of data.

When Coulter Jones was at WNYC, Mayor Michael Bloomberg pushed for more open data, especially concerning education. As a result, Jones began requesting data from all over the city, but he also found that he had to submit the same FOIL request to three or four departments just to locate the correct education information. These agencies, he knew, weren't lacking the data, but he didn't know that each agency called the data something different. Some agencies redacted information that shouldn't have been redacted. Others provided only partial data. Certain agencies gave preferential treatment to researchers who signed an agreement that they would use the data only in studies, while pushing media and public requests to the back of the line. Jones found that requests for less than ten records would generally get filled more quickly. Sometimes other data sets were released before he received the materials he requested.

There was no pattern. Without policy, Jones found, every request was only as strong as the person or department on the other end. "Any move to open data should be viewed as positive, but the data being released proactively isn't really getting at the heart of the data," Jones said. "The data is not useful by its nature and doesn't answer questions right away, like documents. We know there are stories in there, but we don't view stories based on data sets that are released by general governance. The stuff that you want is just not being released on will."[9]

Portals and Problems

Ben Wellington's TEDxNewYork Talk on November 2014 has been viewed more than one million times, mainly because, beyond the title, *How We Found the Worst Place to Park in New York City— Using Big Data*, his use of city records has gained a following. Through TEDx and his blog, *I Quant NY*, Wellington will be the first to tell you there is nothing complex about the questions he asks, which are based mostly on basic human curiosity more than on anything else. Over time, he has also found that these questions are ones that other New Yorkers—but not all—are asking. The cohort that is often remiss, Wellington said, is the government.

The two open-data efforts running parallel in New York—one in the state (Open Data: State of New York), the other in the city (NYC OpenData)—tout the growing number of publicly available data sets from their agencies. Through 2017, both offer more than 1,500 publicly available data sets, which usually have thousands rows of examinable statistics from hundreds of agencies. There is little consistency in which agencies proactively disclose or a timetable according to which data sets must be made available. There is no directive regarding which employee or agency should be contacted if a member of the public has any questions.

Basically, both open-data sites are data dumps, playgrounds for the inquisitive, and points of frustration for the growing community of data scientists and enthusiasts who understand the value and power of data while embracing the potential of what these sets can offer—solutions to large-scale problems or answers to specific questions, such as finding the fire hydrant at the center of Wellington's TEDx Talk. He is part of that community and one of the leading voices in the New York City open-data movement. Like most in the group, he questions the true meaning of "open" and government's hesitation to offer full access to all its information. Wellington is a visiting assistant professor in the City and Regional Planning Program at the Pratt Institute in Brooklyn and a quantitative analyst at the tech company Two Sigma, but his biggest public find was based on a data set that showed the highest-grossing parking ticket locations in New York City.

The highest was on the Lower East Side, part of a curb extension that was painted in a manner that suggested a parking spot but wasn't. In November 2014, Wellington showed the TEDx audience the spot on Google Street View and at the same time presented the findings on his blog. The New York City Department of Transportation responded, and in just a few weeks the spot was repainted.[10] Once Wellington had the data set in hand, he conducted a basic search and in seconds found the reason why the hydrant in that spot was responsible for $33,000 in parking tickets every year.

Two years later, Wellington was still somewhat conflicted. In his TEDx Talk and subsequent blog posts, he shared his enthusiasm about the potential of government completely disclosing all its data in a city that he refers to as one of the most open in the country. Like most in the data community, he still believes the citizens of New York are years away from such complete openness. "The hydrant story is a perfect example. The city had just redesigned all their parking signs—hired a company to come in and redesign the look and feel of all the no-parking signs and make them less confusing. If someone said to me, 'You need these to be less confusing,' what would be the first thing I would do? I would look at places where people would get tickets that shouldn't. That should be the first stop. If you did that, the very first thing you would see is the spot I found—a cursory look—is the number one spot in New York. No one ever did that," Wellington said. "Not a single person thought, 'Let's look at where people are getting confused by our signs before redesigning the entire sign system in New York.' Those kind of things is where open data can help."[11]

Wellington's work on his blog offers a cross-section of findings and follows a basic formula, starting with one large-scale question gleaned from the examination of a large-scale public data set. He presents his findings in a well-written analysis with context and sometimes includes a response from the New York City agency that produced the data. The summer of 2016 offers a snapshot of the kinds of stories Wellington has produced:

- May 11, 2016: The NYPD Was Systematically Ticketing Legally Parked Cars for Millions of Dollars a Year—Open Data Just Put an End to It
- June 30, 2016: Payer or Prayer—a Look at NYC's $650 Million Property Tax Breaks Related to Religion
- July 15, 2016: Open Data Reveals $791 Million Error in Newly Adopted NYC Budget

Some stories are witty; others leave Wellington incredulous. The titles alone offer a summary of the data, but with supporting maps and charts he presents his argument for the issue at hand and the need for more open data. His findings, though, are not based on data sets extracted through the FOIL process. After the parking ticket story, Wellington continued to test the open-data system. He wanted to work exclusively in the public-data space to see what existed and to see if the concept of "open" really applied to New York City. He wanted to see which records are offered without prompting, not through extraction by means of the FOIL process. It was only recently that Wellington began filing FOIL requests with agencies, and by his own admission he hasn't had much luck. Only then did he start to make the argument that the public must distinguish between FOIL and open data. Open data, he explained, is a push model, whereas FOIL is a pull model. The push model suffers from the concept "you only get what you want to get out of this," whereas the pull model suffers from the concept "I don't even know what to ask for, and I don't even know what's there."[12]

Wellington also discovered the paradox that exists between FOIL and the open-data mandates established in New York State and New York City in 2013, and he pointed to a thinly veiled theory tucked into the writing of such legislation that doesn't necessarily come into practice: "All data is public unless there is a reason [for them] not to be." This description fascinates Wellington, he said, because in theory that's not how the concept of open data is supposed to work. Anything that is FOILable, he argued, should be on the open-data portal because the same restrictions that apply to FOIL are built into the open-data laws. "The fact that you can get information that is not on the open-data portal points to the unsurprisingly [sic] loss of the perfect world where all data is just public because it's supposed to be," Wellington said. "And we're so far from that."[13]

Ever since the fire hydrant story, Wellington has remained on the radar of larger media outlets. His blog, written with a distinct voice but always supported by data, is now taken seriously as each new post generates media mention or the findings lead to a larger piece. On April 28, 2014, the *New York Post* extended the hydrant story—one of five news organizations to tell the tale.[14] Wellington's TEDx Talk also highlighted taxi issues and his final thought—perhaps plea—that city government "can do better."[15] Both the hydrant and the taxi anecdotes led to larger media-outlet stories. His methodology was featured in an article in the *Guardian*, a British-based publication with a global audience, that focused on the NYPD's parking ticket errors, which in turn generated a full admission by the NYPD.[16] Wellington has also been tapped by publications to offer further insight, including a *New Yorker* piece published on August 14, 2015, that explains through data why "Uber isn't causing New York City's traffic slowdown."[17]

Wellington appreciates the newfound public interest in his work. It was unexpected, but what he thought might happen across all government agencies because of this interest never fully materialized. He found that the executive branch of New York City's government, the mayor's office, has no interest in his work, but the legislative branch, the city council, does. To Wellington, this discrepancy indicates that the collective governing body considers itself an oversight body for the city, often agreeing with the popular public sentiment that open data and transparency should be synonymous. Once again, he pointed to the theory-versus-practice argument. Agencies perceive the open-data portal, Wellington said, as the minimum bar set by law. When a mandate is an executive action or a response to the release of data, then it is political. In return, Wellington said what city residents have received is the data minimum—a data dump to appease legislators.[18]

For a stretch, the *I Quant NY* blog was the largest driver of traffic to the NYC OpenData portal. No one from the de Blasio administration reached out to discuss his work, and Wellington thought that was indicative of the administration's mentality and leadership on open data. Members of the administration's data analytics team would speak at the same conferences as Wellington, and they would briefly discuss each other's work, but such discussions never occurred through proactive outreach. The promise of more open data seems to be gaining momentum, and Wellington harbors a vision of a utopian city where all agencies open all databases for public consumption. As data literacy grows and more accessible data-cutting tools are created, perhaps full disclosure will happen.

His work is sometimes more of a philosophical struggle for Wellington, who wants to hold off from filing FOIL requests to see which agencies disclose relevant information for a data community to dissect and offer solutions. He would rather see the process be organic than legislative or legal. "I felt that with the analysis I was doing, there was a value-add to an agency. It's a carrot-versus-stick thing. In order for them to say, 'Hey, look, agencies are having these new things happen when they open their data,' they need to open it," Wellington said. "Then another agency would say, 'Hey, I want my agency to get some new things, so I should open my data.' It was kind of a dream that if I get enough people interested in doing this kind of stuff, you don't do it through FOIL. Yep, take a number."[19]

He is also seeing a reverse trend on the government side. Organizations and government agencies have approached him to analyze private data, but he mostly turns down the offers, especially those from government agencies. He said as more academic institutions file FOIL requests to acquire data for research, the government gives these institutions the benefit of those findings instead of giving the responsibility to the agency. The agencies are keeping the data private, which is counterintuitive to the scientific method of building on others' findings. Wellington's response is consistent with others in the data community—please let him know when the data are public.

Part Five

More Perspective,
Looking into the Future

13

State and Fed

Different Levels, Same Issues

The unmistakable voice of Sam Waterston filled the room at Columbia University's Graduate School of Journalism, and as he did so many times as Jack McCoy on *Law & Order*, he attempts in the video being shown to put a complex situation in perspective. He isn't explaining how a crime makes its way through the New York City court system. This time he places the volume of existing federal government documents into context. "Every three seconds some government official creates a new official secret. But it takes decades before some other official decides whether we get to see it," Waterston says on the video. "There are now over twenty-eight million cubic feet of secret papers equivalent in volume to twenty-six Washington Monuments. That's more than five times more paper that's been archived from the entire history of the republic." Graphics roll across the video to illustrate the magnitude of the situation and complement the urgency in Waterston's voice. After a beat, he then punctuates his thought, further outlining the challenge facing the federal government and the tension that exists between agencies and citizens when it comes to public information in the digital age. "The production of electronic classified records is orders of magnitude greater," he says, "the digital equivalent of more than a trillion pages of classified docs every year."[1]

The choice of Waterston to promote a new FOIA project's potential is not a mistake. Even before he served as the sagacious litigator and eventual district attorney on *Law & Order* for sixteen seasons,

Waterston portrayed journalist Sydney Schanberg in the Academy Award–winning film *The Killing Fields* (Roland Joffé, 1984), which documents the Khmer Rouge genocidal regime in Cambodia. He added his time to the FOIA project and participated in the promotional video pro bono, which debuted during Columbia's FOIA@50 conference in June 2016 to usher in the golden anniversary of the law. The video touts the power of History Lab, a joint endeavor between Columbia, the Brown Institute for Media Innovation, and the MacArthur Foundation that serves as a repository for declassified documents, including some of the earliest examples of electronic records.[2] History Lab's principal investigator, Dr. Matthew Connelly, is a professor of international and global history at Columbia, and he follows Waterston's lead on the video, adding that the tools produced within a section of the project, the Declassification Engine, are efforts to capture history as data science. The project has been noted during US Department of State, Central Intelligence Agency, and the National Declassification Center briefings.

The number of offerings at History Lab is vast and connects the past seventy years of American history through the prism of FOIA. As proof of concept, there is a section entitled "America's Most Redacted," a treasure trove of documents from the Eisenhower administration. Cables and itineraries can be found with a few keystrokes, but even though these artifacts are declassified, the heavy tones of black marker still strike through words and identities. Deeper on the History Lab webpage is entry into Hillary Clinton's controversial emails, exchanged when she served as secretary of state, allowing public inspection of the communications within the gathered database. Search by name, time, and date—among other categories—and data science paints a compelling mosaic of contemporary political life, shaped by perceived secrecy and policy.

Secrecy and policy served as a recurring theme for the conference and continues today with every general matter of national and global importance. The entire three-day event at Columbia was also a reminder of how much the law has evolved and how increasingly intertwined technology, resource demands, and societal habits have

fueled public distrust of the government and the growing desire—
and need—to request more information. The issues enveloping the
federal legislation regarding access to public information are very
much the same as those found in New York State. Even though many
experts of open-government legislation across the country agree that
New York's FOIL is stronger than the FOIA, since 2007 federal agencies have taken notice because of additional statutes. All of those at
the FOIA@50 conference, on both the public and government sides
of the debate, agree that more needs to be done to address similar
problems. The reliance is now on cooperation, technology, and, as
always, people. "I would like to see a reduction in the need to make
requests. When the presidential guidelines came out in 2009, we
thought we would quickly reduce the need. We just haven't gotten to
that tipping point, hoping proactive disclosure will allow this," said
Melanie Ann Pustay, the director of the Office of Information Policy
of the US Department of Justice (DOJ). "That's not happening."[3]

As part of the OPEN Government Act of 2007, Congress created the Office of Government Information Services (OGIS), mainly
to resolve FOIA disputes between executive-branch agencies and
requesters of information.[4] The OGIS offers a form of public-records
mediation, a process that does not exist to the same extent in New
York. The question arose of where the OGIS would be housed so
that it would serve as a truly independent and apolitical office, a
discussion similar to the one in New York State in the 1970s. Congress suggested that OGIS be housed with the National Archives in
the executive branch. The George W. Bush administration changed
course, though, creating a line item in the 2008 budget under the
DOJ. The OGIS did not open its doors until September 8, 2009,
months into Obama's presidency, and it remains in the executive
branch as that branch's impartial FOIA ombudsman.[5]

As another layer, a system of checks and balances was created
in the DOJ with the Office of Information Policy, which oversees
compliance with the OPEN Government Act and the development
of guidelines for agencies. The guidelines were first outlined in a
memorandum from a recently elected Barack Obama to all heads of

executive departments and agencies, released on the first day he took office in 2009.[6] In it, he quoted Justice Louis Brandeis's noteworthy comment that "sunlight is said to be the best of disinfectants," which can be found connected to all public-information access laws, state and federal.

At the FOIA@50 conference, Office of Information Policy director Pustay pointed to a passage deeper in the memo that stresses the importance of proactive disclosure with the help of technology after each agency's backlog, the most requested public information, and other nonclassified data are evaluated. "The presumption of disclosure also means that agencies should take affirmative steps to make information public. They should not wait for specific requests from the public," Obama wrote. "All agencies should use modern technology to inform citizens about what is known and done by their Government. Disclosure should be timely."[7] A few months later, US attorney general Eric Holder released guidelines on how proactive disclosure should be implemented.[8] Even seven years later, Pustay and officers in the one hundred agencies in the executive branch have found what public-information officers on the state, county, town, and village levels encounter—the more information released by enhanced digital means, the more information people want.

In measuring FOIA success under the Obama administration, there are matters of perception. In December 2015, the Freedom of the Press Foundation sued the DOJ after its requests for documents from the DOJ went unanswered for more than a year.[9] The documents were eventually handed over and outlined how administration officials had made an effort to redirect the FOIA Oversight and Implementation Act of 2014, which received unanimous support in the House of Representatives by a vote of 410–0.[10] The documents show the administration's opposition to the bill, specifically its concerns that the bill would create an even larger FOIA backlog and budget issues and that managing a universal online portal for requests would be difficult. As the bill reached the Senate, it focused on the redundancies in the exemptions, which includes Exemption 5 (or B5), an arbitrary judgment commonly referred to as the "withhold it because you want to exemption."[11] The bill was strengthened, but when it was passed back to the House of Representatives in December 2014, Speaker of the House John Boehner did not raise it for a final vote, which prompted the Freedom of the Press Foundation's FOIA request for the DOJ documents.[12]

A *Vice News* story published on March 9, 2016, further detailed the fallout from the Freedom of the Press Foundation request, just days before the beginning of Sunshine Week, which trumpets the concept of open government.[13] The account also detailed the DOJ's contentious relationships with OGIS, the agency under the executive branch that creates open-data policy for agencies. Then, a week after the disclosure, the Associated Press released its annual report on FOIA compliance within the one hundred agencies in the executive branch, based on data that can also be found at FOIA.gov, the government's public record keeping of requests. The administration stated that 93 percent of FOIA requests were at least partially fulfilled in 2015, indicating that information that doesn't fall under exemption is open for public inspection.[14] However, 77 percent of the FOIA requests were rejected or only partially fulfilled, a 12 percent increase since 2009.[15]

At FOIA@50, Pustay said that the public must consider that consistent with the number of fulfilled, rejected, or partially fulfilled requests, the number of overall requests has risen every year. Assessments of the number of fulfilled, rejected, or partially fulfilled requests were taken during March 2016 as a different version of the FOIA Oversight and Implementation bill made its way through the House and Senate, landing on President Obama's desk three months later, in June. The White House signed the bill just weeks before FOIA's official fiftieth anniversary.[16] In the amended bill, more power was granted to OGIS to serve as an independent office—still a point of contention between FOIA advocates and detractors for political reasons—and the Office of Management and Budget must create a single portal so FOIA requesters can file and track online. More importantly, Exemption 5 received an overhaul, stipulating now that "government agencies can only withhold records pertaining to internal deliberations for twenty-five years."[17] In the original FOIA, these records and documents related to attorney–client privilege were exempt.

In the shadow of the improved legislation, attendees of the FOIA@50 conference at Columbia continued to welcome debate about the exercise and abuse of privacy and power—none more so than the members of a panel scheduled to discuss the current state of public-records laws on the federal and state levels. COOG executive director Bob Freeman was joined by Miriam Nisbet, the founding director of OGIS; Frederick Sadler, the former FOIA officer and the senior official at the US Food and Drug Administration (FDA); and William Holzerland, the director of information disclosure at the FDA, a position similar to one Sadler once held. (Within a year after the conference, Holzerland became FEMA's senior director of information management.)

The panel discussion laid out the overlapping concerns on the state and federal levels but quickly shifted to specific information desired by smaller communities, both geographical and subject matter. The shift wasn't unexpected, given the panel's composition, and there was acknowledgement of FOIA and FOIL working best when applied to the smallest government factions. What was unexpected was the healthy debate that ensued about the current nature of power held by a chosen few in a governmental landscape that is decidedly much larger than what existed in the 1960s and 1970s, when FOI laws were first implemented. This debate especially concerned issues raised by a request for perceived sensitive information received at the bottom and delivered to the top by order. "I don't think the federal government cares very much," Freeman said. "I think in Washington maybe too many people lost track of where we ought to be." He cited Wikileaks and the admission in declassified documents that weapons were being produced in Iran. Freeman also questioned the interpretation of FOIA by the federal courts, stating that the phrase "unwarranted invasion of personal privacy" (sec. (a)(2)(A); see appendix B) in the law, pointing to the identification of somebody by name, is not simply verbiage because heavy redaction has become commonplace in documents requested under both FOIL and FOIA.[18]

Before the conversation moved on, Nisbet, the first director of OGIS, politely asked moderator Nicholas Lemann, dean emeritus at the Columbia University Graduate School of Journalism, if she could respond to Freeman. "I disagree with you, Bob, completely, about people not caring," Nisbet stated. "From my experience, which is about twenty-five years in the federal government, people who do hold these jobs really do care, and in some instances you have some leadership in the agencies that consider this to be very much 'do it if you can' and 'whatever money we can find.'" She continued without assigning further blame. "Mainly because there is a spotlight on open government and transparency, people who are entrusted, they're frustrated, and the requesters are frustrated. There's hostility, and that's where we are changing the mode of operation." Freeman nodded and added one more thought. "What we see is a great deal of control maintained by executives at the top—mayors, governors. Sometimes it's too late, it's wrong, it's political."[19]

For the next hour or so, the intense discussion continued. At times, it was difficult to discern whether the panel was discussing state or federal issues regarding public information. The anecdotes may have been different, but it was apparent that the same obstacles exist on both levels.

A Million-Dollar Inquiry

Of the more than 4.6 million FOIA requests the US executive branch received from 2009 to 2015, 1.4 million were directed to the Department of Homeland Security (DHS), according to FOIA.gov, the federal online public-records-tracking database. Most of these requests are of a personal nature (e.g., privacy or personnel records). For some other agencies, such as the FDA, the intent is entirely different. The panel discussing public-records laws at FOIA@50 offered insight into how agencies approach FOIA requests—and the difficulty in fulfilling some—and how one agency handles the transition of requests from one FOIA officer to another. It was also a rare opportunity to listen to two FOIA officers speak in very different measures—one retired and off the cuff, the other steeped in process.

When Sadler retired as FOIA officer at the FDA, he left a very different public-records landscape than the one he first entered decades earlier. Digital advancement and the edict from above regarding proactive disclosure forced him to adjust, but requesters' intent has not changed. The agency is also buried in bureaucratic layers, creating a logistics nightmare in both disclosing the requested information that is nonexempt and redacting information that should not be disclosed.

The reason is simple: each request to the FDA holds a financial—and sometimes medical—stake. Sadler estimated that of the FOIA requests to the FDA, 85 percent have commercial interests, or what he refers to as either "industrial espionage" or "information on competitors" or, more bluntly, "students who want us to do their term papers."[20] The remaining requests come from people in the food or medical fields, journalists (6 percent), and individuals working with trade publications. Given the commercial interest associated with any FDA matter, from 2010 to 2016 the agency on average received 9,793 requests annually but at the same time continued to try to clear a backlog, thus fulfilling 10,168 requests every year, according to data from FOIA.gov. The requested records range from one page to hundreds of thousands pages. (As a matter of form, the DOJ, during an annual FOIA audit, asks each agency to clear its ten oldest requests.) Sadler knew that the FDA's review of an application could cost thousands of dollars, but the result of a commercial entity's FOIA request could be worth millions.

Holzerland offered an additional perspective, which also could explain the difference in the majority of requests to either state or federal agencies. "When you're talking about records, you have to think of two buckets—input and output," Holzerland said. "The users [of documents from the FDA] are curious about output, such as medical and patient devices. With other requests [to other agencies], it's about the input, the sausage making, how decisions were arrived at. Their goals are different."[21]

A disconnect also exists at the federal level, as at the state level, between requesters, the timing of requests, and expectations. At the conference, Sadler offered an example that outlines how demand, the law, and the expectations of technology have reached a troubling crossroads. Sadler said he had 134 people working for him at the FDA, stretched across a number of continents. For one request, he may have to consult an expert on the West Coast, or for another he may need a colleague who is performing field operations in India because of the rise of generic drug production there. Or he may have to consult an oncologist on a cancer-related matter. He refers to these colleagues as "subject-matter experts." In order for one of his staff to accurately and carefully fulfill an FOIA request, that person needs at least a year of training, and turnover is sometimes high.

The process at the FDA follows a similar pattern: On day one, his office receives a request. On day twenty-one, the day after the deadline by which his office must legally comply and offer a response to the requester, the FDA may be sued, with Sadler named as the respondent, because the requester did not obtain the records.

Sadler cited two instances when his office wasn't able to supply the requested information on time, the first involving a cardiac pacemaker that failed. Three different FOIA requests arrived on the same day, each asking for twenty-one thousand pages of research documents on the pacemaker. On day twenty-one, by which point the requests had not been fulfilled because of the volume of documents requested, all three requesters sued. On another occasion, a corporate entity requested 1.4 million records on a potential link between autism and pediatric vaccines. The request included both digital records and hard copies, all peppered with heavy medical and scientific jargon. Sadler asked the petitioner to modify the request. The petitioner did not do so and subsequently sued the FDA when it did not meet the mandated deadline. When the agency went to court, the judge asked the requester to modify again, citing the issue of considerable patient-privacy data within the records. The company cut the request by 75 percent, and the FDA complied.

OGIS favors mediation over litigation, but not all citizens are willing to compromise. Also, at times a unique tension grows between requestor, agency, and the interpretation of the law, causing further disagreement about disclosure. Some agencies have developed their own internal practices for disclosure, and Holzerland's previous experience at DHS is an example. He once served as the associate director for disclosure policy at DHS, and in 2009, after Obama and Holder's guidelines were distributed, he said that DHS's policy of heavy redaction "does not square" with the directives. He made this statement in response to an overly redacted email—a product of DHS new standards—that was censored as part of an Associated Press FOIA request in 2009. He was blunt but concise in the email the Associated Press acquired: "This is bananas!"[22] This email was also referenced during a hearing by the US House Committee on Oversight and Government Reform. As one of Holzerland's superior's spoke, committee chairman Darrell Issa (R–CA) flipped to the quote and displayed it on the big screen to underscore the point. "Common sense should usually win. Is it going to put national security at risk? Not all the time," Holzerland commented at the FOIA@50 conference. "But the requester has to be realistic. The human touch works, so call us. What do you need? Sometimes those people are taken aback when we ask for additional contact info, and they ask why. Some documents are just that, paper documents. So you have old school, and then there is Old Testament. We may have to drop them in the mail, so technology hasn't solved everything—yet."[23]

An Agency Snapshot: Homeland Security

Holzerland's former employer, DHS, remains the federal agency that receives the most FOIA requests annually. The year-over-year snapshot based on DOJ data shown in table 1 places the volume of requests in perspective.

Table 1

Number of FOIA Requests Submitted to the US Department
of Homeland Security

Year	Pending as of Start of Fiscal Year (FY)	Received in FY	Processed in FY	Pending as of End of FY
2015 total	117,034	281,138	348,878	49,294
2014 total	67,097	291,242	238,031	120,308
2013 total	38,474	231,534	204,332	65,676
2012 total	51,143	190,589	205,895	35,837
2011 total	18,468	175,656	145,631	48,493
2010 total	27,188	130,098	138,651	18,635
2009 total	84,096	103,093	160,007	27,182
2008 total	83,819	108,952	109,028	83,743

Source: FOIA.org.

A few statistical observations can be made of the FOIA requests
received at DHS (based on the numbers given in table 1):

- There was a 47.5 percent increase in submissions from 2012 to
2015 (190,589 to 281,138).
- There was an overall process increase in requests (46.56 percent) from 2014 to 2015.
- There was an overall rise in clearing requests: pending inquiries
dropped more than 59 percent from 2014 to 2015.

Appeals

With denial of a request comes the appeal process, which prompts
further questions from agency to agency within DHS. For instance:

- Since 2011, the number of appeals received by the US Citizen
and Immigration Services has grown each fiscal year (from
1,180 in 2011 to 1,987 in 2015, a 68.3 percent rise).

- The Customs and Border Protection appeals rose from 346 in 2013 to 1,735 in 2015, a 401 percent increase.
- Introduced in 2011, US Immigration and Customs Enforcement appeals more than doubled from 288 in 2012 to 599 in 2015.[24]

If future FOIA-related legislation winds through Congress, Sadler suggested that lawmakers consider amending the law regarding the requirement to route personal inquiries through DHS. Some individual requesters are simply asking for their own immigration records. The DOJ has a number of tracking mechanisms in place to assess quality control, and initial hypotheses about immigration requests have proven true. With 30 percent of all FOIA requests to the executive branch running through DHS, according to the website FOIA.gov, bottlenecks have increased, reshuffling federal resources to one agency and diluting resources to other agencies.

Also, in an effort to avoid litigation, Pustay said, the DOJ instructs agencies to develop a tracking log, and she went as far as to say that they should "assume [each] request will go to litigation."[25] Agency logs exist for all requests, follow-up, and interaction with the requester. If the request does go to litigation, the log will serve as documentation. Currently, there is no digital tracking log in New York State.

In an effort to streamline processes called for by the new legislation, the government has created FOIA.gov, so that requested data are made public, but it has also created the FOIA Online website, which shows tracking of each bill. However, because it is not a federal mandate, the operation is disjointed, with only some agencies providing information. Pustay also relies on the common academic and government maxim that all agencies should be brought onboard to the same level: in theory, the system should work; in practice, it's not so easy.

Exemptions

Through 2016, there were fourteen possible exemptions under FOIA. The most extensive, Exemption 7, which has six parts, focuses on law enforcement. Since 2010, a few patterns in applying exemptions have existed from year to year, but overall such application varies from agency to agency, including DHS. According to FOIA.gov, the most widely used exemptions within DHS from 2008 to 2015 were:

Exemption 2 exempts from mandatory disclosure records that are "related solely to the internal personnel rules and practices of an agency." (See appendix B for the text of these exemptions.)

Overall, this exemption was used 17,807 times in 2011, but the number dropped to 480 in 2012. Then its use more than doubled from 2014 to 2015, from 325 times to 822 a year later.

Exemption 6 protects information about individuals in "personnel and medical files and similar files" when the disclosure of such information "would constitute a clearly unwarranted invasion of personal privacy."

From 2014 to 2015, the use of this exemption increased from 89,953 to 178,929 times.

Exemption 7 of the FOIA, as amended, protects from disclosure "records or information compiled for law enforcement purposes, but only to the extent that the production of such law enforcement records or information: . . . (C) could reasonably be expected to constitute an unwarranted invasion of personal privacy."

From 2014 to 2015, the use of exemption (C) jumped from 108,259 to 193,239 times, and the use of exemption (E) jumped from 108,398 times to 193,826 times.

(E) would disclose techniques and procedures for law enforcement investigations or prosecutions, or would disclose guidelines for law enforcement investigations or prosecutions if such disclosure could reasonably be expected to risk circumvention of the law.

"There is no correlation between the number of exemptions that you use and the volume of material that is withheld," Pustay stated at the conference, "and we've been really focusing on partial releases of information, which means multiple exemptions being cited within a request." Her last thought is consistent with a prevailing public concern and government refrain: "It's important to protect personal privacy."[26]

Technology

As the second day of the FOIA@50 conference drew to a close, the audience continued to raise questions about government accuracy, efficiency, and privacy. All the questions were asked within the context of technology, with most of them focused on automation, electronic redaction, and exemptions that can be deciphered by artificial intelligence based on prior case law.

Both Sadler and Holzerland, speaking from their experience at the FDA, told the audience that as technology companies develop new software, either the FDA or another agency in the executive branch would be more than willing to test it. As of now, the technology that both the government and public desire simply does not exist. "I can set the program to redact Fred's name or any combination with a Maryland address with an employee of the federal government with cancer treatment, and it won't catch everything. There will still be three hundred people who would know it was me," Sadler offered as an example. "It is contextual in order to make the determination."[27]

Other problems include how one law directly affects another and how there is little recognition of a law's future widespread impact upon passage. Section 508 of the Rehabilitation Act of 1973 (29 U.S.C. §794d) requires the federal government to ensure that the electronic and information technology that it develops, procures, maintains, or uses is accessible to persons with disabilities. Sadler was quick to point out at the conference that it is against the law to put any item on a government website that cannot be enabled by a voice synthesizer. In New York State, advisory opinions rendered by COOG since 1993 can be found online. On the federal level, with additional photos and other visual items, the FDA and other agencies can either make a choice—devote resources to complying with the law or find a technology vendor who has developed the technology. Sadler estimated that 20 percent more requested documents would be posted online if this technology were to exist, and in the process the number of requests and responses necessary would decrease.

The tension that exists between the requester and the agency remains cemented in the fact that technology is moving substantially faster than government—or, perhaps more accurately, than legislation. As budgets remain stagnant for federal agencies, the sliver devoted to research and development to expedite the FOIA process to please the public while complying with the law is almost nonexistent. Sadler, still speaking openly, also said that what the government can pay vendors for their software is much lower than what is needed to develop software that can perform the necessary functions correctly and legally in redacting and judging whether to fulfill the request. The technology vendor's product would generate more revenue on the open market. Private enterprises also continue to recognize the value of public information, creating an even greater demand to capitalize on opportunity. Nisbet noted the increase in the number of businesses asking for more data, but in the same breath she mentioned the innovative approaches companies are taking in fields such as health, transportation, and finance, three areas central to American life regionally and nationally in the first two decades of the twenty-first century.

As technology accomplishes more, expectations change. Sometimes the product being presented to the government was born out of an initial FOIA request to identify a problem, and in return companies have created products for greater market consumption. This process unlocked by public-records requests—from inquiry to acquisition to viable end product—is not lost on government officials, and the panel at FOIA@50 was in universal agreement that the steps taken so far are only the beginning of realizing the greater fiscal and societal potential of compiling public data. Finding a common ground between the public and government, systemically and legally, remains more difficult to envision.

14

Transparency

Defining the Future of "Open"

Perhaps Dan Melton did all he could not to interrupt the speakers at the Personal Democracy Forum workshop on open government held in 2014, but more than an hour into the session he offered a rare clarification from the perspective of a technology vendor. It was not in defense of the client but an explanation to a room of transparency advocates and, to a larger extent, to the people of New York City.

Melton, who at the time served as deputy chief technology officer of the digital company Granicus, stood up during a discussion featuring Manhattan Borough president Gale A. Brewer and New York City council member Ben Kallos. He told the audience that he represented the technology vendor that Kallos repeatedly blamed for impeding progress because the city was stuck in contracts with large vendors for what Kallos considered limited software for enhanced citizen engagement, public-meeting efficiency, and records management. Granicus offers the Legistar platform as the digital engine that powers New York City government, and cities as large as Chicago and as small as Ann Arbor use the product. Kallos did his best to explain the limitations of the platform and his desire for an application programming interface (API), a tool used to build additional software or programs based on the API developer's original code—essentially building blocks needed for communication, which, more importantly, would open data to a larger, undefined audience.[1]

Melton outlined the central issue for New York City, which to other cities and clients never was a problem. "We actually have the ability for notifications by keyword, RSS [really simple syndication], and various other feeds currently available to all clients at Granicus that use Legistar. New York asked us to turn it off over ten years ago. We can turn it on in five seconds, and everyone here will have access to that, and many other cities already do that," Melton said. "We just need the clerk of NYC to ask for that, and we'd be happy to do that." Melton explained that the Legistar system was developed in 1999 behind a firewall to prevent access to updates that would allow APIs and cloud-based applications.[2] It was an admission Kallos most likely did not expect. The system and thinking, among other things, were outdated. Melton further explained that his company is not a closed vendor, and an objective has always been to give data to citizens.

In the years since the exchange, the Personal Democracy Forum has gained traction, and web developers across New York City and the country have built thousands of digital tools from APIs that offer a trove of government information and data, which are then used to solve civic problems by presenting information in user-friendly ways. Some APIs are better built than others, and these efforts have not gone unnoticed by municipalities that once treated technology and digital communication as an afterthought. For most large American cities, these digital initiatives are now priorities. The give-and-take between Kallos and Melton also underscored the issues that exist between tech-savvy legislators and veteran governing bodies with different definitions of government transparency. In the mixing of a culture of openness with defiance, a tension has built for decades. What has changed, though, is the technology, which presumably tips the scales in favor of advocates.

The accessibility to open data and information has reached an inflection point, and digital advancement has given new strength to New York's Freedom of Information Law, but at what level remains debatable. Technology has enabled citizens and government to move at a much faster speed, but the culture within many large, bureaucratic institutions changes at a much different pace. "An elected official's job is to get reelected. Any legislation that undermines their chances of winning may cause a legislator to pause if information coming to light reflects poorly upon them," said Kallos, who began serving his first term representing New York's 5th District on Manhattan's Upper East Side in 2014. "They ask, 'Will transparency help or hurt me in my career?' If folks move to a default of open, this doesn't happen."[3]

Even though that moment at the Personal Democracy Forum 2014 was viewed as a positive step, Kallos still wasn't satisfied with the degree of access citizens have through Legistar or the capability allowed by the city. In the months after the forum, one of Kallos's former constituents from his district moved to San Francisco and told Kallos about a city supervisor named Mark Farrell who had similar ideas. Farrell had also met the same level of resistance from public agencies and lawmakers when he advocated for the release of more information to citizens. As Kallos retold the story, he reached out to Farrell to compare notes, and the two found identical challenges.

The biggest problem, Kallos explained, was what he refers to as "inertia." "No one gets fired from their job which they've done the same way for fifty years, but people can get fired when doing something new."[4] Kallos and Farrell's ultimate goal is to improve how citizens can access, produce, and maintain public information—basically everything that is considered a public record under New York State's FOIL. But they don't want to focus on just one state. They established the Free Law Founders, a coalition of technologists, clerks, and lawmakers created to find solutions and best practices for opening all public information in states that face similar challenges to doing just that.[5] The members of the group are diverse in age, geography, race, and gender. The coalition's objective is also to leverage market power, and most of its members govern or work in technologically progressive hubs—New York, Chicago, and San Francisco. The thinking, according to Kallos, is part of an older business model: approaching a vendor and upselling to make more money to underline the profit motive and in the process make more money. Instead of money, though, the focus is data.

Kallos and Farrell wanted to bring like-minded thinkers into the same room, and through 2017 twenty-eight individuals were part of this nationwide coalition. They also believe in competition and detest nonprofits that identify the same problem they do but that fail to get on the same page. If there were one set of data that all within a certain sector could use and access, Kallos argued, would this create stronger government efficiencies? "I'm OK with open-source projects, but that means we have to set some open standards, compare documents, and build one system for everyone," Kallos said. "And I know that takes time—that's why an API is important. You don't have to go to one site. It's the same API pulling for all agencies, feeding one system for the public."[6]

Kallos's view of open data working in conjunction with FOIL was formed a decade ago when he was statewide coordination committee chair for the New York Democratic Lawyers Council, and it continued to develop when he served as chief of staff for New York State assemblyman Jonathan Bing. In 2007, he noticed the state party had a list of twelve million voters, but the party then received a file from New York State officials listing only ten million.[7] The state's database, built primarily on a spreadsheet, was "flat and ugly," and Kallos wanted to understand the two-million voter discrepancy, which is sometimes referred to as a "voter purge," a concept that was seen on the federal level in 2008 in connection with Barack Obama and in 2016 with Vermont senator Bernie Sanders, who ran in the Democratic presidential primary.[8] Then Kallos taught himself MySQL, an open-source data-management computer program, and other tools to make sense of the issue, which Kallos eventually did.

Two years later, in 2009, as Bing's chief of staff, Kallos realized voting records for the state Senate and Assembly were not online and that there was no public legislative retrieval system. He filed a FOIL request for legislative documents, and the clerk said the legislature was not subject to FOIL when Kallos asked for an enumerated list of items. He looked at the exemption but argued that voting records were not a specifically enumerated list, so he received the information. Then he wanted to explore outside income for each legislator, so he filed another FOIL request. After resistance, Kallos received the records. These items were now officially public and had begun appearing on various government watchdog websites.[9]

As a result of proactive disclosure, both voting records and outside income are now commonly found on sites that don't require the use of FOIL. Most sites are powered by APIs provided by state agencies—and produced by the same practices—and are becoming some of the most commonly used databases of information on the state and city levels. This standard was not set immediately after Kallos's initial inquiry. Mostly because of Governor Cuomo's Executive Order No. 95 (2013), the state agencies, not New York City or other municipalities, are required to upload these data. Kallos did not overlook this change. Now he is on the inside as a lawmaker, and the challenge is not technology but rather convincing his fellow councilmembers to see the potential of open data. "Most change in government takes five years at a minimum, which is a sad reality, and it opens up the opportunity to let the private [sector] leave the public sector in the dust on a lot of things," Kallos said. "I wouldn't underestimate a legislator to learn and engage on a topic that is important to them; however, the topic of government and transparency after a good day's work isn't particularly popular right now."[10]

Systems

Just as state and federal agencies are a delicate and interwoven complexity, so is the law that the same agencies are required to comply with but only occasionally do. The larger question exists whether the issue with compliance emanates from the bottom, local government, or from the cultural approaches to both FOIL and FOIA at the highest level of government power.

For David Sobel, senior counsel at the Electronic Frontier Foundation (EFF), the problems with compliance with public-records laws have only become worse since the Ronald Reagan era, when Sobel first began leaning on government to disclose more information in the public interest. Then he served as co-counsel in the challenge to government secrecy concerning detentions after September 11, 2001, and now his efforts with EFF focus on government surveillance. According to Sobel, the connection between the public and government with respect to public records is symbiotic—the two diverse organisms live together, but the relationship is not necessarily beneficial to both. Over three decades, Sobel explained, there hasn't been much change in how government perceives and responds to any public-records request. He believes that a bureaucratic mindset exists that is philosophically opposed to the level of transparency desired by those who file inquiries.

Sobel continued to dissect the issue's core—there are systemic and substantial legal obstacles to complete transparency. In the course of his more than thirty years of both filing and litigating requests, he didn't see that much progress in improving either system. The most basic obstacle encountered at every level of government affects requestors across the board, whether the average citizen or a journalist who is more sophisticated in submitting requests or a public-interest group that has the legal resources to challenge any unfulfilled query or appeal.

The biggest system issue, Sobel explained, is the delay any requester encounters. "I've almost never seen a response in twenty days [the time allowed by law either to acknowledge the record exists or deny a request for information]. I've seen twenty weeks or twenty months more frequently than I see twenty days," Sobel said. "That's a problem that's been consistent. If that's fixed, things change, but I'm not confident. How do you change that culture that has been built up and passed on for decades?"[11]

EFF deals with the substantial legal obstacles that Sobel described. The same privacy that lawmakers use as shields against public-records requests is sometimes different than the privacy EFF is concerned with as a nonprofit that defends civil liberties and as part of its mission statement—"to ensure that rights and freedoms are enhanced and protected as our use of technology grows." Although EFF advocates for matters involving file sharing, encryption, and open-source software, it also has the resources to outlast government's delay in fulfilling requests. From anonymity to the Digital Millennium Copyright Act (DMCA) of 1998, EFF is in position to litigate but recognizes the same inefficiencies felt on all levels of government—some of which have played a central role in some New York State FOIL requests, specifically the matter of email retention and privacy laws.

EFF's white paper *Who Has Your Back? 2015: Protecting Your Data from Government Requests* outlines antiquated policies, such as the Electronic Communications Privacy Act of 1986. It discusses the issue of email retention ("acknowledge that email stored more than six months deserves identical protections to email stored less than six months") and digital communication ("Congress is even on the precipice of making things far worse, considering proposals that would mandate government backdoors into the technology we rely on to digitally communicate").[12]

The paper focuses on federal legislation, but local and state governments interpret matters differently, especially with respect to FOIL requests for digital communication inside and outside a state agency. Sobel outlined the deficiencies facing federal agencies, but he very well could have been describing issues in New York State. Federal agencies don't have enough resources to keep pace with and fulfill FOIA requests in a timely manner, but, then again, he argued, they don't seek additional resources. FOIA is not a specific line item in an agency budget, but no study has ever been conducted on any budgetary aspect of FOIA. Never has an agency approached Congress publicly to request additional FOIA support. Congress also proposes new FOIA requirements, but it doesn't provide additional money for support.

A good example can be found in the aftermath of the terrorist attacks on September 11, 2001, and the legal powers granted by the USA PATRIOT Act of 2001. Although governing bodies were quick to implement new legislation, there was little concern about the resources that would be needed to satisfy both the rise in requests for information as well as the government and the public interest, so that more than fifteen years after the attacks a volatile and costly mix of requests, litigation, and government involvement still exists. As Sobel explained, quite a bit of FOIA litigation is devoted to privacy matters particular to sections of the PATRIOT Act. The EFF and other privacy advocates believe that heightened public interest is countered by an increased sensitivity on part of the courts when parties litigate. The courts then argue that what is requested would impede antiterrorism efforts and affect both sides of the equation—government and the public—but the EFF counters that this information is in the public interest, especially when the government is exercising its enhanced power.

In the end, because of the sensitivity of holding what is perceived as public information, the courts, Sobel explained, are willing to side with the agency. He doesn't expect much to change, perhaps only if there are system-wide mandates. "With the caveat that we're speaking at the federal level, it's hard to assess. I don't know if there's been a lot of meaningful change in respect to the recent legislation; nothing that is groundbreaking," Sobel said. "I have to take a long view, and I know you can hope for change, but I know everyone is not in position to the same extent to take as much time as we do to fight something."[13]

Sunlight and Shadows

In terms of processes and transparency on the state level, the institutional scorecard generated by the Sunlight Foundation, a nonprofit that advocates the use of technology for greater government accountability and transparency, has become a destination to gauge how open state governments are each year. There is some hint of bias, but the methodology is sound, and the assessment baselines are consistent. In just four years, some states have improved public-information laws and systems either through executive mandate or small amendments that strengthen the original law. In the Sunlight Foundation scorecard for 2016, New York and ten other states received an A, but New England states such as Maine and Rhode Island received a D. Massachusetts—which passed a series of open-government measures

during its legislative session for 2016, some of which include language reminiscent of New York's provisions—is one of four states
that received an F, along with Nebraska, Alabama, and Kentucky.

The states were evaluated based on Sunlight's Ten Principles for
Opening Up Government Information, which include timeliness,
record costs, and ease of physical or electronic access.[14] Even with
mounting concern about the effectiveness of New York's FOIL, public-information advocates can interpret the findings in one of two
ways—New York is progressive in disclosure, or a large faction of
state governments have transparency problems. "States are much
more complicated than large cities, and there are varying degrees
of autonomy that's enjoyed by individual departments with data-
release possibilities," said Emily Shaw, a former senior analyst at
the Sunlight Foundation and now a senior implementation adviser at
Johns Hopkins University's GovEx center. "We're really focused on
answering the question of how do you bring states into this system
of full data publication. Cities are increasingly moving toward more
proactive disclosure, and larger cities with tech-savvy populations
are looking to put as much government online as they can—but we
know there are challenges."[15]

Similar to Kallos's mission to provide a universal API for city and
state government, up until the end of 2016 the Sunlight Foundation
offered an example of how effective an open-data policy has become
on all levels of government. Its Tools and Projects section described
large-scale projects on everything from congressional spending to an
expansive political spending database that allows users to examine
the flow of money through lawmaking levels of the federal government. Seven projects offered APIs, and the response quantitatively
and qualitatively illustrated the reach and influence of an organization's opening of public information. Through 2016, more than
twenty-eight thousand API keys used by other organizations to pull
Sunlight's data produced more than 1.35 million daily API calls.
When the foundation shuttered Sunlight Labs, its major projects
were taken on by other organizations such as *ProPublica* and the
Center for Responsive Politics.

Shaw described the organizational acknowledgment that public-information advocates see across respective states.[16] Sunlight's push for more open data on the state level was a new objective that focused on education within agencies in an effort to convince local government there is more promise than problems with opening data. Shaw recognized the issues within large, bureaucratic institutions with thousands of agencies, much like New York State and New York City. There are imbalances within some data portals because agencies that are more receptive to posting data online—and in a more immediate manner—are disclosing more information for public inspection that may not necessarily be useful for an entire citizenry. There are also significant pushes for real-time data because some agencies have disclosed only information that is now outdated by a year or two. Shaw's argument is that some agencies may be missing opportunities for economic development, and others may be limiting their potential for improved safety measures and increased transparency, both of which are public-perception issues. When discussing cities, Shaw used Seattle as an example, which publicly presents an almost real-time police-generated crime map.

Shaw said the law enforcement area of public data remains the most controversial, especially with respect to public-information laws, given privacy concerns. "We know there are large numbers of data holders that have been exempt as a whole, and some aspects of government are getting a total pass, along with government services that are contracted out that don't get included," Shaw said. "These are big missing pieces. Does this mean nobody pays attention, and people don't get scrutinized? It removes some aspects of government functions. That's not good."[17]

Sunlight's strategy also included advocating for more proactive disclosure that would not be deemed, as Shaw put it, "inherently controversial,"[18] especially with any form of electronic communication that may prove costly to review and redact for both a petitioner and the government. As Shaw explained, the strategy pushes the concept of transparency forward in a wide but shallow as opposed to narrow and deep manner. Data that may not be deemed politically dangerous can be useful to the public for longitudinal research, meaning there is potential for solutions and discovery among a general populous.

The organization's strategy also called for states to take the lead from cities, not the other way around. Shaw's rationale is rooted in the perception that cities are less political than states and are not necessarily partisan places. Individuals in city administration are also held more accountable by their constituency based on how they do their jobs, as opposed to how a large legislative body or a network of state agencies is perceived. With open data, more public inspection in cities means more accountability. Sunlight and Shaw's research shows that a public perception of openness and trustworthiness exists in cities where data are more readily available. Whether this concept trickles into state governments is the challenge; it may take Sunlight years to convince lawmakers that this approach is worthwhile.

These are small steps Sunlight encourages municipalities to take and part of a larger plan for system-wide change and a raised level of transparency. Shaw knows that it remains a challenge for people to get the information they really want—the information that government is least likely to release—especially email or other electronic correspondence that would expose the inner workings of government or that were intended to be secret. Most agencies, Shaw rationalized, develop with internal goals in mind to keep the organization running, not with necessarily external measures to satisfy a public's want for information. "We've always had these ideas that everything is being reviewed on the state government level, and it's not," Shaw said. "It's basically the thinking that if we don't hear about problems, there are none. That's definitely not what we want."[19]

Building the Network

On the state level, the concerns facing FOIL advocates and the general public in New York are consistent throughout the United States. Extracting data from the federal government continues to become problematic, especially in matters of security. An example can be found in the Pentagon's push to draft another exemption in 2017.[20]

But extracting information on the local and state level, where public-information laws work the best, has also run into more obstacles. The difference is that a federal amendment will draw larger interest because of the immediacy and breadth of national media outlets. Most local matters draw only small interest from a depleted press corps or advocacy groups that are drawing some attention but whose prominence is growing.

Networks that share best practices are becoming more organized, offering educational workshops and extending legal resources that focus primarily on public-records laws exclusive to each state. Investigative Reporters and Editors, based at the University of Missouri, has been providing these services for media for more than a decade, and the National Freedom of Information Coalition (NFOIC), of which Reinvent Albany is a member, is a nonpartisan alliance of state and regional affiliates that promotes collaboration between advocacy and media groups in the name of open government. The network has hosted information summits since 2006, and technological advancements have allowed even greater collaboration, but as is the case for most groups attempting to unlock government's trove of information, legislative resistance has created issues for the NFOIC—a perpetual problem with defining what constitutes government transparency almost two decades into the twenty-first century. "The themes are consistent across the nation, and now we're seeing those differences at a wider level because of stronger electronic communication sharing," said Dan Bevarly, NFOIC's executive director. "I equate it with a small nuclear arms race—everyone is trying to one-up the other, especially on the legislative side in the wrong direction."[21]

Bevarly offered a running list of competitive actions taken: agencies unnecessarily redacting more; legislatures creating more exemptions in FOI laws; removal of law enforcement officers' names from reports; repeal of laws that have been on the books for decades, simply for political purposes; and growing concern regarding the retention of police body-camera video. At the start of 2017, the NFOIC had thirty-three affiliates, including an advocacy group in Washington, DC, and the New England First Amendment Coalition, which counts all six states in the region as members. There are two affiliates in Florida, whose Sunshine Law, some argue, is one of the strongest public-information statutes in the country. Similar to the Sunlight Foundation, the NFOIC works with government agencies for educational and compliance purposes in an effort to bridge the decades-long chasm that exists between government and the public. Both are grantees of the Knight Foundation, which has funded at least a dozen FOI initiatives, including FOIA Machine, cofounded by *Wall Street Journal* data reporter Coulter Jones.

Even though the NFOIC does explore the differences between state laws, the watchdog organizations within its membership function outside of government, recognizing that COOG remains unique in its role as both watchdog and state agency. As the public and media outcry grows louder on matters of public-records access and transparency, government offices have tried to find solutions in many of the same ways that some people in New York have searched for stronger FOIL and COOG oversight. States now work to walk back decisions made decades ago either to close similar agencies or to dilute their purpose. For instance, the NFOIC's research found that

- Indiana has a state public-access counselor, which is a separate agency. The attorney serves in an educational and mediation-type role, issuing opinions as to whether state or local agencies are in violation of the state's Open Door Law or Access to Public Records Act. The opinions are not binding, but a citizen armed with such an opinion can take an agency to court, and if successful in the lawsuit, the citizen will receive reasonable attorneys' fees and court costs as long as he or she tried the Public Records Act first to convince the government unit to comply.
- Virginia established the Freedom of Information Advisory Council within the Division of Legislative Services in 2000. The council serves more of an ombudsman role, not a watch-dog one. Its opinions are advisory only. Its two most important functions are its by-request training sessions (more than fifty a

year) and its study framework that brings stakeholders together on a regular basis to look at proposals submitted by legislators and to initiate legislative proposals itself.

- Tennessee has the Office of Open Records Counsel, but the office's mission is not to serve as a watchdog. The office serves a passive role instead, answering questions from government entities and citizens about the public-records and open-meetings law. It mostly provides help through education about the laws. The Open Records Counsel occasionally will write a letter to a government official after a complaint from a citizen, but it has made clear that it is not an "advocacy" agency there to hold government accountable for compliance with the public-records law. The only legislation that the Open Records Counsel has been involved in to date was a proposal to increase fees to inspect public records.

- Iowa has an independent executive-branch agency, the Iowa Public Information Board, but its operation is more similar to Tennessee's approach than to New York's. The Iowa agency responds to citizen, media, and government questions and complaints.

- Maine has had a Freedom of Access Act ombudsman in the attorney general's office since 2010. The ombudsman—one person, a lawyer—serves only in an advisory capacity but can ask the attorney general to take action against an agency that flagrantly violates the law. The office also reports annually to the legislature on complaints and compliance.

- In 2011, the District of Columbia created an executive-branch agency called the Office of Open Government. The office has one main enforcement assignment—policing compliance with DC's Open Meetings Act. It does training, issues rules, and adjudicates complaints, and it may bring suit to enforce the law. The law chiefly covers boards and commissions as well as the legislature (the DC Council) but has notable omissions, including the committees of such bodies. DC's public-records law also applies to both the executive branch and the legislative branch.

The office is able to issue advisory opinions and recommend changes in law.

In addition, steps have been taken, Bevarly noted, for watchdog organizations and government to work together. One such step is the Florida First Amendment Foundation, which, with the support of local governments in the state, created an online compliance test for agencies to gauge their competency in complying with the state law. An 80 percent threshold is necessary to pass the test. The existence of this test hasn't stopped lawmakers from abusing their powers, though. Florida's Sunshine Law also offers attorneys' fees, which came into larger focus on August 7, 2015. In an effort to settle seven public-records lawsuits that dealt with members of his staff allegedly shielding their email accounts from the law, Florida governor Rick Scott paid a Tallahassee lawyer $700,000 to settle all the cases—all on the taxpayers' dime. It was the first time in Florida that a sitting governor and attorney general have been sued and settled allegations of violations of the Sunshine Law. It was the second time Scott ended a lawsuit with taxpayer money.[22]

Less than a year later, public-information watchdogs in the state were challenged again, this time by the state legislature. An attorneys' fees bill was proposed, giving judges more discretion in awarding fees to the plaintiff in the event of a victory in court. The case involved the Jacksonville Police and Fire Pension Fund and its refusal to release records relating to payment. State lawmakers produced a bill that would essentially change one word—*shall* to *may* in the Sunshine Law.[23] The bill did not gain passage, but the Florida Supreme Court ruled that agencies must pay when in violation of the Sunshine Law.[24] Bevarly anticipated that the same story would be heard in the future, but in a different state.

A Continuing Process

As Beverly outlined the consistent concerns across state lines, New York lawmakers decided to resuscitate one of the two bills Governor

Cuomo had vetoed in December 2015—a revival seldom seen in state government without an incident prompting it. An attorneys' fees bill in New York would rival bills passed in California, Colorado, New Jersey, and other states, but events in Florida demonstrate that even in states where open-records law are strengthened with the threat of fiscal repercussions, such laws are still violated with fees paid by public dollars. Nevertheless, it is believed that the threat of awarding attorneys' fees to a FOIL petitioner serves as a deterrent.

That is what Senator Patrick Gallivan and Assemblymember Amy Paulin hoped during the New York legislative session of 2017. A bipartisan bill, similar to the one vetoed in December 2015, made its way through the Assembly in May 2017 (A02750-A, passing by a 135–1 vote) and gained unanimous approval in the Senate on June 5, 2017 (S02392-A, passing by a 62–0 margin). Unlike other states that adopted similar attorneys' fees legislation, New York added a two-tier system—on the strength of the terms *may* and *shall*—allowing some flexibility in interpretation by the courts but mandating payment after a lengthy legal process. The proposed bill stated that if an agency fails to respond to a request or appeal, the court, as outlined in the first tier of the proposed legislation, can decide whether to award ("may"). The second tier, however, mandates the award of fees ("shall") when the FOIL petitioner "has substantially prevailed and the court finds that the agency has no reasonable basis for denying access."[25]

When the 2017 legislative session ended, the bill, like all others that gained approval from both chambers, would eventually be sent to the governor. Yet again one of the strongest transparency amendments in recent New York State history awaited approval by the Cuomo administration, and, once again, advocates had to wait until after Thanksgiving for a decision. With some reluctance, citing judiciary discretion and provisions that exempt the legislature, the governor signed the attorneys' fees bill on December 13, 2017.[26]

15

The Administration

In less than two years, Alphonso David found himself in the thicket of New York's business and directly involved in the most pressing issues facing the state. After all, as counsel to Governor Andrew Cuomo, he must lead an office responsible for legal advisement to the highest government official in New York and his administration. Since David took the position at the beginning of the governor's second term in 2015, some of the most high-profile issues concerning the administration have also become the most controversial—from the investigation into the Buffalo Billion project to the SAFE Act to a proposed measure for New York to boycott companies that do the same with Israel, an ongoing global issue that always has a direct impact on the country and Wall Street.[1]

In terms of communication, David has remained proactive in either clarifying or refuting public accounts—which was not done in the past with such depth and immediacy. In terms of FOIL, the SAFE Act and the Buffalo Billion remain at the center of media inquiries that will most likely continue because of their widespread impact statewide. With respect to the SAFE Act, a statement from David on July 11, 2015, asked for patience on the part of gun shops and owners across New York in regard to the creation of a database to conduct background checks prior to any purchase of ammunition. In a measured tone, David outlined what is necessary to implement a legal and compliance system that is also safe and efficient, especially considering that the SAFE Act is legislation without precedent.[2] Language related to the openness of the database records was not included in the statement. That was a matter for the judiciary at the close of 2017; two hours south of Albany, the *Journal News* still awaited Putnam County's pistol-permit owner data.

This statement from David involved legislation. Another statement from him involved an investigation. On April 29, 2016, David issued a joint statement with Bart M. Schwartz, who was hired by the administration to launch an independent investigation into the business dealings of the Buffalo Billion project after the US attorney for the Southern District of New York, Preet Bharara, opened a federal inquiry. Schwartz had served as chief of the criminal division in the US Attorney General's Office. In the statement, David wrote that the administration would fully cooperate with that office. The decision to retain Schwartz was an attempt to allay any concerns regarding the nanotechnology-driven project that is part of the Buffalo Billion project and may serve as the catalyst in revitalizing upstate New York's manufacturing base. In the same statement, Schwartz publicly announced that "the state has reason to believe that in certain programs and regulatory approvals, they may have been defrauded by improper bidding and failures to disclose potential conflicts of interest by lobbyists and former state employees."[3] The focus was diverted from the administration and directed toward the individuals who were now part of the federal probe.

Even as subpoenas were issued to the governor's office and three companies central to the project, including SolarCity, the statement never mentioned by name Alain Kaloyeros, president and CEO of SUNY Polytechnic and vice president of FMSC—both connected to the Buffalo Billion project. On May 2, 2016, David issued a letter to SUNY officials that Schwartz would review and approve all decisions by SUNY Polytechnic Institute and SUNY Research Foundation. Also, Kaloyeros was stripped of all authority.[4] The administration then distanced itself from the man many believed to be at one time the savior of a new age of New York manufacturing. Weeks later, the US Attorney General's Office seized Kaloyeros's iPhone as another probe was launched to investigate Todd Howe, who served as Kaloyeros's informal chief of staff, advising the SUNY head on almost all matters related to the project.[5] Howe is also a registered lobbyist whose professional relationship with the governor has lasted three decades. He first registered with JCOPE in December 2015.[6]

The Cuomo administration has distanced itself from Kaloyeros, Howe, and Joseph Percoco, who, along with Howe, was at the center of Bharara's investigation. Federal agents raided Percoco's Westchester home the same week in May 2016 and confiscated records, and a relationship that began during the first Cuomo administration began to sour. The federal agents were looking for evidence that alleged Percoco and his wife received kickbacks from companies that conducted business with the state.[7] Then, on September 22, 2016, federal corruption charges were announced against ten aides, appointees, and developers, including Howe, Percoco, and Kaloyeros, who was charged with three felony counts in the state case brought forth by New York State attorney general Eric Schneiderman's office and with a count of wire-fraud conspiracy in the federal case by Bharara. In total, the ten faced a combined thirty-seven felony counts of bribery, extortion, and fraud.[8] Even though an unsealed seventy-nine-page criminal complaint outlined Percoco and Howe's alleged plan, the subsequent press conference offered more details on the ten defendants but did not connect the investigation to the governor's office. When asked about such a connection, Bharara said, "There are no allegations of any wrongdoing or misconduct by the governor, anywhere in this complaint."[9] (On March 11, 2017, the Trump administration fired Bharara, along with forty-six other US attorneys, after he refused to resign.[10])

The larger investigation in New York State started—and proliferated—with a FOIL request. It remains to be seen what will come from the investigation, but the promised FOIL reform has yet to materialize, and this failure may be attributed to the inherent nature of New York politics—specifically the struggle between the executive office and the legislature. Even when the attorneys' fees bill was signed on December 13, 2017, the governor emphasized his desire for an "updated" FOIL provision to include more direct language pertaining to the legislature.[11]

When asked about FOIL, David said in an interview in August 2016 that it is outdated in a number of ways and that a consistent model does not exist. He cannot speak to noncompliance by any particular agency, but he also acknowledged that a disconnect remains between the branches. Past efforts to engage the legislature on transparency and FOIL matters, he said, were met with no response, and reform proposed by the Cuomo administration was never considered as a whole. The veto message on December 12, 2015, David said, speaks for itself. "If the legislature is interested in modifying the FOIL law, they should first make the legislature subject to provisions of the FOIL law that currently they're not subject to," he explained. "When we legislate public policy, at least we're trying to do it in a way that achieves a broader goal, and from our perspective the goal would be if you are looking to increase transparency and provide greater access to information for the public, do so in a way that's consistent."[12]

David acknowledged the difficulties in creating efficient and fair systems and then implementing those same networks, much like the complexities that exist within all levels of government. With respect to compliance, a centralized reporting system similar to New York City's data portal has been discussed, but only for documenting that a FOIL request exists and that an agency is currently reviewing the inquiry. As for full compliance in fulfilling records requests, no legislation is currently being proposed that will take such a step—none that would address the widespread reform the Cuomo administration and David are proposing.

As the year 2016 neared its end, large-scale FOIL issues remained part of a disjointed narrative. Assemblyman David Buchwald's FOIL appeal bill—which, by all accounts, remains a positive step for reform—sat in the pipeline before being signed on November 29. An investigation continued into a project that is hailed as the economic driver for a region that has felt the impact of globalization. In courtrooms across the state, FOIL petitioners continued to wait for the judiciary's ruling whether public records should be made available and attorneys' fees awarded when a judge decides in favor of the plaintiff. In the inboxes and queues of more than ten thousand agencies across New York State and New York City, FOIL requests awaited to be answered and either rejected or fulfilled.

In conversation, David said that FOIL requests across all agencies overseen by the executive branch do not go to the second floor of the state capitol for review, as was suggested by media members and watchdog agencies who have discussed various FOIL protocols with public-information officers at those same agencies. David said that only requests directed to the executive chamber are handled by his staff.[13] The chamber maintains a FOIL log, which lends some insight into the decision-making processes at the highest level of state government and publicly discloses the names of petitioners who for either communication or political or business reasons seek information that only the executive chamber possesses. A FOIL log also reveals either the crush of requests that an office receives or the breadth of requested records—perhaps some made on a political fishing expedition—that may require months of review or redaction.

The executive chamber FOIL log is also a public document. It shows that during 2015, a relatively tame year by Albany standards, 288 public-records requests were submitted to the executive chamber. The log shows spikes in requests during newsworthy events (such as the Clinton Correctional Facility prison breaks and Governor Cuomo's trip to Cuba) and is filled with businesses requesting data for fiscal gain, attorneys searching to strengthen their cases, and lobbyists asking for internal communications between key political players. In its entirety, the log for 2015 shows an almost even split between FOIL requests received during the legislative session, which ended June 25, and requests received in the subsequent months, when lawmakers did not meet in Albany.

The log also shows the steady flow of requests from members of the media—from the *New York Times* to *Politico* to the *Wall Street Journal*—who are holding the highest office in the state accountable, each experiencing varying degrees of success in the pursuit of public information. The executive-chamber attorneys, however, said they do not keep track of the number of FOIL requests that were either filled or partially filled or simply denied.

The FOIL Log—Part I

Perhaps it's symbolic that the press room at the state capitol sits one floor above the governor's office. Thick marble separates the levels, and the barrier between the inner workings of state government and the public through the media is sometimes considered just as thick.

Due to the downsizing of traditional media outlets, the Albany press corps has diminished, but its appetite for news remains just as insatiable. High-quality, public-policy reporting is some of the costliest for newsroom budgets, and media in Albany now consist of a hybrid of traditional outlets from New York City, such as the *New York Times*, the *New York Daily News*, and the *New York Post*, and new digital pillars such as *Politico*. Although hybrid in nature, they are still present on the third floor of the capitol—the halls are lined with historical photos, and journalists fill desks and stand in corners conducting interviews with aides and lawmakers. The rhythms of the capitol are persistent, and so is the reporting in and out of the legislative session. The media's continued presence is also apparent in the FOIL log for 2015.

During that calendar year, the media accounted for 34.38 percent of all FOIL requests to the executive chamber. The most prolific media requester of public information in 2015 was *New York Times* reporter Thomas Kaplan, who submitted eleven requests, mostly for internal communications specific to devices, cell phone numbers, and email accounts. Kaplan covered Albany for five years for the *New York Times* before reporting on the presidential elections of 2016. He was followed by David Sirota, an author and investigative editor with the *International Business Times* and *MuckRock*, known for his relentless and sometimes controversial political reporting on the national level. Sirota's eight requests cut a wide swath—for information regarding everything from charter schools to lobbyists, property at the World Trade Center, and Hudson River PCBs, a recurring environmental issue in New York State. The FOIL requests from state and national media are an affirmation of a press corps still exercising its use of the process to inform the public of all matters relating to government—and to the agencies it oversees.

When Richard Matt and David Sweat escaped from Clinton Correctional Facility on June 6, 2015, ten FOIL requests were filed for inner communication between the governor's office that day and key state personnel so that a fact-driven narrative could be constructed. As a follow-up in the subsequent week, Jolene Greene, a producer for Local 22 WVNY and Local 44 WFFF, filed a FOIL request for the disciplinary records of the prison's superintendent, Steve Racette, who was later suspended and then retired in the wake of the escape.

Other requests highlight deeper investigative reporting beyond the daily beat of the capitol. *New York Post* reporter Kirstan Conley furthered the media's pursuit of information as the Buffalo Billion project story grew. *Wall Street Journal* reporter Mike Vilensky looked deeper in the Empire State Development Corporation. *Politico* reporter Josefa Velasquez submitted a FOIL request on August 31, 2015, for any communication between the state's sixty-two district attorneys, on the one hand, and the governor's office and Alphonso David, on the other, regarding Executive Order No. 147, which appoints the New York State attorney general as a special prosecutor in matters relating to the deaths of unarmed civilians caused by law enforcement officers. The information added context to her reporting that showed that the state's district attorneys believed the decision was "deeply flawed."[14] Overall, all requests serve as an essential media practice of deeper reporting or a practice of checks and balances on newsworthy events.

The media are not the only group requesting information from the executive chamber. An analysis of requesters shows a balance between citizens, the media, and legal communities, but there are also inquiries regarding real estate and business within the state, including a blanket request from SmartProcure, which is attempting to make government contracting and spending more efficient.

Table 2

Source of FOIL Requests Submitted to the New York State
Executive Chamber, 2015

Source	Number of Requests	Percentage of Total Requests
Media	99	34.38
Individuals	79	27.43
Businesses	27	9.38
Attorneys	26	9.03
Advocacy groups	16	5.56
Other	13	4.51
Inmates	10	3.47
Lobbyists/Political	10	3.47
Super political action committees	8	2.77
Total	288	100.00

Source: FOIL log, New York State Executive Chamber.

Table 2 shows the breakdown of sources of inquiries to the New York State executive chamber divided into nine categories by profession or intent of request.

The "other" category includes FOIL requests that were either completely redacted or sent to the incorrect office, highlighting communication issues in the system or petitioner error. Some requests showed variance in the petitioner's language; others were looking for something larger (four requests for any emails to and from to Hillary Clinton); and some underscored the resource issue that exists on the government's end with respect to the time needed to locate and deliver records.

In the executive chamber, the staff assigned to fielding and fulfilling FOIL requests is paltry, as is the case in all state agencies. More than 85 percent of the 288 requests sent to the governor's office in 2015 included pointed questions, with the request seeking either a single document or specific communication via email or memo, and 22.92 percent mentioned the governor by name. One in three requested part or full communication—either digital or paper—from key aides or from their respective email accounts. In addition, forty-one requests (14.24 percent) were multipart and usually highlighted communication between government employees—elected, hired, or appointed.

Fulfilling these requests involves contacting multiple state agencies, working with attorneys, and levying decisions about the disclosure of records in compliance with all state and federal laws. It also involves months of communication, which means time for the government and waiting for the petitioner. Michael Kink, on behalf of the advocacy group Strong Economy for All Coalition, filed a request on April 17, 2015, for all email communication to and from particular people from January 1, 2012, until the day of his inquiry. Organizing names into two columns, he requested communication from twenty-seven people in column A to thirty-nine people in column B—1,053 possible combinations. This request was considered voluminous, but the government had to do the search.

The practice of submitting large-scale, multilayered requests is not uncommon, though, and it is engaged in by citizens, attorneys, and journalists alike. The need for Eliot Brown, a real estate reporter for the *Wall Street Journal*, to submit a voluminous request was the result of a previous FOIL denial from the executive chamber. Brown's reporting delves deep into the intricacies of the commercial and residential markets and how the state's real estate complexities, especially New York City's, often spill into the global economy.

Brown's reporting in 2015 and 2016 included a closer examination of the federal program EB-5, which Congress created in 1990 to stimulate the US economy through job creation and capital investment by foreign investors ("EB-5" is the abbreviated reference to the employment-based fifth-preference visa that participants receive). The program allows developers to secure low-cost financing for major projects. For aspiring immigrants, a $500,000 investment in certain projects that can create ten jobs per investor has been enticing since the law's creation. The $20 billion Hudson Yards development in Manhattan, as Brown has reported, benefits from this infusion of capital.[15]

The federal law in the visa program was aimed at economically challenged areas, but Brown found that within the past few years New York City real estate developers have been using EB-5 to construct luxury skyscrapers, including a nine-hundred-foot structure slated for completion by 2020 along "billionaires' row" bordering Central Park. Steve Witkoff, the developer, argued that even though the $500,000 investment secures a green card for the investor as part of EB-5, it also creates middle-class jobs. He said he is also compliant with the law.[16]

Brown found that for developers to comply with this program, the practice of gerrymandering is sometimes used in what is referred to as "targeted employment areas," which are defined mostly by census tracts and evaluated by statisticians in the Department of Labor as part of the New York State Department of Economic Development. The EB-5 program doesn't specify the size of the targeted employment areas, allowing government flexibility in defining the tracts for real estate developers. The determination of whether an area can be designated a targeted employment area, predicated on unemployment data, is required for an EB-5 ruling. In the case of the luxury skyscrapers, the tract where they were being built linked the development on the south side of Central Park to a public-housing project in East Harlem—a considerable geographical gap even by New York City's standards, extending almost the length of the park.[17]

On December 15, 2015, Brown submitted a FOIL request for all emails during the previous calendar year between anyone in the executive chamber and anyone with a related .com address that contained "EB-5" in the subject line or text. The request served as an anomaly amid the Albany daily routine but was only one of a few requests that transcended city and state business and the private and public sectors. The request was denied, and Brown was told that no such record exists, prompting him to submit another FOIL request on December 23, 2015, for emails between individuals listed in column A (sixteen people in the private sector) and individuals listed column B (seven people in the public sector). Column A included Witkoff and, among others, Bruce Ratner, the billionaire developer overseeing the Harbor Yards project. Column B included Bill Mul-row, who replaced Lawrence Schwartz as the governor's secretary, and Joseph Percoco, the aide who is now under state and federal indictments. With 112 possible combinations, the request took three months to complete. For Brown, the results offered some context essential for his coverage area for the *Wall Street Journal* but not groundbreaking information that would provide further insight to the importance of the EB-5 program in New York or for reforming it in Congress, which seeks to close the loopholes.[18]

Brown then went in another direction and filed a FOIL request on June 13, 2016, to Empire State Development, asking about the process for deciding the target employment area specific to the area surrounding the Nordstrom Tower at 217 West Fifty-Seventh Street. As the city's tallest proposed residential structure at more than 1,500 feet, the tower will alter the view from Central Park and open in 2019 as a mixed-use building, with a Nordstrom store on the ground level. It will be built by Extell Development Company, which broke ground in 2014 and had eleven active projects in New York City at the time, covering 5.7 million square feet. (The company faced scrutiny in 2013 when it was found that one of its proposed luxury buildings located at 40 Riverside Boulevard on the Upper West Side was planned to have two entrances—one for the fifty-five low-income units facing away from the Hudson River and another for the remaining tenants.[19])

A few weeks after making the second FOIL request, Brown received letters from Empire State Development that showed how EB-5 and government data pave the way for developers and foreign funding, essential for projects such as the Nordstrom development. The estimate used by the statistician at the New York State Department of Labor in Albany, Joseph Bifaro Jr., included data from the US Census (tract boundaries in 2010 and American Community Survey five-year estimated labor force in 2014) and the New York Department of Labor (annual average for the local area unemployment statistics). In Bifaro's estimation, the block group in which the complex is slated for construction yields an unemployment rate of

2.0 percent. In order for the project to meet the target employment area for EB-5 investment, the block group must reach an unemployment rate of 8.0 percent.

Since the law does not define the target employment area, with some reclassification a new tract was developed, extending north to East Harlem and thus allowing the block group to be assessed at an 8.2 percent unemployment rate, surpassing the threshold necessary to qualify for the Department of Economic Development EB-5 program. A few days later, Kay Alison Wilkie, the program administrator, sent a letter to Extell's director, Erika Banach, confirming the new tract.

The program's affirmative response did not surprise Brown because he had already sought the information he desired from another agency and knew that letters between the state and developers existed as a matter of practice. What surprised Brown was that with considerable real estate developments rising across New York City, no information existed on the highest level, as revealed by the response to his FOIL request for emails between anyone in the executive chamber and anyone with a related .com address that contained the name "EB-5" in the subject line or text.[20]

Brown has found mixed results in using FOIL and does not use it often, given the scope of his beat. Through each process, he raised questions, mostly about disconnect, the technological challenges, and the overall strength of the legislation. "They claimed they don't have the technological ability on the first request they denied. I redid their request, went through email accounts that I specified and directly to people I was interested in, and just following their wish. That made more work for them—doesn't make sense," Brown said. "They did fulfill that one, to my surprise, but my sense of FOIL in New York is this—the state has the legal ability to withhold whatever they want, and it varies from agency to agency."[21]

The FOIL Log—Part II

On the shores of Lake Ontario, north of Buffalo, sits the town of Somerset, a rural community with a population of 2,600. With a strong mix of farmers and retirees, the town holds on to its distinctive landmarks, such as the Golden Hill State Park Marina and Campground, which has been named one of the top-one-hundred parks in the United States, and the Thirty Mile Point Lighthouse, which can be found on the National Register of Historic Places. Now Somerset finds itself at the center of contention between state plans, renewable energy, and the rights and preservation of a small New York town.

On August 1, 2016, the New York State Public Service Commission approved the state's Clean Energy Standard, a plan focused on using clean energy, combatting climate change, and reducing air pollution. The plan is progressive, with the administration calling for New York to be a national and global leader on this front. The Clean Energy Standard will require 50 percent of New York's electricity to come from renewable energy sources, such as wind and solar, by 2030.[22] The plan is aggressive and ambitious, receiving praise from a number of sectors. Also, in the announcement of the approval, Public Service Commission chair Audrey Zibelman noted the fact that the plan will generate "billions of dollars in private investment for new renewable power supplies, developing new jobs and new green choices for consumers."[23]

The release, though, did not mention the proposal for the development of more than three hundred wind plants across the state in that time, one of which will be located in Somerset's backyard.

The plan called for sixty to seventy wind turbines in Lake Ontario, just off the shores of Somerset, with each turbine standing five hundred to seven hundred feet. In design, the wind farm would rival the skylines of Rochester, Buffalo, and Toronto. To compound environmental matters, the proposed wind farm sits in the middle of a primary migratory bird route, meaning wildlife habits and patterns will drastically change if the turbines are constructed. Farmers have already been approached by energy companies to lease their land, and the town began holding monthly meetings regarding the project.

The town also issued a public survey, which showed that 67 percent of its residents opposed the project. In Yates, the bordering town that is also part of the proposal, that number hit 70 percent. The survey also asked about tax reductions and other financial and environmental benefits. Those numbers decreased in terms of opposition, but the support for the project never grew to more than 30 percent and then only when a question about solar farms was asked. The approval number for that specific aspect grew to 40 percent, but this meant farmers must lease their land, causing other environmental concerns.[24]

The wind-plant project is led by the Virginia-based company Apex Clean Energy, which states that two hundred megawatts could power fifty-three thousand homes, while also addressing other health and environmental risks.[25] Apex estimates the initiative, labeled "Lighthouse Wind," will generate $1.6 million in tax revenue to local governments and help create jobs.

Given Somerset's location—the northernmost part of Niagara County—the company also knows that the area is one of best wind resources in the state.[26] "With all of this, the idea here is to have an uninterrupted line of wind farms from one end of New York to other," said Benjamin Wisniewski, an attorney with Lippes Mathias Wexler Friedman LLP. "Maybe that's the right thing to do with energy production, but it's going to impact the people that live there."[27]

Wisniewski's firm, which includes former New York State attorney general Dennis C. Vacco as a partner, represents Somerset and is leading the legal fight against the state and Apex. Even though the opposition's argument is strengthened by the environmental factors associated with the Lighthouse Wind project, the issue focuses more on the town's rights. Somerset may have a say in the project, but not necessarily a choice.

Article 10 of the New York State Public Service Law, which permits major electric-generating facilities in New York, has gone through different iterations since 2000. The law applies to any facility with twenty-five-megawatt-generating capability or more and emphasizes shared economic benefit between provider and town. It also called for the creation of the New York State Board on Electric

Generation Siting and the Environment, which comprises five members appointed by the government and two ad hoc members, designated by the Senate and Assembly. Given the board's composition, a municipality has some representation but in many ways no control of its land. A municipality is allowed to participate in the process of making a decision about a facility, but it does not have veto power, and ultimately the board decides the fate of a project.

Wisniewski argued that some municipalities may overwhelmingly approve a project or choose to reject one, but stripping their choice is central to the Lighthouse Wind project case. In subsequent editorials on the project, Vacco presented two arguments—Article 10 wrongfully limits municipalities' constitutional home-rule power, and wind and solar energy developers believe Article 10 strips municipalities of their control over land usage and zoning. He also asks a larger question: "Such central control also flies in the face of legal precedent. If towns in New York can ban fracking, why can't they ban industrial wind energy production?"[28]

As part of the fact-finding process, Wisniewski submitted a FOIL request to the executive chamber on October 27, 2015. Perhaps more so than any other request submitted to the chamber in 2015, Wisniewski's six-part inquiry was the most detailed and direct. Aside from communication between government officials and Apex, he requested all emails, plans, and written documents that were transmitted regarding the Lighthouse Wind project as well as all proposed, ongoing, or completed studies of it. At the same time, he submitted FOIL requests to the New York State Department of Public Service (DPS) and DEC. As part of Article 10 and a standard practice for any project with environmental impact, studies are conducted by the company proposing the plan. Wisniewski and his firm were looking for more information on behalf of Somerset.

In time, Wisniewski received a response from the executive chamber—the records he requested didn't exist. He did, however, receive information from DPS and DEC, but it did not include any health or environmental studies. What compounds matters, Wisniewski said, is the inclusion of a private business in the equation. "It does become problematic when a private third party becomes involved because they're going to object to disclosure—they'll say it's business confidential information, and it's overbroadly used in my opinion," Wisniewski said. "In terms of FOIL, I'm not surprised by inconsistency. When I receive no response, I would just think, 'No response, and you're holding out.' But if I get something from one and not the other, either I'm completely wrong and nothing happened, or someone is probably not providing what I requested."[29]

Through the FOIL requests he made to the state agencies, Wisniewski and his firm did receive copies of emails between the DPS and DEC. The most telling was an exchange in September 2015 that discusses the *Lake Ontario Migratory Bird Stopover Technical Report*. With input from several environmental groups and agencies, including the US Fish and Wildlife Service, the exchange highlighted the negative long-range fiscal and environmental cost to municipalities as well as the dangers posed to hundreds of thousands of birds that migrate through the corridor and call the shores home. The US Fish and Wildlife Service ended the report with a conclusion: "US FWS Region 4 Guidance specifies the Niagara Escarpment as an area where siting of wind turbine projects should be avoided."[30]

Wisniewski noted that the deadline to meet the administration's mandate, the year 2030, is not too far in the future, and his firm is already representing more towns, which means there are more meetings and more studies to be conducted. Somerset is taking additional steps. On November 11, 2016, it approved its budget, which called for the doubling of attorneys' and engineer fees for 2017. Of the $2.9 million town budget, $300,000 was earmarked to fight the Lighthouse Wind project. In comparison, the town's line item for economic development shrank to $10,000.[31]

Resource concerns, both time and fiscal, weigh on Wisniewski. As he and his firm try to find the necessary information, he is mindful of the cost, but he also knows meetings are being held and communication is necessary even for the project to advance. Developers have to propose studies, design the studies, and be critical of the conclusions. Even as he outlined the necessary communication within agencies, he underscored the value and purpose of information for all parties involved and punctuated his thoughts with an identification of what exists at the core of the issue—if the town is not present at project meetings to voice its own concerns, then the town and its residents will effectively never have a chance to do so.

16

FOIL Analysis and Review

In Their Words

Seventy-four people shared in interviews their experiences with New York's Freedom of Information Law, all of them dissecting contemporary challenges and offering solutions. This chapter highlights some of the larger themes they discussed and offers further analysis on a number of topics.

On Media: Eve Burton

From a newsroom budgetary perspective, the in-depth policy or investigative reporting (sometimes referred to as enterprise reporting) remains the costliest because of the time and expertise needed to produce quality and accurate journalism. Given the current media landscape, compounded by technological advancements that have eroded traditional business models, the trimming of newsrooms and institutional knowledge has led to questions about the future of accountability journalism. Eve Burton, senior vice president and general counsel for Hearst as well as one of the country's preeminent public-records attorneys who has spent time in both traditional print and broadcast newsrooms, has seen the change firsthand. A casualty of an industry in flux, she noted, is usually top-level reportage:

> The industry does not fund litigation, so when you don't exercise a muscle, it's less usable. There isn't a robust industry to protect our constitutional rights like it once did. The first

227

moment we realized this within the news industry is when it was decided by the bear out west—Google—that it can just take clippings of stories. People know the story now throughout the industry. Google told newspapers, "We can shoot back to your site, and you can have a larger audience and share." It was correct in all aspects, effectively trading a dollar of revenue for twenty-five cents. We were never able to return.

In a world of aggregation, all those companies are looking for content, and FOIL is meant for serious content and stories, not just simple aggregation. We're not living in a world where there is a want for that every day. FOIL doesn't get used as much. So for that to change, a cultural shift is needed, and we're seeing what is happening right now when all those factors add up. It's not good.[1]

On Email Correspondence: John Kaehny

When the framers of FOIL first introduced the new law, they were aware that technology would undoubtedly affect the statute. Perhaps what was not known at the time were the pace and means by which information would be shared in the digital age. Just as in all aspects of law, in FOIL interpretation matters. The proliferation and availability of video and data have emerged as significant issues, but the struggle between what constitutes the difference between an inter- and intraoffice communication—akin to the memo of yesteryear—remains at the forefront of some controversies. Advocacy groups such as Kaehny's Reinvent Albany, of which he is executive director, continue to debate semantics and perception:

> Conceptually FOIL has a tough time with email—Is it a memo or a phone call? Right now, it seems it's more a phone call than a memo. How do we deal with emails with sitting officials?"
>
> Take this "agents of the city" issue with the mayor. It was an attempt by the de Blasio administration to be explicit, to make the mayor of New York City's email account open but

then say "agents of the city" falls into a different category. It's
as if they are saying they should be praised for being open—
incorrect, everything but. It completely subverts FOIL. It's arbitrary. These happen to all be lobbyists, which is problematic.
There is no exemption, but they get to say there is? There's no
real high-level discussion or informed discussion on emails, and
there needs to be.[2]

On Taking the Next Step: Bill Mahoney

The penalties for violating FOIL remain inconsistent in New York,
even as other states have adopted clearer language, especially on
matters involving attorneys' fees. Because FOIL is a civil and not a
criminal statute, the more significant penalty for violating it is usually incurred in the court of public opinion. This penalty, however,
has not deterred lawmakers and public officials from breaking the
law and abusing FOIL.

The larger questions—and perhaps the most challenging—are:
How do elected officials draft legislation that would force the disclosure of public information in an expeditious and cost-efficient manner,
and, in turn, how can a lawmaking body whose members sometimes
defy the statute pass such a bill? Journalists such as Bill Mahoney,
campaign-contribution reporter for *Politico*, understand the financial
constraints some agencies face, but ethical standards remain questionable as the media attempt to produce stories in the public interest:

In theory it's [FOIL is] written beautifully, but if an agency
wants to stonewall you from getting information, it's still difficult for you to fight it. If they tell you they don't have it, and
if you know they do, it can be costly and time-consuming. So
what do you do, start charging low-level bureaucrats with felo-
nies? That would be overboard.

What we have now seems like it's not going as far as it
should. Some advocates have pushed reforms to reclaim costs.
That's a gamble, provided you actually win the case. For

whatever reason, you're on the hook. So it's got to be more than just creating the expectation that if it's not burdening an agency unreasonably, then they work to make information available to the public. That's more of cultural change in places that are resistant to cultural change. So I don't know how you would bring that about because changing culture in government is difficult, but it would help.[3]

On Volume and Policies: Brian Curran

Every FOIL request passes through the hands of someone in government, regardless of the size of the municipality or the agency. Over time, either public-information officers or attorneys can recognize the volume of the request or the sensitivity of the records being requested based on the FOIL petitioner's name alone. According to Brian Curran, corporation counsel for the City of Rochester, offices like his are caught between traditional means of rendering a decision on disclosure and new challenges, mainly with respect to video. What has remained, though, is the process by which some offices decide what to disclose. Each request fits into a category, and so does each requestor.

I think there is a general need for FOIL to deal with issue of voluminous requests. Since there is no real limit in New York FOIL law, there's a discussion that comes up in the city that we always get requests, and we can't charge them for all this work. For video, this will be even more burdensome. There may be a massive request for all these videos.

It will be useful if the state looks at some of the exemption categories and clarif[ies] them with [respect to] video footage and personal privacy. Basically, when and how do you apply certain exemptions? There is a different reaction with documents than video. Take, for example, one of the most common requests. Police are called to a private residence for some incident that occurred. Other people reside there. We always had a police report, a piece of paper after the incident. Now we're going to have two or three officers with footage. People will react differently to a report than video in someone's house. This will be a prime example, and we don't have a good answer on that. This involves some serious policy and practical issues, not just legal.

This is further complicated by the fact that you have three categories of FOIL filers—the citizen, the media, and lawyers and litigants. Some of the reporters use FOIL quite aggressively for the purpose of searching for stories, so those can be overwhelming to deal with, but, on the other hand, they represent a powerful public need for disclosure. For lawyers and litigants— this area can use some clarification on the policy side. There are rules pertaining to discovery, and there are lawyers that try to end-run those rules when the city is a participant in the case. They make the case that they can get information in FOIL that they can't get in discovery. Third, there are people with an agenda—people who make a practice to find things to criticize the government for, no matter what. They will file extensive requests frequently, and this means time and effort. I have some concern that this can become a real issue with body cameras.[4]

On Complexities of Changing Media and Technology: Michael J. Grygiel

With technological advancements, filing information has never been easier, but a problem exists between the means by which agencies categorize records and growing privacy concerns, whether they are justified or reactionary. According to Michael J. Grygiel, a media attorney, this problem may cause further challenges—for the guardians of government information, lawmakers, and the media.

Because of the increasingly complicated regulatory environment that we all inhabit and the demands on state government, when agencies continue to accumulate information—which they are able to do more easily now to collect information and data because of centralized technological developments and because society in many ways is becoming more complex—the regulatory impulse, if anything, has in my judgment increased dramatically in the last decade or decade and a half. This means there is a much greater repository of information that both the state and municipal government levels are collecting, so the question for journalists and news organizations is, How best can they access this information in order to deliver newsworthy information to their readers and viewers?[5]

On Future Legislation: Patrick Gallivan

When analyzing and drafting proposed legislation, partisan politics aside, a legislator must balance the interests of his or her constituency and larger, sometimes much more complex past, present, and unforeseen future societal issues. As much as lawmakers are held accountable, they must also weigh the actions of multiple stakeholders, including citizens and fellow elected officials and their actions. It is a difficult position, New York State senator Patrick Gallivan explained, but he often uses the past to guide his judgment in navigating contemporary issues.

I couldn't necessarily pick apart the law line by line, but I see three potential issues.

First, an ongoing challenge is government's compliance with the law. We have to ensure the government at any level, with the same intent for any individual request, is trained to comply. The governor has to put a premium on this. You hear the media complain about nonconformity with the law, but I never heard the government complain that we're not conforming. Sure, sometimes you get an expense, a fishing expedition, but there are ways to prevent fishing expeditions to cut down on government waste.

Second, there's some issues with context within the FOIL laws, especially with technology and law enforcement. There is ongoing discussion about exemptions to discuss where the line should be drawn on information in performance evaluations—Is it right for discussion, and when can it be discussed? This is considerable in the law enforcement community.

Lastly, what happens when the law of the land changes? In the context of body cameras, what happens if a case reaches the Supreme Court on the federal level? There's no discussion about establishing policy on this, and this conceivably can happen. This is polarizing and will have an effect. Look at Baltimore. Look at Ferguson.[6]

On Law Enforcement Exemptions: Brendan Lyons

Debate continues regarding FOIL exemptions and law enforcement's use of language related to exemption when weighing whether to fulfill a request, but as we move further into the twenty-first century, scientific ingenuity and forensic evidence are also changing the nature of the job. The social complexities that the original FOIL language highlights are now reaching new levels. When chemical composition and identity fall under FOIL's privacy provision, the quest for truth ends—Or does it begin? It's a larger question contemplated by journalists such as Brendan Lyons, the investigations editor for the *Albany Times Union.*

The New York State Police crime lab is under scrutiny, facing criticism because of the traditional way DNA analysis is done. We always thought and accepted DNA analysis was bullet proof because the FBI expert gets up there and says there is only a one in a million chance that the guy up there is not the guy who left blood on this knife. Now, you're starting to see other crime labs where the analyst knows who the subject is and then builds their analysis around building the profile around that person. It's like the tail wagging the dog. It's problematic. Mistakes have been made.

There are crimes that can be solved, and it's mix DNAtology. What's changed is this guy out of Pittsburgh who built computer programs that do DNA analysis and now are bullet-proof. It's $5 million, this program. Analysts say you can rerun work that you've already done in order to fact-check perhaps innocent people or guilty people walking around out there. Suddenly the posture of the state police became different. And ultimately people were fired, analysts were targeted. There were accusations that twenty analysts cheated on a qualifying test for this program. State police said, "We're done with TrueAllele [the program in question]; we spent $5 million, but we're going in another direction." The guy who runs the company, Mark Perlin, has accused the state police of creating this whole scandal in an effort to get rid of TrueAllele.

So we wanted to check two months of DNA reports from a random date a few years ago from the state. We FOILed for the information, very detailed, with assistance from people who knew how to ask for the information and how it was kept and where it can be located. And in an unusual response—normally the state police will take two years or more to respond to a FOIL; they'll acknowledge it but drag it out—they responded within a week or two. They said sorry, this executive law, which Pataki passed in the '90s, exempts all DNA records from disclosure, and we can't get around that. We're trying to figure out how, and I don't think we can. We were going to have all these DNA labs recheck all the data in a random sampling of cases. Let's look at a two-month snapshot. I didn't know about the executive law. I hate that; they threw it right back in my face.

At a time in the '90s, people were skittish about DNA. It's hard to redact the identifying information because, in fact, DNA is identifying. I don't know if we can. You can get DNA records if the person gives you that. The problem is the prison guys: everyone is innocent, right? Basically, we wanted to answer the question: "Is the way we perform DNA analysis flawed?" And we can't prove it because we couldn't get the records to check it. Point being, technology is changing the game; the law should probably follow if it has the potential to right a wrong.[7]

On Strength of Law: Jim Heaney

When the strength of a law is examined, questions often arise about the statute's relevance, timeliness, and, perhaps above all, effectiveness. For someone such as *Investigative Post* executive director and editor Jim Heaney, who has exercised FOIL in some capacity for more than thirty years, these questions often arise every time he files a request. Strength of a statute and its associated consequences are sometimes built on one highly visible public precedent—which bodes well for FOIL petitioners but becomes problematic for the government. Some question whether just implementing stiffer penalties would lead to more widespread compliance.

> I think there are two big problems with the law right now—there needs to be something written in to compel a more timely response to requests; and, two, more importantly, there has to be teeth built in to impose meaningful consequences on government officials who violate the law. If you have a minimum extreme to make a point, if there is a minimum jail sentence to honor the FOIL law, those people who drag their feet have something to fear. The bureaucrat is told to turn over the documents, and if they drag their feet, what are the consequences? Make them pay a fine. It's civil—not criminal. Has anyone taken on a meaningful fine? Make it easier for plaintiffs to recover attorneys' fees and attach a consequence to a person in government not following the law.[8]

On Process: Cezary Podkul

Once the FOIL request leaves the petitioner's hand, the trust is now with the government. Since no central database exists to gauge the availability of the records in question, and the state has not created a central reporting clearinghouse similar to New York City's, often only conjecture remains. Journalists such as Cezary Podkul of *ProPublica* (now of the *Wall Street Journal*) who use FOIL and FOIA on the federal level will remain persistent in making their requests but skeptical of the process:

> The Department of State has a consumer-complaint database for businesses. It's a structured database, and I just wanted the consumer complaints. They wanted to charge me hundreds of dollars. It took them a year to redact it by hand. They also wanted me to shrink the request, and I told them no, I don't [want to].
>
> I believe if anything will happen, it would have to be if a governor is strong on FOIL. But here's the problem that I found out after a conversation I had with an FOI officer at a state agency: every FOIL request goes through a review process through the governor's office. It's deemed politically sensitive. It's like the Politboro.[9]

On Government Responsiveness: David Grandeau

How do you ensure that government officials and agencies fulfill a request for a record if exemptions do not deem the record unavailable? Possible solutions are often presented to COOG, advocacy groups, and lawmakers. Some are practical, and almost all are covered in bureaucratic red tape. Others are extreme or perhaps classified. The question of compliance, however, remains on the minds of people close to Albany, such as David Grandeau, the former executive director of the Temporary Commission on Lobbying and now in private practice.

> I've been around state agencies, and when they get a FOIL request the first reaction is—we don't have to respond to this. It's cultural because of the type of people that go into government. They're paranoid. They distrust anyone asking them questions. When I was there, if you want the info, you can have it. It doesn't affect me. I'll give you my check, my resume, you can have my letters, you can have my phone messages—I don't care.

So what I'm saying is get rid of FOIL altogether because it gives government a reason to deny information. Start requiring government to be responsive to the requests of the citizenry, and get the media to write that story. Get the media to change their culture so they're writing the story about what government is hiding, because people love to read what government is hiding.

I'll give you an example. When Cuomo was attorney general, he was providing Spitzer people information about Joe Bruno's travel—this is Troopergate.[10] There came a point in Troopergate when they put out a report. It's half-assed. They never got the testimony of key people, never got the testimony of the governor's counsel. Cuomo said, "We don't have the ability to get that information." All Andrew Cuomo had to do was tell the media, "We are going to subpoena so-and-so to appear for a deposition in three days, the deposition is going to be held at such and such location, and if they don't appear that means they have information and they don't want to tell us." Put that in the media for two days; they all would have to show up. They have to. It's a perp walk. If they no-showed, they had to have do[ne] something wrong, and you go from there. That's how you can get information.[11]

On the System: Karl Sleight

As with elected officials who experience FOIL from multiple angles, other government employees who enter the private sector after years of serving the people of New York State—and vice versa—see all sides of the statute. This is particularly true for attorneys such as Karl Sleight, the former executive director of the State Ethics Commission and now in private practice. In a detailed story, he explains the importance of FOIL but also the trappings of the law and the culture of government agencies.

I can show you how—and detail how—the system needs fixing based on one case. We filed a FOIL request with the state tax department for documentation on one individual. The state tax department ignored the request—ignored [it] repeatedly. They did not respond. At the same time on a parallel track, we were working on a criminal appeal. A few days before [former technology firm CFO Richard Saxton[12]] was scheduled to be sentenced, we get a last trickle of documents from the FOIL request that, in my opinion, showed that Mr. Saxton had no intent to commit a crime. That documentation was huge evidence in the case.

We made a motion request, and the judge denied it. Appellate Division justice John C. Egan Jr.—here in Albany—then actually signed an emergency order to keep [Saxton] out of jail pending the results of the case. The case had been to the Appellate Division five times based on FOIL issues and criminal issues. At the end of the day, we weren't successful on a postconviction motion, and Mr. Saxton served four months in jail—ninety days—and he was on probation for five years, but his FOIL case continued because we wanted to get the documents, and there was a significant cost, as you can imagine, with a private law firm on a FOIL case going to the Appellate Division—having to sue the tax department, the tax department has to get an appeal, the Appellate Division has to render a decision, it got sent back to the trial court in Albany, there was a hearing, you have to prepare for a hearing, and then it was appealed again because there was an award of attorneys' fees. There was an appeal because the award of attorneys' fees were so paltry—$20,000, and we won the FOIL case, which was rare, and if you're doing this work, you know it's even more rare to get attorneys' fees.

Because the government fought us so significantly and made us appeal and fought us at every turn and didn't turn over the documents, those attorneys' fees were over $100,000. By the time we were done, over $150,000. It went to the Appellate Division; they said the trial court judge erred because he picked a number out of the air. We just got a decision last week that now it's up to $45,000.

That case is just remarkable. The judge talked about the Herculean effort of us and Mr. Saxton to get these records and how bad the tax department was and then basically said, "We'll give you ten cents on the dollar." No law firm in their right mind would open up a practice group on FOIL cases. There's zero incentive because your chances of ever getting paid—even close to what you should be paid compared to some other matter—won't happen. But in our case, we took a particular interest because there was such an unjust situation. The system is set up to disincentivize or prevent private citizens from using the tools available to them with FOIL because you just can't make that kind of investment.

The documentation we needed? Mr. Saxton reached out in April 2007 to the tax department and told them that our company didn't pay our taxes, and we need to make the adjustments. He's ultimately charged with falsifying business records—business records being the tax records. A critical element in the case was this—What was Mr. Saxton's intent?

If you call the tax department, and you're having an open dialogue, and there are tax department records that are showing you're doing that, really, it runs contrary to the notion that you're trying to be secretive and falsifying business records because you don't falsify business records and have a conversation with the government at the same time. If we had that information and were able to show it to the jury, there is no doubt in my mind that Mr. Saxton would never have been convicted, and that is ultimately the only crime he was convicted of.[13]

On Ethics Reform in New York: Peter Bienstock

In terms of ethics, discussions continue regarding the level of corruption that exists on all levels of government in New York State. Even though steps have been taken to deter government employees, political appointees, and elected officials from questionable behavior, completely eradicating the problem seems to remain a futile exercise. Since FOIL is not *the* ethics law but *an* ethics law, account-ability remains paramount, forcing people to revert to a central ques-tion: What would happen if the government were to disclose? The same question surfaces every few years—or whenever a new scandal arises—according to Peter Bienstock, the former executive director of the Commission on Government Integrity.

Access to public records is part of ethics reform, and it has to do with money. Any receipt of money by government, there's no basis to exempt from FOIL. I'm talking idealistically, so none of this will be enacted because New York is New York. Any check in and out should be a matter of public record. I'm not sure what the argument against that would be. First of all, all employees, hired or elected, they're being paid taxpayer money. I think that it's important to know and always keep in mind. Then, any government expenditure is open to taxpayer money. I don't know what the counterargument would be, either. Everything works slowly on this, like there needs to be a discussion, so what's the argument against real-time data for disclosure of all dollars coming in and out? Why would you need to FOIL this? Why would you have to wait? But we do.

It was very disappointing in terms of actual change because these are the same conversations we're having now that we had years ago. We wrote twenty-something cogent, persuasive reports, and they collect dust more so than any other thing on the shelf. They are as cogent and persuasive as they were twenty years ago, and we still have corruption. And that's sad.[14]

APPENDIXES

NOTES

INDEX

The Freedom of Information Law

Public Officers Law, Article 6
Sections 84–90
Freedom of Information Law

§84. Legislative declaration.
The legislature hereby finds that a free society is maintained when government is responsive and responsible to the public, and when the public is aware of governmental actions. The more open a government is with its citizenry, the greater the understanding and participation of the public in government.

As state and local government services increase and public problems become more sophisticated and complex and therefore harder to solve, and with the resultant increase in revenues and expenditures, it is incumbent upon the state and its localities to extend public accountability wherever and whenever feasible.

The people's right to know the process of governmental decision-making and to review the documents and statistics leading to determinations is basic to our society. Access to such information should not be thwarted by shrouding it with the cloak of secrecy or confidentiality. The legislature therefore declares that government is the public's business and that the public, individually and collectively and represented by a free press, should have access to the records of government in accordance with the provisions of this article.

§85. Short title. This article shall be known and may be cited as the "Freedom of Information Law."

§86. Definitions. As used in this article, unless the context requires otherwise.

1. "Judiciary" means the courts of the state, including any municipal or district court, whether or not of record.

2. "State legislature" means the legislature of the state of New York, including any committee, subcommittee, joint committee, select committee, or commission thereof.

3. "Agency" means any state or municipal department, board, bureau, division, commission, committee, public authority, public corporation, council, office or other governmental entity performing a governmental or proprietary function for the state or any one or more municipalities thereof, except the judiciary or the state legislature.

4. "Record" means any information kept, held, filed, produced or reproduced by, with or for an agency or the state legislature, in any physical form whatsoever including, but not limited to, reports, statements, examinations, memoranda, opinions, folders, files, books, manuals, pamphlets, forms, papers, designs, drawings, maps, photos, letters, microfilms, computer tapes or discs, rules, regulations or codes.

5. "Critical infrastructure" means systems, assets, places or things, whether physical or virtual, so vital to the state that the disruption, incapacitation or destruction of such systems, assets, places or things could jeopardize the health, safety, welfare or security of the state, its residents or its economy.

§87. Access to agency records.

1. (a) Within sixty days after the effective date of this article, the governing body of each public corporation shall promulgate uniform rules and regulations for all agencies in such public corporation pursuant to such general rules and regulations as may be promulgated by the committee on open government in conformity with the provisions of this article, pertaining to the administration of this article.

(b) Each agency shall promulgate rules and regulations, in conformity with this article and applicable rules and regulations promulgated pursuant to the provisions of paragraph (a) of this subdivision, and pursuant to such general rules and regulations as may be promulgated by the committee on open government in conformity with the provisions of this article, pertaining to the availability of records and procedures to be followed, including, but not limited to:

i. the times and places such records are available;

ii. the persons from whom such records may be obtained; and

iii. the fees for copies of records which shall not exceed twenty-five cents per photocopy not in excess of nine inches by fourteen inches, or the actual cost of reproducing any other record in accordance with the provisions of paragraph (c) of this subdivision, except when a different fee is otherwise prescribed by statute.

c. In determining the actual cost of reproducing a record, an agency may include only:

i. an amount equal to the hourly salary attributed to the lowest paid agency employee who has the necessary skill required to prepare a copy of the requested record;

ii. the actual cost of the storage devices or media provided to the person making the request in complying with such request;

iii. the actual cost to the agency of engaging an outside professional service to prepare a copy of a record, but only when an agency's information technology equipment is inadequate to prepare a copy, if such service is used to prepare the copy; and

iv. preparing a copy shall not include search time or administrative costs, and no fee shall be charged unless at least two hours of agency employee time is needed to prepare a copy of the record requested. A person requesting a record shall be informed of the estimated cost of preparing a copy of the record if more than two hours of an agency employee's time is needed, or if an outside professional service would be retained to prepare a copy of the record.

2. Each agency shall, in accordance with its published rules, make available for public inspection and copying all records, except that such agency may deny access to records or portions thereof that:

(a) are specifically exempted from disclosure by state or federal statute;

(b) if disclosed would constitute an unwarranted invasion of personal privacy under the provisions of subdivision two of section eighty-nine of this article;

(c) if disclosed would impair present or imminent contract awards or collective bargaining negotiations;

(d) are trade secrets or are submitted to an agency by a commercial enterprise or derived from information obtained from a commercial enterprise and which if disclosed would cause substantial injury to the competitive position of the subject enterprise;

(e) are compiled for law enforcement purposes and which, if disclosed, would:

i. interfere with law enforcement investigations or judicial proceedings;
ii. deprive a person of a right to a fair trial or impartial adjudication;
iii. identify a confidential source or disclose confidential information relating to a criminal investigation; or
iv. reveal criminal investigative techniques or procedures, except routine techniques and procedures;

(f) if disclosed could endanger the life or safety of any person;

(g) are inter-agency or intra-agency materials which are not:

i. statistical or factual tabulations or data;
ii. instructions to staff that affect the public;
iii. final agency policy or determinations; or
iv. external audits, including but not limited to audits performed by the comptroller and the federal government; or

(h) are examination questions or answers which are requested prior to the final administration of such questions;

(i) if disclosed, would jeopardize the capacity of an agency or an entity that has shared information with an agency to guarantee the security of its information technology assets, such assets encompassing both electronic information systems and infrastructures; or

* (j) are photographs, microphotographs, videotape or other recorded images prepared under authority of section eleven hundred eleven-a of the vehicle and traffic law.

* NB Repealed December 1, 2014

* (k) are photographs, microphotographs, videotape or other recorded images prepared under authority of section eleven hundred eleven-b of the vehicle and traffic law.

* NB Repealed December 1, 2014

* (l) are photographs, microphotographs, videotape or other recorded images produced by a bus lane photo device prepared under authority of section eleven hundred eleven-c of the vehicle and traffic law.
* NB Repealed September 20, 2015

3. Each agency shall maintain:

(a) a record of the final vote of each member in every agency proceeding in which the member votes;
(b) a record setting forth the name, public office address, title and salary of every officer or employee of the agency; and
(c) a reasonably detailed current list by subject matter, of all records in the possession of the agency, whether or not available under this article. Each agency shall update its subject matter list annually, and the date of the most recent update shall be conspicuously indicated on the list. Each state agency as defined in subdivision four of this section that maintains a website shall post its current list on its website and such posting shall be linked to the website of the committee on open government. Any such agency that does not maintain a website shall arrange to have its list posted on the website of the committee on open government.

4. (a) Each state agency which maintains records containing trade secrets, to which access may be denied pursuant to paragraph (d) of subdivision two of this section, shall promulgate regulations in conformity with the provisions of subdivision five of section eighty-nine of this article pertaining to such records, including, but not limited to the following:

(1) the manner of identifying the records or parts;
(2) the manner of identifying persons within the agency to whose custody the records or parts will be charged and for whose inspection and study the records will be made available;
(3) the manner of safeguarding against any unauthorized access to the records.

(b) As used in this subdivision the term "agency" or "state agency" means only a state department, board, bureau, division, council or office and any public corporation the majority of whose members are appointed by the governor.

(c) Each state agency that maintains a website shall post information related to this article and article six-A of this chapter on its website. Such information shall include, at a minimum, contact information for the persons from whom records of the agency may be obtained, the times and places such records are available for inspection and copying, and information on how to request records in person, by mail, and, if the agency accepts requests for records electronically, by e-mail. This posting shall be linked to the website of the committee on open government.

5. (a) An agency shall provide records on the medium requested by a person, if the agency can reasonably make such copy or have such copy made by engaging an outside professional service. Records provided in a computer format shall not be encrypted.

(b) No agency shall enter into or renew a contract for the creation or maintenance of records if such contract impairs the right of the public to inspect or copy the agency's records.

§88. Access to state legislative records.

1. The temporary president of the senate and the speaker of the assembly shall promulgate rules and regulations for their respective houses in conformity with the provisions of this article, pertaining to the availability, location and nature of records, including, but not limited to:

(a) the times and places such records are available;

(b) the persons from whom such records may be obtained;

(c) the fees for copies of such records, which shall not exceed twenty-five cents per photocopy not in excess of nine inches by fourteen inches, or the actual cost of reproducing any other record, except when a different fee is otherwise prescribed by law.

2. The state legislature shall, in accordance with its published rules, make available for public inspection and copying:

(a) bills and amendments thereto, fiscal notes, introducers' bill memoranda, resolutions and amendments thereto, and index records;

(b) messages received from the governor or the other house of the legislature, and home rule messages;

(c) legislative notification of the proposed adoption of rules by an agency;

(d) transcripts or minutes, if prepared, and journal records of public sessions including meetings of committees and subcommittees and public hearings, with the records of attendance of members thereat and records of any votes taken;

(e) internal or external audits and statistical or factual tabulations of, or with respect to, material otherwise available for public inspection and copying pursuant to this section or any other applicable provision of law;

(f) administrative staff manuals and instructions to staff that affect members of the public;

(g) final reports and formal opinions submitted to the legislature;

(h) final reports or recommendations and minority or dissenting reports and opinions of members of committees, subcommittees, or commissions of the legislature;

(i) any other files, records, papers or documents required by law to be made available for public inspection and copying.

3. Each house shall maintain and make available for public inspection and copying:

(a) a record of votes of each member in every session and every committee and subcommittee meeting in which the member votes;

(b) a record setting forth the name, public office address, title, and salary of every officer or employee; and

(c) a current list, reasonably detailed, by subject matter of any records required to be made available for public inspection and copying pursuant to this section.

§89. General provisions relating to access to records; certain cases. The provisions of this section apply to access to all records, except as hereinafter specified:

1. (a) The committee on open government is continued and shall consist of the lieutenant governor or the delegate of such officer, the secretary of state or the delegate of such officer, whose office shall act as secretariat for the committee, the commissioner of the office of general services or the

delegate of such officer, the director of the budget or the delegate of such officer, and seven other persons, none of whom shall hold any other state or local public office except the representative of local governments as set forth herein, to be appointed as follows: five by the governor, at least two of whom are or have been representatives of the news media, one of whom shall be a representative of local government who, at the time of appointment, is serving as a duly elected officer of a local government, one by the temporary president of the senate, and one by the speaker of the assembly. The persons appointed by the temporary president of the senate and the speaker of the assembly shall be appointed to serve, respectively, until the expiration of the terms of office of the temporary president and the speaker to which the temporary president and speaker were elected. The four persons presently serving by appointment of the government for fixed terms shall continue to serve until the expiration of their respective terms. Thereafter, their respective successors shall be appointed for terms of four years. The member representing local government shall be appointed for a term of four years, so long as such member shall remain a duly elected officer of a local government. The committee shall hold no less than two meetings annually, but may meet at any time. The members of the committee shall be entitled to reimbursement for actual expenses incurred in the discharge of their duties.

(b) The committee shall:

i. furnish to any agency advisory guidelines, opinions or other appropriate information regarding this article;

ii. furnish to any person advisory opinions or other appropriate information regarding this article;

iii. promulgate rules and regulations with respect to the implementation of subdivision one and paragraph (c) of subdivision three of section eighty-seven of this article;

iv. request from any agency such assistance, services and information as will enable the committee to effectively carry out its powers and duties; and

v. develop a form, which shall be made available on the internet, that may be used by the public to request a record; and

vi. report on its activities and findings regarding articles six and seven of this chapter, including recommendations for changes in the law, to the governor and the legislature annually, on or before December fifteenth.

2. (a) The committee on open government may promulgate guidelines regarding deletion of identifying details or withholding of records otherwise available under this article to prevent unwarranted invasions of personal privacy. In the absence of such guidelines, an agency may delete identifying details when it makes records available.

(b) An unwarranted invasion of personal privacy includes, but shall not be limited to:

i. disclosure of employment, medical or credit histories or personal references of applicants for employment;
ii. disclosure of items involving the medical or personal records of a client or patient in a medical facility;
iii. sale or release of lists of names and addresses if such lists would be used for solicitation or fund-raising purposes;
iv. disclosure of information of a personal nature when disclosure would result in economic or personal hardship to the subject party and such information is not relevant to the work of the agency requesting or maintaining it;
v. disclosure of information of a personal nature reported in confidence to an agency and not relevant to the ordinary work of such agency; or
vi. information of a personal nature contained in a workers' compensation record, except as provided by section one hundred ten-a of the workers' compensation law; or
vii. disclosure of electronic contact information, such as an e-mail address or a social network username, that has been collected from a taxpayer under section one hundred four of the real property tax law.

(c) Unless otherwise provided by this article, disclosure shall not be construed to constitute an unwarranted invasion of personal privacy pursuant to paragraphs (a) and (b) of this subdivision:

i. when identifying details are deleted;
ii. when the person to whom a record pertains consents in writing to disclosure;
iii. when upon presenting reasonable proof of identity' a person seeks access to records pertaining to him or her; or

iv. when a record or group of records relates to the right, title or interest in real property, or relates to the inventory, status or characteristics of real property, in which case disclosure and providing copies of such record or group of records shall not be deemed an unwarranted invasion of personal privacy, provided that nothing herein shall be construed to authorize the disclosure of electronic contact information, such as an e-mail address or a social network username, that has been collected from a taxpayer under section one hundred four of the real property tax law".

2-a. Nothing in this article shall permit disclosure which constitutes an unwarranted invasion of personal privacy as defined in subdivision two of this section if such disclosure is prohibited under section ninety-six of this chapter.

3. (a) Each entity subject to the provisions of this article, within five business days of the receipt of a written request for a record reasonably described, shall make such record available to the person requesting it, deny such request in writing or furnish a written acknowledgment of the receipt of such request and a statement of the approximate date, which shall be reasonable under the circumstances of the request, when such request will be granted or denied, including, where appropriate, a statement that access to the record will be determined in accordance with subdivision five of this section. An agency shall not deny a request on the basis that the request is voluminous or that locating or reviewing the requested records or providing the requested copies is burdensome because the agency lacks sufficient staffing or on any other basis if the agency may engage an outside professional service to provide copying, programming or other services required to provide the copy, the costs of which the agency may recover pursuant to paragraph (c) of subdivision one of section eighty-seven of this article. An agency may require a person requesting lists of names and addresses to provide a written certification that such person will not use such lists of names and addresses for solicitation or fund-raising purposes and will not sell, give or otherwise make available such lists of names and addresses to any other person for the purpose of allowing that person to use such lists of names and addresses for solicitation or fund-raising purposes. If an agency determines to grant a request in whole or in part, and if circumstances prevent disclosure to the person

requesting the record or records within twenty business days from the date of the acknowledgement of the receipt of the request, the agency shall state, in writing, both the reason for the inability to grant the request within twenty business days and a date certain within a reasonable period, depending on the circumstances, when the request will be granted in whole or in part. Upon payment of, or offer to pay, the fee prescribed therefor, the entity shall provide a copy of such record and certify to the correctness of such copy if so requested, or as the case may be, shall certify that it does not have possession of such record or that such record cannot be found after diligent search. Nothing in this article shall be construed to require any entity to prepare any record not possessed or maintained by such entity except the records specified in subdivision three of section eighty-seven and subdivision three of section eighty-eight of this article. When an agency has the ability to retrieve or extract a record or data maintained in a computer storage system with reasonable effort, it shall be required to do so. When doing so requires less employee time than engaging in manual retrieval or redactions from non-electronic records, the agency shall be required to retrieve or extract such record or data electronically. Any programming necessary to retrieve a record maintained in a computer storage system and to transfer that record to the medium requested by a person or to allow the transferred record to be read or printed shall not be deemed to be the preparation or creation of a new record.

(b) All entities shall, provided such entity has reasonable means available, accept requests for records submitted in the form of electronic mail and shall respond to such requests by electronic mail, using forms, to the extent practicable, consistent with the form or forms developed by the committee on open government pursuant to subdivision one of this section and provided that the written requests do not seek a response in some other form.

4. (a) Except as provided in subdivision five of this section, any person denied access to a record may within thirty days appeal in writing such denial to the head, chief executive or governing body of the entity, or the person therefor designated by such head, chief executive, or governing body, who shall within ten business days of the receipt of such appeal fully explain in writing to the person requesting the record the reasons for further denial, or provide access to the record sought. In addition, each

agency shall immediately forward to the committee on open government a copy of such appeal when received by the agency and the ensuing determination thereon. Failure by an agency to conform to the provisions of subdivision three of this section shall constitute a denial.

(b) Except as provided in subdivision five of this section, a person denied access to a record in an appeal determination under the provisions of paragraph (a) of this subdivision may bring a proceeding for review of such denial pursuant to article seventy-eight of the civil practice law and rules. In the event that access to any record is denied pursuant to the provisions of subdivision two of section eighty-seven of this article, the agency involved shall have the burden of proving that such record falls within the provisions of such subdivision two. Failure by an agency to conform to the provisions of paragraph (a) of this subdivision shall constitute a denial.

(c) The court in such a proceeding: (i) may assess, against such agency involved, reasonable attorney's fees and other litigation costs reasonably incurred by such person in any case under the provisions of this section in which such person has substantially prevailed, [when: i. the agency had no reasonable basis for denying access; or ii.] and when the agency failed to respond to a request or appeal within the statutory time; and (ii) shall assess, against such agency involved, reasonable attorney's fees and other litigation costs reasonably incurred by such person in any case under the provisions of this section in which such person has substantially prevailed and the court finds that the agency had no reasonable basis for denying access.

5. (a) (1) A person acting pursuant to law or regulation who, subsequent to the effective date of this subdivision, submits any information to any state agency may, at the time of submission, request that the agency except such information from disclosure under paragraph (d) of subdivision two of section eighty-seven of this article. Where the request itself contains information which if disclosed would defeat the purpose for which the exception is sought, such information shall also be excepted from disclosure.

(1-a) A person or entity who submits or otherwise makes available any records to any agency, may, at any time, identify those records or portions thereof that may contain critical infrastructure information, and request that the agency that maintains such records except such information from disclosure under subdivision two of section eighty-seven of this article. Where the request itself contains information which if disclosed would defeat the purpose for which the exception is sought, such information shall also be excepted from disclosure.

(2) The request for an exception shall be in writing and state the reasons why the information should be excepted from disclosure.

(3) Information submitted as provided in subparagraphs one and one-a of this paragraph shall be excepted from disclosure and be maintained apart by the agency from all other records until fifteen days after the entitlement to such exception has been finally determined or such further time as ordered by a court of competent jurisdiction.

(b) On the initiative of the agency at any time, or upon the request of any person for a record excepted from disclosure pursuant to this subdivision, the agency shall:

(1) inform the person who requested the exception of the agency's intention to determine whether such exception should be granted or continued;

(2) permit the person who requested the exception, within ten business days of receipt of notification from the agency, to submit a written statement of the necessity for the granting or continuation of such exception;

(3) within seven business days of receipt of such written statement, or within seven business days of the expiration of the period prescribed for submission of such statement, issue a written determination granting, continuing or terminating such exception and stating the reasons therefor; copies of such determination shall be served upon the person, if any, requesting the record, the person who requested the exception, and the committee on open government.

(c) A denial of an exception from disclosure under paragraph (b) of this subdivision may be appealed by the person submitting the information and a denial of access to the record may be appealed by the person requesting the record in accordance with this subdivision.

(1) Within seven business days of receipt of written notice denying the request, the person may file a written appeal from the determination of

the agency with the head of the agency, the chief executive officer or governing body or their designated representatives.

(2) The appeal shall be determined within ten business days of the receipt of the appeal. Written notice of the determination shall be served upon the person, if any, requesting the record, the person who requested the exception and the committee on public access to records. The notice shall contain a statement of the reasons for the determination.

(d) A proceeding to review an adverse determination pursuant to paragraph (c) of this subdivision may be commenced pursuant to article seventy-eight of the civil practice law and rules. Such proceeding, when brought by a person seeking an exception from disclosure pursuant to this subdivision, must be commenced within fifteen days of the service of the written notice containing the adverse determination provided for in subparagraph two of paragraph (c) of this subdivision.

(e) The person requesting an exception from disclosure pursuant to this subdivision shall in all proceedings have the burden of proving entitlement to the exception.

(f) Where the agency denies access to a record pursuant to paragraph (d) of subdivision two of section eighty-seven of this article, the agency shall have the burden of proving that the record falls within the provisions of such exception.

(g) Nothing in this subdivision shall be construed to deny any person access, pursuant to the remaining provisions of this article, to any record or part excepted from disclosure upon the express written consent of the person who had requested the exception.

(h) As used in this subdivision the term "agency" or "state agency" means only a state department, board, bureau, division, council or office and any public corporation the majority of whose members are appointed by the governor.

6. Nothing in this article shall be construed to limit or abridge any otherwise available right of access at law or in equity of any party to records.

7. Nothing in this article shall require the disclosure of the home address of an officer or employee, former officer or employee, or of a retiree of a public employees' retirement system; nor shall anything in this article

require the disclosure of the name or home address of a beneficiary of a public employees' retirement system or of an applicant for appointment to public employment; provided however, that nothing in this subdivision shall limit or abridge the right of an employee organization, certified or recognized for any collective negotiating unit of an employer pursuant to article fourteen of the civil service law, to obtain the name or home address of any officer, employee or retiree of such employer, if such name or home address is otherwise available under this article.

8. Any person who, with intent to prevent public inspection of a record pursuant to this article, willfully conceals or destroys any such record shall be guilty of a violation.

9. When records maintained electronically include items of information that would be available under this article, as well as items of information that may be withheld, an agency in designing its information retrieval methods, whenever practicable and reasonable, shall do so in a manner that permits the segregation and retrieval of available items in order to provide maximum public access.

§90. Severability.
If any provision of this article or the application thereof to any person or circumstances is adjudged invalid by a court of competent jurisdiction, such judgment shall not affect or impair the validity of the other provisions of the article or the application thereof to other persons and circumstances.

APPENDIX B

The Freedom of Information Act

5 U.S. Code § 552—Public information; agency rules, opinions, orders, records, and proceedings

(a) Each agency shall make available to the public information as follows:

(1) Each agency shall separately state and currently publish in the Federal Register for the guidance of the public—

(A) descriptions of its central and field organization and the established places at which, the employees (and in the case of a uniformed service, the members) from whom, and the methods whereby, the public may obtain information, make submittals or requests, or obtain decisions;

(B) statements of the general course and method by which its functions are channeled and determined, including the nature and requirements of all formal and informal procedures available;

(C) rules of procedure, descriptions of forms available or the places at which forms may be obtained, and instructions as to the scope and contents of all papers, reports, or examinations;

(D) substantive rules of general applicability adopted as authorized by law, and statements of general policy or interpretations of general applicability formulated and adopted by the agency; and

(E) each amendment, revision, or repeal of the foregoing.

Except to the extent that a person has actual and timely notice of the terms thereof, a person may not in any manner be required to resort to, or be adversely affected by, a matter required to be published in the Federal Register and not so published. For the purpose of this paragraph, matter reasonably available to the class of persons affected thereby is deemed published in the Federal Register when incorporated by reference therein with the approval of the Director of the Federal Register.

(2) Each agency, in accordance with published rules, shall make available for public inspection and copying—

> (A) final opinions, including concurring and dissenting opinions, as well as orders, made in the adjudication of cases;
> (B) those statements of policy and interpretations which have been adopted by the agency and are not published in the Federal Register;
> (C) administrative staff manuals and instructions to staff that affect a member of the public;
> (D) copies of all records, regardless of form or format, which have been released to any person under paragraph (3) and which, because of the nature of their subject matter, the agency determines have become or are likely to become the subject of subsequent requests for substantially the same records; and
> (E) a general index of the records referred to under subparagraph (D);

unless the materials are promptly published and copies offered for sale. For records created on or after November 1, 1996, within one year after such date, each agency shall make such records available, including by computer telecommunications or, if computer telecommunications means have not been established by the agency, by other electronic means. To the extent required to prevent a clearly unwarranted invasion of personal privacy, an agency may delete identifying details when it makes available or publishes an opinion, statement of policy, interpretation, staff manual, instruction, or copies of records referred to in subparagraph (D). However, in each case the justification for the deletion shall be explained fully in writing, and the extent of such deletion shall be indicated on the portion of the record which is made available or published, unless including that indication would harm an interest protected by the exemption in subsection (b) under which the deletion is made. If technically feasible, the extent of the deletion shall be indicated at the place in the record where the deletion was made. Each agency shall also maintain and make available for public inspection and copying current indexes providing identifying information for the public as to any matter issued, adopted, or promulgated after July 4, 1967, and required by this paragraph to be made available or published. Each agency shall promptly publish, quarterly or more frequently, and distribute (by sale or otherwise) copies of each index or supplements thereto unless it determines by order published in the Federal Register that the publication would be unnecessary and impracticable, in which case the agency shall nonetheless provide copies of such index on request at a cost not to exceed the direct cost of duplication. Each agency shall make the index referred to in subparagraph (E) available by computer telecommunications by December 31, 1999. A final order, opinion, statement of policy, interpretation, or staff manual or instruction that affects a member of the public may be relied on, used, or cited as precedent by an agency against a party other than an agency only if—

> (i) it has been indexed and either made available or published as provided by this paragraph; or
> (ii) the party has actual and timely notice of the terms thereof.

(3)(A) Except with respect to the records made available under paragraphs (1) and (2) of this subsection, and except as provided in subparagraph (E), each agency, upon any request for records which (i) reasonably describes such records and (ii) is made in accordance with published rules stating the time, place, fees (if any), and procedures to be followed, shall make the records promptly available to any person.

> (B) In making any record available to a person under this paragraph, an agency shall provide the record in any form or format requested by the person if the record is readily reproducible by the agency in that form or format. Each agency shall make reasonable efforts to maintain its records in forms or formats that are reproducible for purposes of this section.
> (C) In responding under this paragraph to a request for records, an agency shall make reasonable efforts to search for the records

in electronic form or format, except when such efforts would significantly interfere with the operation of the agency's automated information system.

(D) For purposes of this paragraph, the term "search" means to review, manually or by automated means, agency records for the purpose of locating those records which are responsive to a request.

(E) An agency, or part of an agency, that is an element of the intelligence community (as that term is defined in section 3(4) of the National Security Act of 1947 (50 U.S.C. 401a(4))) [1] shall not make any record available under this paragraph to—

> (i) any government entity, other than a State, territory, commonwealth, or district of the United States, or any subdivision thereof; or
> (ii) a representative of a government entity described in clause (i).

(4)(A)(i) In order to carry out the provisions of this section, each agency shall promulgate regulations, pursuant to notice and receipt of public comment, specifying the schedule of fees applicable to the processing of requests under this section and establishing procedures and guidelines for determining when such fees should be waived or reduced. Such schedule shall conform to the guidelines which shall be promulgated, pursuant to notice and receipt of public comment, by the Director of the Office of Management and Budget and which shall provide for a uniform schedule of fees for all agencies.

> (ii)Such agency regulations shall provide that—

> > (I) fees shall be limited to reasonable standard charges for document search, duplication, and review, when records are requested for commercial use;
> > (II) fees shall be limited to reasonable standard charges for document duplication when records are not sought for commercial use and the request is made by an educational or noncommercial scientific institution, whose

purpose is scholarly or scientific research; or a representative of the news media; and

(III) for any request not described in (I) or (II), fees shall be limited to reasonable standard charges for document search and duplication.

In this clause, the term "a representative of the news media" means any person or entity that gathers information of potential interest to a segment of the public, uses its editorial skills to turn the raw materials into a distinct work, and distributes that work to an audience. In this clause, the term "news" means information that is about current events or that would be of current interest to the public. Examples of news-media entities are television or radio stations broadcasting to the public at large and publishers of periodicals (but only if such entities qualify as disseminators of "news") who make their products available for purchase by or subscription by or free distribution to the general public. These examples are not all-inclusive. Moreover, as methods of news delivery evolve (for example, the adoption of the electronic dissemination of newspapers through telecommunications services), such alternative media shall be considered to be news-media entities. A freelance journalist shall be regarded as working for a news-media entity if the journalist can demonstrate a solid basis for expecting publication through that entity, whether or not the journalist is actually employed by the entity. A publication contract would present a solid basis for such an expectation; the Government may also consider the past publication record of the requester in making such a determination.

(iii) Documents shall be furnished without any charge or at a charge reduced below the fees established under clause (ii) if disclosure of the information is in the public interest because it is likely to contribute significantly to public understanding of the operations or activities of the government and is not primarily in the commercial interest of the requester.

(iv) Fee schedules shall provide for the recovery of only the direct costs of search, duplication, or review. Review costs shall

include only the direct costs incurred during the initial examination of a document for the purposes of determining whether
the documents must be disclosed under this section and for the
purposes of withholding any portions exempt from disclosure
under this section. Review costs may not include any costs
incurred in resolving issues of law or policy that may be raised
in the course of processing a request under this section. No fee
may be charged by any agency under this section—

> (I) if the costs of routine collection and processing of the
> fee are likely to equal or exceed the amount of the fee; or
> (II) for any request described in clause (ii) (II) or (III) of
> this subparagraph for the first two hours of search time
> or for the first one hundred pages of duplication.

(v) No agency may require advance payment of any fee unless
the requester has previously failed to pay fees in a timely fashion, or the agency has determined that the fee will exceed $250.
(vi) Nothing in this subparagraph shall supersede fees charge-
able under a statute specifically providing for setting the level
of fees for particular types of records.
(vii) In any action by a requester regarding the waiver of fees
under this section, the court shall determine the matter de
novo: Provided, That the court's review of the matter shall be
limited to the record before the agency.
(viii) An agency shall not assess search fees (or in the case of
a requester described under clause (ii)(II), duplication fees)
under this subparagraph if the agency fails to comply with
any time limit under paragraph (6), if no unusual or exceptional circumstances (as those terms are defined for purposes
of paragraphs (6)(B) and (C), respectively) apply to the processing of the request.

(B) On complaint, the district court of the United States in the
district in which the complainant resides, or has his principal
place of business, or in which the agency records are situated, or
in the District of Columbia, has jurisdiction to enjoin the agency

from withholding agency records and to order the production of any agency records improperly withheld from the complainant. In such a case the court shall determine the matter de novo, and may examine the contents of such agency records in camera to determine whether such records or any part thereof shall be withheld under any of the exemptions set forth in subsection (b) of this section, and the burden is on the agency to sustain its action. In addition to any other matters to which a court accords substantial weight, a court shall accord substantial weight to an affidavit of an agency concerning the agency's determination as to technical feasibility under paragraph (2)(C) and subsection (b) and reproducibility under paragraph (3)(B).

(C) Notwithstanding any other provision of law, the defendant shall serve an answer or otherwise plead to any complaint made under this subsection within thirty days after service upon the defendant of the pleading in which such complaint is made, unless the court otherwise directs for good cause shown.

[(D) Repealed. Pub. L. 98–620, title IV, § 402(2), Nov. 8, 1984, 98 Stat. 3357.]

(E)(i)The court may assess against the United States reasonable attorney fees and other litigation costs reasonably incurred in any case under this section in which the complainant has substantially prevailed.

(ii)For purposes of this subparagraph, a complainant has substantially prevailed if the complainant has obtained relief through either—

(I) a judicial order, or an enforceable written agreement or consent decree; or
(II) a voluntary or unilateral change in position by the agency, if the complainant's claim is not insubstantial.

(F)(i) Whenever the court orders the production of any agency records improperly withheld from the complainant and assesses against the United States reasonable attorney fees and other

litigation costs, and the court additionally issues a written finding that the circumstances surrounding the withholding raise
questions whether agency personnel acted arbitrarily or capri-
ciously with respect to the withholding, the Special Counsel shall
promptly initiate a proceeding to determine whether disciplinary action is warranted against the officer or employee who was
primarily responsible for the withholding. The Special Counsel,
after investigation and consideration of the evidence submitted,
shall submit his findings and recommendations to the administrative authority of the agency concerned and shall send copies of the
findings and recommendations to the officer or employee or his
representative. The administrative authority shall take the correc-
tive action that the Special Counsel recommends.

(ii)The Attorney General shall—

(I) notify the Special Counsel of each civil action
described under the first sentence of clause (i); and
(II) annually submit a report to Congress on the number
of such civil actions in the preceding year.

(iii) The Special Counsel shall annually submit a report to
Congress on the actions taken by the Special Counsel under
clause (i).

(G) In the event of noncompliance with the order of the court, the
district court may punish for contempt the responsible employee,
and in the case of a uniformed service, the responsible member.

(5) Each agency having more than one member shall maintain and
make available for public inspection a record of the final votes of each
member in every agency proceeding.
(6)(A)Each agency, upon any request for records made under paragraph (1), (2), or (3) of this subsection, shall—

(i) determine within 20 days (excepting Saturdays, Sundays, and
legal public holidays) after the receipt of any such request whether

to comply with such request and shall immediately notify the person making such request of such determination and the reasons therefor, and of the right of such person to appeal to the head of the agency any adverse determination; and

(ii) make a determination with respect to any appeal within twenty days (excepting Saturdays, Sundays, and legal public holidays) after the receipt of such appeal. If on appeal the denial of the request for records is in whole or in part upheld, the agency shall notify the person making such request of the provisions for judicial review of that determination under paragraph (4) of this subsection.

The 20-day period under clause (i) shall commence on the date on which the request is first received by the appropriate component of the agency, but in any event not later than ten days after the request is first received by any component of the agency that is designated in the agency's regulations under this section to receive requests under this section. The 20-day period shall not be tolled by the agency except—

> (I) that the agency may make one request to the requester for information and toll the 20-day period while it is awaiting such information that it has reasonably requested from the requester under this section; or
> (II) if necessary to clarify with the requester issues regarding fee assessment. In either case, the agency's receipt of the requester's response to the agency's request for information or clarification ends the tolling period.

(B)(i) In unusual circumstances as specified in this subparagraph, the time limits prescribed in either clause (i) or clause (ii) of subparagraph (A) may be extended by written notice to the person making such request setting forth the unusual circumstances for such extension and the date on which a determination is expected to be dispatched. No such notice shall specify a date that would result in an extension for more than ten working days, except as provided in clause (ii) of this subparagraph.

(ii) With respect to a request for which a written notice under clause (i) extends the time limits prescribed under clause (i) of subparagraph (A), the agency shall notify the person making the request if the request cannot be processed within the time limit specified in that clause and shall provide the person an opportunity to limit the scope of the request so that it may be processed within that time limit or an opportunity to arrange with the agency an alternative time frame for processing the request or a modified request. To aid the requester, each agency shall make available its FOIA Public Liaison, who shall assist in the resolution of any disputes between the requester and the agency. Refusal by the person to reasonably modify the request or arrange such an alternative time frame shall be considered as a factor in determining whether exceptional circumstances exist for purposes of subparagraph (C).

(iii) As used in this subparagraph, "unusual circumstances" means, but only to the extent reasonably necessary to the proper processing of the particular requests—

(I) the need to search for and collect the requested records from field facilities or other establishments that are separate from the office processing the request;

(II) the need to search for, collect, and appropriately examine a voluminous amount of separate and distinct records which are demanded in a single request; or

(III) the need for consultation, which shall be conducted with all practicable speed, with another agency having a substantial interest in the determination of the request or among two or more components of the agency having substantial subject-matter interest therein.

(iv) Each agency may promulgate regulations, pursuant to notice and receipt of public comment, providing for the aggregation of certain requests by the same requestor, or by a group of requestors acting in concert, if the agency reasonably believes that such requests actually constitute a single request, which would otherwise satisfy the unusual circumstances specified in this subparagraph, and the requests involve clearly related matters. Multiple requests involving unrelated matters shall not be aggregated.

(C)(i) Any person making a request to any agency for records under paragraph (1), (2), or (3) of this subsection shall be deemed to have exhausted his administrative remedies with respect to such request if the agency fails to comply with the applicable time limit provisions of this paragraph. If the Government can show exceptional circumstances exist and that the agency is exercising due diligence in responding to the request, the court may retain jurisdiction and allow the agency additional time to complete its review of the records. Upon any determination by an agency to comply with a request for records, the records shall be made promptly available to such person making such request. Any notification of denial of any request for records under this subsection shall set forth the names and titles or positions of each person responsible for the denial of such request.

(ii) For purposes of this subparagraph, the term "exceptional circumstances" does not include a delay that results from a predictable agency workload of requests under this section, unless the agency demonstrates reasonable progress in reducing its backlog of pending requests.

(iii) Refusal by a person to reasonably modify the scope of a request or arrange an alternative time frame for processing a request (or a modified request) under clause (ii) after being given an opportunity to do so by the agency to whom the person made the request shall be considered as a factor in determining whether exceptional circumstances exist for purposes of this subparagraph.

(D)(i) Each agency may promulgate regulations, pursuant to notice and receipt of public comment, providing for multitrack processing of requests for records based on the amount of work or time (or both) involved in processing requests.

(ii) Regulations under this subparagraph may provide a person making a request that does not qualify for the fastest multitrack processing an opportunity to limit the scope of the request in order to qualify for faster processing.
(iii) This subparagraph shall not be considered to affect the requirement under subparagraph (C) to exercise due diligence.

(E)(i) Each agency shall promulgate regulations, pursuant to notice and receipt of public comment, providing for expedited processing of requests for records—

(I) in cases in which the person requesting the records demonstrates a compelling need; and
(II) in other cases determined by the agency.

(ii)Notwithstanding clause (i), regulations under this subparagraph must ensure—

(I) that a determination of whether to provide expedited processing shall be made, and notice of the determination shall be provided to the person making the request, within 10 days after the date of the request; and
(II) expeditious consideration of administrative appeals of such determinations of whether to provide expedited processing.

(iii) An agency shall process as soon as practicable any request for records to which the agency has granted expedited processing under this subparagraph. Agency action to deny or affirm denial of a request for expedited processing pursuant to this subparagraph, and failure by an agency to respond in a timely manner to such a request shall be subject to judicial review under paragraph (4), except that the judicial review shall be based on the record before the agency at the time of the determination.

(iv) A district court of the United States shall not have jurisdiction to review an agency denial of expedited processing of a request for records after the agency has provided a complete response to the request.

(v) For purposes of this subparagraph, the term "compelling need" means—

(I) that a failure to obtain requested records on an expedited basis under this paragraph could reasonably be expected to pose an imminent threat to the life or physical safety of an individual; or

(II) with respect to a request made by a person primarily engaged in disseminating information, urgency to inform the public concerning actual or alleged Federal Government activity.

(vi) A demonstration of a compelling need by a person making a request for expedited processing shall be made by a statement certified by such person to be true and correct to the best of such person's knowledge and belief.

(F) In denying a request for records, in whole or in part, an agency shall make a reasonable effort to estimate the volume of any requested matter the provision of which is denied, and shall provide any such estimate to the person making the request, unless providing such estimate would harm an interest protected by the exemption in subsection (b) pursuant to which the denial is made.

(7)Each agency shall—

(A) establish a system to assign an individualized tracking number for each request received that will take longer than ten days to process and provide to each person making a request the tracking number assigned to the request; and

(B) establish a telephone line or Internet service that provides information about the status of a request to the person making the request using the assigned tracking number, including—

(i) the date on which the agency originally received the request; and

(ii) an estimated date on which the agency will complete action on the request.

(b)This section does not apply to matters that are—

(1)(A) specifically authorized under criteria established by an Executive order to be kept secret in the interest of national defense or foreign policy and (B) are in fact properly classified pursuant to such Executive order;
(2) related solely to the internal personnel rules and practices of an agency;
(3) specifically exempted from disclosure by statute (other than section 552b of this title), if that statute—

(A)(i) requires that the matters be withheld from the public in such a manner as to leave no discretion on the issue; or
(ii) establishes particular criteria for withholding or refers to particular types of matters to be withheld; and
(B) if enacted after the date of enactment of the OPEN FOIA Act of 2009, specifically cites to this paragraph.

(4) trade secrets and commercial or financial information obtained from a person and privileged or confidential;
(5) inter-agency or intra-agency memorandums or letters which would not be available by law to a party other than an agency in litigation with the agency;
(6) personnel and medical files and similar files the disclosure of which would constitute a clearly unwarranted invasion of personal privacy;
(7) records or information compiled for law enforcement purposes, but only to the extent that the production of such law enforcement records or information (A) could reasonably be expected to interfere with enforcement proceedings, (B) would deprive a person of a right to a fair trial or an impartial adjudication, (C) could reasonably be expected to constitute an unwarranted invasion of personal privacy, (D) could reasonably be expected to disclose the identity of a confidential source, including a State, local, or foreign agency or authority

or any private institution which furnished information on a confidential basis, and, in the case of a record or information compiled by criminal law enforcement authority in the course of a criminal investigation or by an agency conducting a lawful national security intelligence investigation, information furnished by a confidential source, (E) would disclose techniques and procedures for law enforcement investigations or prosecutions, or would disclose guidelines for law enforcement investigations or prosecutions if such disclosure could reasonably be expected to risk circumvention of the law, or (F) could reasonably be expected to endanger the life or physical safety of any individual;

(8) contained in or related to examination, operating, or condition reports prepared by, on behalf of, or for the use of an agency responsible for the regulation or supervision of financial institutions; or

(9) geological and geophysical information and data, including maps, concerning wells.

Any reasonably segregable portion of a record shall be provided to any person requesting such record after deletion of the portions which are exempt under this subsection. The amount of information deleted, and the exemption under which the deletion is made, shall be indicated on the released portion of the record, unless including that indication would harm an interest protected by the exemption in this subsection under which the deletion is made. If technically feasible, the amount of the information deleted, and the exemption under which the deletion is made, shall be indicated at the place in the record where such deletion is made.

(c)(1) Whenever a request is made which involves access to records described in subsection (b)(7)(A) and—

(A) the investigation or proceeding involves a possible violation of criminal law; and

(B) there is reason to believe that (i) the subject of the investigation or proceeding is not aware of its pendency, and (ii) disclosure of the existence of the records could reasonably be expected to interfere with enforcement proceedings, the agency may, during only such time as that circumstance continues, treat the records as not subject to the requirements of this section.

(2) Whenever informant records maintained by a criminal law enforcement agency under an informant's name or personal identifier are requested by a third party according to the informant's name or personal identifier, the agency may treat the records as not subject to the requirements of this section unless the informant's status as an informant has been officially confirmed.

(3) Whenever a request is made which involves access to records maintained by the Federal Bureau of Investigation pertaining to foreign intelligence or counterintelligence, or international terrorism, and the existence of the records is classified information as provided in subsection (b)(1), the Bureau may, as long as the existence of the records remains classified information, treat the records as not subject to the requirements of this section.

(d) This section does not authorize withholding of information or limit the availability of records to the public, except as specifically stated in this section. This section is not authority to withhold information from Congress.

(e)(1) On or before February 1 of each year, each agency shall submit to the Attorney General of the United States a report which shall cover the preceding fiscal year and which shall include—

(A) the number of determinations made by the agency not to comply with requests for records made to such agency under subsection (a) and the reasons for each such determination;

(B)(i) the number of appeals made by persons under subsection (a)(6), the result of such appeals, and the reason for the action upon each appeal that results in a denial of information; and

(ii) a complete list of all statutes that the agency relies upon to authorize the agency to withhold information under subsection (b)(3), the number of occasions on which each statute was relied upon, a description of whether a court has upheld the decision of the agency to withhold information under

each such statute, and a concise description of the scope of
any information withheld;

(C) the number of requests for records pending before the agency
as of September 30 of the preceding year, and the median and
average number of days that such requests had been pending
before the agency as of that date;
(D) the number of requests for records received by the agency and
the number of requests which the agency processed;
(E) the median number of days taken by the agency to process different types of requests, based on the date on which the requests
were received by the agency;
(F) the average number of days for the agency to respond to a
request beginning on the date on which the request was received
by the agency, the median number of days for the agency to
respond to such requests, and the range in number of days for the
agency to respond to such requests;
(G) based on the number of business days that have elapsed since
each request was originally received by the agency—

  (i) the number of requests for records to which the agency
  has responded with a determination within a period up to
  and including 20 days, and in 20-day increments up to and
  including 200 days;
  (ii) the number of requests for records to which the agency
  has responded with a determination within a period greater
  than 200 days and less than 301 days;
  (iii) the number of requests for records to which the agency
  has responded with a determination within a period greater
  than 300 days and less than 401 days; and
  (iv) the number of requests for records to which the agency
  has responded with a determination within a period greater
  than 400 days;

(H) the average number of days for the agency to provide the
granted information beginning on the date on which the request
was originally filed, the median number of days for the agency to

provide the granted information, and the range in number of days for the agency to provide the granted information;

(I) the median and average number of days for the agency to respond to administrative appeals based on the date on which the appeals originally were received by the agency, the highest number of business days taken by the agency to respond to an administrative appeal, and the lowest number of business days taken by the agency to respond to an administrative appeal;

(J) data on the 10 active requests with the earliest filing dates pending at each agency, including the amount of time that has elapsed since each request was originally received by the agency;

(K) data on the 10 active administrative appeals with the earliest filing dates pending before the agency as of September 30 of the preceding year, including the number of business days that have elapsed since the requests were originally received by the agency;

(L) the number of expedited review requests that are granted and denied, the average and median number of days for adjudicating expedited review requests, and the number adjudicated within the required 10 days;

(M) the number of fee waiver requests that are granted and denied, and the average and median number of days for adjudicating fee waiver determinations;

(N) the total amount of fees collected by the agency for processing requests; and

(O) the number of full-time staff of the agency devoted to processing requests for records under this section, and the total amount expended by the agency for processing such requests.

(2) Information in each report submitted under paragraph (1) shall be expressed in terms of each principal component of the agency and for the agency overall.

(3) Each agency shall make each such report available to the public including by computer telecommunications, or if computer telecommunications means have not been established by the agency, by other electronic means. In addition, each agency shall make the raw statistical data used in its reports available electronically to the public upon request.

(4) The Attorney General of the United States shall make each report which has been made available by electronic means available at a single electronic access point. The Attorney General of the United States shall notify the Chairman and ranking minority member of the Committee on Government Reform and Oversight of the House of Representatives and the Chairman and ranking minority member of the Committees on Governmental Affairs and the Judiciary of the Senate, no later than April 1 of the year in which each such report is issued, that such reports are available by electronic means.

(5) The Attorney General of the United States, in consultation with the Director of the Office of Management and Budget, shall develop reporting and performance guidelines in connection with reports required by this subsection by October 1, 1997, and may establish additional requirements for such reports as the Attorney General determines may be useful.

(6) The Attorney General of the United States shall submit an annual report on or before April 1 of each calendar year which shall include for the prior calendar year a listing of the number of cases arising under this section, the exemption involved in each case, the disposition of such case, and the cost, fees, and penalties assessed under subparagraphs (E), (F), and (G) of subsection (a)(4). Such report shall also include a description of the efforts undertaken by the Department of Justice to encourage agency compliance with this section.

(f)For purposes of this section, the term—

(1) "agency" as defined in section 551(1) of this title includes any executive department, military department, Government corporation, Government controlled corporation, or other establishment in the executive branch of the Government (including the Executive Office of the President), or any independent regulatory agency; and

(2) "record" and any other term used in this section in reference to information includes—

(A) any information that would be an agency record subject to the requirements of this section when maintained by an agency in any format, including an electronic format; and

(B) any information described under subparagraph (A) that is maintained for an agency by an entity under Government contract, for the purposes of records management.

(g)The head of each agency shall prepare and make publicly available upon request, reference material or a guide for requesting records or information from the agency, subject to the exemptions in subsection (b), including—

(1) an index of all major information systems of the agency;
(2) a description of major information and record locator systems maintained by the agency; and
(3) a handbook for obtaining various types and categories of public information from the agency pursuant to chapter 35 of title 44, and under this section.

(h)(1) There is established the Office of Government Information Services within the National Archives and Records Administration.

(2)The Office of Government Information Services shall—

(A) review policies and procedures of administrative agencies under this section;
(B) review compliance with this section by administrative agencies; and
(C) recommend policy changes to Congress and the President to improve the administration of this section.

(3) The Office of Government Information Services shall offer mediation services to resolve disputes between persons making requests under this section and administrative agencies as a non-exclusive alternative to litigation and, at the discretion of the Office, may issue advisory opinions if mediation has not resolved the dispute.

(i) The Government Accountability Office shall conduct audits of administrative agencies on the implementation of this section and issue reports detailing the results of such audits.

(j) Each agency shall designate a Chief FOIA Officer who shall be a senior official of such agency (at the Assistant Secretary or equivalent level).

(k)The Chief FOIA Officer of each agency shall, subject to the authority of the head of the agency—

> (1) have agency-wide responsibility for efficient and appropriate compliance with this section;
> (2) monitor implementation of this section throughout the agency and keep the head of the agency, the chief legal officer of the agency, and the Attorney General appropriately informed of the agency's performance in implementing this section;
> (3) recommend to the head of the agency such adjustments to agency practices, policies, personnel, and funding as may be necessary to improve its implementation of this section;
> (4) review and report to the Attorney General, through the head of the agency, at such times and in such formats as the Attorney General may direct, on the agency's performance in implementing this section;
> (5) facilitate public understanding of the purposes of the statutory exemptions of this section by including concise descriptions of the exemptions in both the agency's handbook issued under subsection (g), and the agency's annual report on this section, and by providing an overview, where appropriate, of certain general categories of agency records to which those exemptions apply; and
> (6) designate one or more FOIA Public Liaisons.

(l) FOIA Public Liaisons shall report to the agency Chief FOIA Officer and shall serve as supervisory officials to whom a requester under this section can raise concerns about the service the requester has received from the FOIA Requester Center, following an initial response from the FOIA Requester Center Staff. FOIA Public Liaisons shall be responsible for assisting in reducing delays, increasing transparency and understanding of the status of requests, and assisting in the resolution of disputes.
(Pub. L. 89–554, Sept. 6, 1966, 80 Stat. 383; Pub. L. 90–23, § 1, June 5, 1967, 81 Stat. 54; Pub. L. 93–502, §§ 1–3, Nov. 21, 1974, 88 Stat. 1561–1564; Pub. L. 94–409, § 5(b), Sept. 13, 1976, 90 Stat. 1247; Pub. L. 95–454, title IX, § 906(a)(10), Oct. 13, 1978, 92 Stat. 1225; Pub. L.

98–620, title IV, § 402(2), Nov. 8, 1984, 98 Stat. 3357; Pub. L. 99–570, title I, §§ 1802, 1803, Oct. 27, 1986, 100 Stat. 3207–48, 3207–49; Pub. L. 104–231, §§ 3–11, Oct. 2, 1996, 110 Stat. 3049–3054; Pub. L. 107–306, title III, § 312, Nov. 27, 2002, 116 Stat. 2390; Pub. L. 110–175, §§ 3, 4(a), 5, 6(a)(1), (b)(1), 7(a), 8–10(a), 12, Dec. 31, 2007, 121 Stat. 2525–2530; Pub. L. 111–83, title V, § 564(b), Oct. 28, 2009, 123 Stat. 2184.)

APPENDIX C

Notable FOIL Cases

Cirale v. 80 Pine Street Corporation, 35 NY2d 113, 359 NYS2d 1 (1974)
Court of Appeals held that executive privilege exists despite passage of FOIL.

Dillon v. Cahn, 79 Misc.2d 300, 359 NYS2d 981 (1974)
First FOIL decision; records of district attorneys are covered by FOIL.

Farrell v. Village Board of Trustees, 372 NYS2d 905 (1975)
Police officers' reprimands available; led to passage of section 50-a of the New York State Civil Rights Law.

Burke v. Yudelson, 368 NYS2d 779, aff'd 51 AD2d 673, 378 NYS2d 165 (1976)
Landmark decision involving the "any person" principle and citing the COPAR resolution.

Zuckerman v. New York State Board of Parole, 385 NYS2d 811, 53 AD2d 405 (1976)
Finding that state agency regulations cannot be more restrictive than FOIL.

Dunlea v. Goldmark, 380 NYS2d 496, aff'd 54 AD2d 446, aff'd 43 NY2d 754 (1977)
Set definition of statistical or factual tabulations or data.

Sheehan v. City of Binghamton, 59 AD2d 808 (1977)
Made police blotters available.

Westchester Rockland v. Mosczydlowski, 58 AD2d 234 (1977)
Allowing exemption from FOIL only if records are prepared solely for litigation.

Warder v. Board of Regents, 410 NYS2d 742 (1978)
Personal notes taken during meeting are "records" subject to rights of access.

Zaleski v. Hicksville Union Free School District, Board of Education of Hicksville Union Free School, Supreme Court, Nassau County, NYLJ, Dec. 27, 1978

> Tape-recording of open meeting is considered an accessible "record"; the fee is the cost of cassette.

Doolan v. BOCES, 422 NYS2d 927, 48 NY2d 341 (1979)

> Found that FOIL is a governmental obligation, not a gift or waste, and rejected executive privilege.

Fink v. Lefkowitz, 63 AD2d 610 (1978); modified in 47 NY2d 567 (1979)

> Key Court of Appeals decision regarding investigative techniques and procedures.

People v. Ystueta, 99 Misc.2d 1105, 418 NYS2d 508 (1979)

> First decision involving tape-recording meetings; found that bylaw with blanket prohibition is invalid.

Herald Company v. School District of City of Syracuse, 430 NYS2d 460 (1980)

> Unproven charges against public employee are deniable.

Steinmetz v. Board of Education, East Moriches, Supreme Court, Suffolk County, NYLJ, October 30, 1980

> No exemption regarding personnel records; content determines rights of access.

Westchester-Rockland v. Kimball, 50 NY2d 575 (1980)

Court of Appeals

> Volunteer fire companies subject to FOIL despite status as not-for-profit corporations.

Geneva Printing Company and Donald C. Hadley v. Village of Lyons, Supreme Court, Wayne County, March 25, 1981

> "Confidential" settlement agreements with public employees are available.

Kwitny v. McGuire, 53 NY2d 968 (1981)

> Gun-license applications are available under Penal Law, despite FOIL exception.

Polansky v. Regan, 440 NYS2d 356, 81 AD2d 102 (1981)

> Estimates and recommendations in form of numbers are available as "statistical information."

Murray v. Troy Urban Renewal Agency, Supreme Court, Rensselaer County, April 24, 1980, rev'd 84 AD2d 612, 56 NY2d 888 (1982)

Appraisal deniable prior to sale based on impairment of contract award.
Morris v. Martin, Chairman of the State Board of Equalization and Assessment, 440 NYS2d 365, 82 AD2d 965, reversed 449 NYS2d 712, 55 NY2d 1026 (1982)

Local enactment is not a "statute" that exempts records from disclosure.
Short v. Board of Managers of Nassau County Medical Center, 57 NY2d 399 (1982)

If statute exempts a class of records, they are exempt in entirety; no redaction.
Babigian v. Evans, 427 NYS2d 699, aff'd 97 AD2d 992 (1983)

The Office of Court Administration is not a court but rather an "agency" subject to FOIL.
Feldman v. Town of Bethel, 106 AD2d 695 (1984)

Although a person has the right to tape-record meeting, he or she has no right to create public inconvenience, annoyance, or alarm.
Johnson Newspapers Corporation v. Stainkamp, 94 AD2d 825, 61 NY2d 958 (1984)

Identities of persons arrested are available unless charges were dismissed.
King v. Dillon, Supreme Court, Nassau County, December 19, 1984

Minutes of open meetings used for law enforcement are available.
M. Farbman & Sons v. New York City Health and Hospitals Corporation, 62 NY2d 75 (1984)

Confirmation of "any person" rule; pendency of litigation is irrelevant to FOIL.
Johnson Newspapers Corporation v. Call, 115 AD2d 335 (1985)

"Preference" of subject is irrelevant to disclosure; law controls.
Mitchell v. Board of Education of the Garden City Union Free School District, 113 AD2d 924 (1985)

Use of unobtrusive, handheld tape recorder cannot be prohibited, even though recordings can be edited or replayed.
Xerox Corporation v. Town of Webster, 65 NY2d 131, 490 NYS2d 488 (1985)

Court of Appeals Records prepared by consultant retained by agency are to be considered intra-agency materials.
Capital Newspapers v. Burns, 109 AD2d 92, aff'd 67 NY2d 562 (1986)

Police officer attendance records public, despite Civil Rights Law §50-a.

Konigsberg v. Coughlin, 68 NY2d 245 (1986)

Provides guidelines regarding the "reasonably describe" standard.

McGraw-Edison v. Williams, 509 NYS2d 285 (1986)

Inadvertent disclosure of deniable records does not create right of access.

Metro-ILA Pension Fund v. Waterfront Commission of New York Harbor, Supreme Court, New York County, NYLJ, Dec. 16, 1986

A bistate agency is not subject to FOIL.

Nalo v. Sullivan, 125 AD2d 311 (1986)

An agency is not required to list or justify denial of access to each record withheld.

Capital Newspapers Division of the Hearst Corporation v. Whalen, 69 NY2d 246 (1987)

"Corning papers" found to be "records" subjected to rights conferred by FOIL.

Sheehan v. City of Syracuse, 521 NYS2d 207 (1987)

Fee in excess of twenty-five cents is invalid if prescribed by local law, not by statute.

Citizens for Alternatives to Animal Labs v. Board of Trustees, 92NY2d 357 (1998)

Limited applicability of FOIL to Cornell University.

Fisher & Fisher v. Davison, Supreme Court, New York County, NYLJ, October 6, 1988

Unreasonably voluminous request.

Kerr v. Koch, Supreme Court, New York County, NYLJ, Feb. 1, 1988

New York City mayor's appointment calendar is available.

Prisoners' Legal Services of New York v. New York State Department of Correctional Services, 73 NY2d 26 (1988)

Grievances and records of rules violation by correction officers are subject to Civil Rights Law section 50-a.

Smithson v. Ilion Housing Authority, 130 AD2d 965 (1987), aff'd 72 NY2d 1034 (1988)

Secret ballot voting is improper.

American Society for the Prevention of Cruelty to Animals v. New York State Department of Agriculture and Markets, Supreme Court, Albany County, May 10, 1989

A business address is not "personal," and requesting it is not "unwarranted invasion of personal privacy."

Moore v. Santucci, 543 NYS2d 103, 151 AD2d 677 (1989)

> Records need not be disclosed a second time; they are available if introduced in judicial proceeding.

Barrett v. Morgenthau, 144 AD2d 1040, 74 NY2d 907 (1990)

> Failure to inform a person of the right to appeal enables that person to sue.

Brownstone Publishers, Inc. v. New York City Department of Finance, 167 AD2d 166 (1990)

> Applicant can choose electronic media over paper printout.

Miller v. Hewlett-Woodmere Union Free School District #14, Supreme Court, Nassau County, NYLJ, May 16, 1990

> The recommendation adopted becomes the final determination.

Whitehead v. Morgenthau, 552 NYS2d 518 (1990)

> No fee waiver is required, even if the request is made by indigent inmate.

American Society for the Prevention of Cruelty to Animals v. Board of Trustees of SUNY, 582 NYS2d 983, 79 NY2d 927 (1992)

> Court of Appeals held that entity outside coverage of the OML because its powers "derive solely from federal law." Also held that a "consensus" is a "judgment arrived at by most of those concerned by some sort of allocution by each member. Whether by "formal written ballot or informal oral expression, it is a vote" that must be recorded to comply with FOIL.

Second case: American Society for the Prevention of Cruelty to Animals v. Board of Trustees of State University of New York, 584 NYS2d 198, 184 AD2d 508 (1992)

> FOIL applies owing to the definition of the term "record," even though OML does not apply.

Hanig v. State Department of Motor Vehicles, 79 NY2d 106 (1992)

> Reasonable-person standard regarding unwarranted invasion of personal privacy.

Planned Parenthood of Westchester, Inc. v. Town Board of Town of Greenburgh, 587 NYS2d 461 (1992)

> Mugshots are available unless there is a dismissal of charges.

Gannett Company Inc. v. City Clerk's Office, City of Rochester, 596 NYS2d 968; aff'd 197 AD2d 919 (1993)

> Basic marriage license information is available.

Mitzner v. Goshen Central School District Board of Education and Superintendent Colistra, Supreme Court, Orange Co, April 15, 1993

Held that "bare-bones" resolutions and minutes that merely ratify action of president of board are inadequate.

Professional Standards Review Council of America Inc. v. New York State Department of Health, 597 NYS2d 829, 193 AD2d 937 (1993)

Rating sheets in the form of numbers are available as statistical information, but narratives are deniable.

Russo v. Nassau County Community College, 81 NY2d 690 (1993)

Films used in public college class are available.

Buffalo Broadcasting Company, Inc. v. New York State Department of Correctional Services, 552 NYS2d 712, 155 AD2d 106 (1990)

Not-for-profit corporation under government control is subject to FOIL.

Buffalo Teachers Federation v. Buffalo Board of Education, 549 NYS2d 541, 156 AD2d 1027 (1990)

Home addresses may be disclosed even though deniable.

Community Board 7 of Borough of Manhattan v. Schaeffer, 570 NYS 2d 769; affirmed, 83 AD 2d 422; reversed on other grounds, 84 NY 2d 148 (1994)

If there is no "inequality of knowledge," negotiation records are available.

Leeds v. Burns, 613 NYS2d 46, 205 AD2d 540 (1994)

No award of attorneys' fees can be made when there is a pro se nonlawyer litigant.

Murtha v. Leonard, 210 AD2d 411, 620 NYS2d 101 (1994)

Limitation of time to inspect rejected; may inspect during regular business hours.

Peloquin v. Arsenault, 616 NYS2d 716 (1994)

Board could not prohibit videotaping simply because doing so is "distasteful."

Town of Moriah v. Cole—Layer Tumble Company, 606 NYS2d 822, 200 AD2d 879 (1994)

Vote to commence litigation in executive session was valid, but failure to prepare minutes constituted failure to comply.

Weston v. Sloan, 84 NY2d 462 (1994)

Records regarding mailings of state senator are available.

Cross-Sound Ferry v. Department of Transportation, 634 NYS2d 575, 219 AD2d 346 (1995)

A contract award can be given when an agency chooses, not when all sign-offs are obtained.

Encore College Bookstores, Inc. v. Auxiliary Service Corporation of the State University, 87 NY2d 410 (1995)

Record kept "for" agency; trade-secret exception.

Orange County Publications v. Kiryas Joel Union Free School District, 724 NYS2d 167, 282 AD2d 604 (2001)

General description of services rendered by attorneys is available.

Gould, Scott and DeFelice v. New York City Police Department, 653 NYS2d 54, 89 NY2d 267 (1996)

Court of Appeals rejected "blanket denial"; gave direction re inter/ intra-agency exception.

Daily Gazette Company v. City of Schenectady, 93 NY2d 145 (1999)

Upheld New York State Civil Rights Law section 50-a in "egg-throwing" case.

Kwasnik v. City of New York and City University of New York, 691 NYS2d 525, 262 AD2d 171 (1999)

Portions of résumés relevant to position are available.

Mantica v. New York State Department of Health, 699 NYS2d 1, 94 NY2d 58 (1999)

Court of Appeals found that patients may obtain their own medical records under FOIL.

Pittari v. Pirro, 258 AD2d 202 (1999)

Generic denial regarding interference with judicial proceeding proper.

Stoll v. New York State College of Veterinary Medicine at Cornell University, 94 NY2d 162, 101 NYS2d 316 (1999)

Records unique to Cornell's statutory colleges are subject to FOIL.

VanNess v. Center for Animal Care and Control, Supreme Court, New York County, January 28, 1999

Government-created not-for-profit corporation is subject to FOIL; there is no right to inspect when portions are deniable.

County of Suffolk v. First American Real Estate Solutions, U.S. Court of Appeals, 2nd Circuit, 261 F.3rd 179 (2001)

Agencies may claim copyright protection, but only if conditions are met.

Newsday v. Empire State Development Corporation, 98 NY2d 359, 746 NYS2d 855 (2002)

Record from court to agency is an agency record subject to FOIL.

Daily News, L.P. v. New York City Office of Payroll Administration, 781 NYS2d 3, 9 AD3d 308 (2003)

Leave to appeal denied. Ages (not dates of birth) of public employees' are public.

Csorny v. Shoreham-Wading River Central School District, 759 NYS2d 513, 305 AD2d 83 (2003)

Claim of "intimidation" insufficient to prohibit use of video recording during meeting.

Buono v. Brodsky, Supreme Court, Albany County, December 30, 2004

Distinction between FOIL and subpoena; rejection of "executive privilege."

Newsday v. New York State Department of Transportation, 5NY3d 84, 833 NE2d 201 (2005)

Disclosure under federal statute precluding discovery in litigation does not preclude FOIL.

New York Times v. City of New York Fire Department, 4 NY3d 477, 796 NYS2d 302 (2005)

Recordings from Twin Towers denied in consideration of privacy of surviving family members; agency staff criticisms and suggestions deniable, even though not part of deliberative process; oral histories by employees are intended to be historical record and so are available.

Archdeacon v. Town of Oyster Bay, Supreme Court, Nassau County, NYLJ, Feb. 28, 2006

Financial disclosure statement is available for inspection and copying.

Baynes v. Fairport Central School District, Supreme Court, Monroe County, November 1, 2006

Union's records on school district computer are covered by FOIL.

Capital Newspapers v. Bruno and Silver, Supreme Court, Albany County, October 23, 2006

Member item information is available; attorneys' fees awarded.

Data Tree, LLC v. Romaine, 9 NY3d 454, 880 NE2d 10 (2007)

Extraction of data not creation of record; no "unwarranted invasion of personal privacy" when no direct solicitation.

Markowitz v. Serio, 11 NY3d 44, 893 NE2d 110 (2008)

Competitive harm must be proven, not speculative.

New York State Rifle and Pistol Association, Inc. v. Kelly, 863 NYS2d 439, 55 AD3d 222 (2008)

List of names and addresses sought for solicitation deniable.

Bly v. City of Yonkers, Supreme Court, Westchester County, March 17, 2009

Agency could not meet burden of proof relative to blanket denial regarding unsolved murder in 1952.

Verizon N.Y., Inc. v. Devita, 879 NYS2d 140, 60 AD3d 956 (2009)

Agency may disclose if exception applies and there has been a reasoned decision to do so.

West Harlem Business Group v. Empire State Development Corporation, 13 NY 3d 882 (2009)

Court of Appeals found that agency did not meet burden of proof owing to "superficial" determinations.

Hearst Corporation v. Research Foundation of the State of New York, Supreme Court, Albany County, September 17, 2010

Foundation subject to FOIL; issue remains unclear statewide.

Irwin v. Onondaga County Resource Recovery Agency, 70 AD3d 314, 895 NYS 2d 262 (2010)

Metadata constitute a "record."

New York State United Teachers v. Brighter Choice Charter School, 15 NY3d 560 (2010)

Charter schools subject to FOIL, but list of names of employees denied owing to concerns about solicitation.

Schenectady County Society for the Prevention of Cruelty to Animals v. Mills, 74 AD3d 1417, 904 NYS2d 511 (2010)

Disclosure of names and business addresses of licensed veterinarians; public agency must disclose in part.

Town of Waterford v. New York State Department of Environmental Conservation, 77 AD3d 224, 906 NYS2d 651 (2010)

Communications between state and federal agency is not interagency materials.

Harbatkin v. New York City Department of Records and Information Services, 19 NY3d 373, 948 NYS2d 220 (2012)

Informants' identities protected when given promise of confidentiality but may become available with passage of time.

Hernandez v. Office of the Mayor of the City of New York, 100 AD3d 555, 955 NYS2d 7 (1st Dept 2012)

> Email between mayor and nominee for chancellor not interagency or intra-agency communication because nominee not yet employed in that or other public position.

Lesher v. Hynes, 19 NY3d 57, 945 NYS2d 214 (2012)

> Generic denials of law enforcement records proper when investigation is ongoing, but records may be available in relation to "cold cases"; must meet burden of proof.

Madera v. Elmont Public Library, 101 AD3d 726, 957 NYS2d 129 (2nd Dept 2012)

> Voluntary disclosure of report to third party constituted waiver of ability to withhold as intra-agency material or attorney–client privilege.

Porco v Fleischer, 100 AD3d 639, 953 NYS2d 282 (2nd Dept 2012)

> Requesting EZ Pass data not identifiable to specific customers is not an unwarranted invasion of privacy.

Stevens and Zirilli v. New York State Thruway Authority, 86 F3d 289 (2012)

> Request of names and addresses of employees of private companies that contract with agencies reported under prevailing wage requirements is deniable as unwarranted invasion of personal privacy.

Weslowski v Vanderhoef, 98 AD3d 1123, 951 NYS2d 538 (3rd Dept 2012)

> No justification for fees that included charges for search or verification of electronic records with paper copies; agency not permitted to charge for "extraordinary effort" but required only to make reasonable effort.

Hearst Corporation v. New York State Police, 109 AD3d, 966 NYS2d 557 (3rd Dept 2013)

> Civil Rights Law section 50-a exemption regarding police officers' personnel records continues after officers' retirement.

Legal Aid Society v. New York State Department of Corrections, 105 AD3d 1120, 962 NYS2d 773 (3rd Dept 2013)

> Award of attorneys' fees proper when applicant subjected to unreasonable delays and denials of access.

Loevy & Loevy v. New York Police Department, Supreme Court, New York County, October 10, 2013

> Blanket denial regarding "cold case" inconsistent with FOIL.

Regenhard v. City of New York, 102 AD3d 612, 959 NYS2d (1st Dept, 2013)

> Names and home addresses of families or representatives of victims of terrorist attacks of September 11, 2001, deniable.

Empire Center for New York State Policy v. Teachers' Retirement System of City of New York, 103 AD3d 1009, (3d Dept 2014)

> Court of Appeals found that names of retirees are accessible; beneficiaries are persons designated by retirees to receive pension following death of retirees.

Gannett Satellite Information Network, Inc. v. County of Putnam and Office of Putnam County Clerk, Supreme Court, Westchester County (March 5, 2014)

> First decision under SAFE Act confirmed that names and addresses of licensees who do not choose to "opt out" of disclosure are accessible.

APPENDIX D

Sample FOIL Requests

The sample FOIL requests included here were provided by New York State's Committee on Open Government.

Requesting Records (Sample)

Records Access Officer
Name of Agency
Address of Agency
City, NY, ZIP code

Re: Freedom of Information Law Request

Records Access Officer:

Under the provisions of the New York Freedom of Information Law, Article 6 of the Public Officers Law, I hereby request records or portions thereof pertaining to [or "containing the following"] _____ [attempt to identify the records in which you are interested as clearly as possible]. If my request appears to be extensive or fails to reasonably describe the records, please contact me in writing or by phone at _____.

If there are any fees for copying the records requested, please inform me before filling the request [or "please supply the records without informing me if the fees are not in excess of $____"].

As you know, the Freedom of Information Law requires that an agency respond to a request within five business days of receipt of a request. Therefore, I would appreciate a response as soon as possible and look forward to hearing from you shortly. If for any reason any portion of my request is denied, please inform me of the reasons for

the denial in writing and provide the name and address of the person
or body to whom an appeal should be directed.

Sincerely,

Signature

Name

Address

City, State, ZIP code

Requesting Records via Email (Sample)

It has been suggested that agencies create an email address dedicated to the
receipt of requests. It is recommended that you review the website of the
agency maintaining the records that you seek to locate its email address and
its records-access officer.

The subject line of your request should be "FOIL Request."

Dear Records Access Officer:

Please email the following records if possible [include as much
detail about the record as possible, such as relevant dates, names,
descriptions, etc.]:

OR

Please advise me of the appropriate time during normal business
hours for inspecting the following records prior to obtaining copies [include as much detail about the records as possible, including
relevant dates, names, descriptions, etc.]:

OR

Please inform me of the cost of providing paper copies of the following records [include as much detail about the records as possible,
including relevant dates, names, descriptions, etc.]:

AND/OR

If all of the requested records cannot be emailed to me, please
inform me by email of the portions that can be emailed and advise

me of the cost for reproducing the remainder of the records requested ($0.25 per page or actual cost of reproduction).

If the requested records cannot be emailed to me due to the volume of records identified in response to my request, please advise me of the actual cost of copying all records onto a CD or floppy disk.

If my request is too broad or does not reasonably describe the records, please contact me via email so that I may clarify my request, and when appropriate inform me of the manner in which records are filed, retrieved, or generated.

If it is necessary to modify my request, and an email response is not preferred, please contact me at the following telephone number: _____ .

If for any reason any portion of my request is denied, please inform me of the reasons for the denial in writing and provide the name, address. and email address of the person or body to whom an appeal should be directed.

Sincerely,

Signature

Name

Address (if records are to be mailed)

Appeal a Written Denial (Sample)

Name of Agency Official

Appeals Officer

Name of Agency

Address of Agency

City, NY, ZIP code

Re: Freedom of Information Law Appeal

Dear _____ :

I hereby appeal the denial of access regarding my request, which was made on _____ [date] and sent to _____ [records-access officer, name and address of agency].

The records that were denied include: _____ [describe the records that were denied to the extent possible and, if possible, offer reasons for disagreeing with the denial—for example, by attaching an opinion of the Committee on Open Government acquired from its website].

As required by the Freedom of Information Law, the head or governing body of an agency or whoever is designated to determine appeals is required to respond within ten business days of the receipt of an appeal. If the records are denied on appeal, please explain the reasons for the denial fully in writing, as required by law.

In addition, please be advised that the Freedom of Information Law directs that all appeals and the determinations that follow be sent to the Committee on Open Government, Department of State, One Commerce Plaza, 99 Washington Ave., Albany, New York 12231.

> Sincerely,
> Signature
> Name
> Address
> City, State, ZIP code

Appeal a Denial Due to an Agency's Failure to Respond in a Timely Manner (Sample)

FOIL Appeals Officer
Name of Agency
Address of Agency
City, NY, ZIP code

Re: Freedom of Information Law Appeal

Dear _____:

I requested [describe the records] by written request made on _____ [date]. More than five business days have passed since the receipt of the request without my having received a response.

OR

Although the receipt of the request was acknowledged, and I was informed that a response would be given by _____ [date], no response has been given. Consequently, I consider the request to have been denied, and I am appealing on that basis.

As required by the Freedom of Information Law, the head or governing body of an agency or whoever is designated to determine appeals is required to respond within ten business days of the receipt of an appeal. If the records are denied on appeal, please explain the reasons for the denial fully in writing, as required by law.

In addition, please be advised that the Freedom of Information Law directs that all appeals and the determinations that follow be sent to the Committee on Open Government, Department of State, One Commerce Plaza, 99 Washington Ave., Albany, New York 12231.

                    Sincerely,
                        Signature
                        Name
                        Address (City, State, ZIP code)

Notes

1. A Brief History of New Yorkers' Right to Know

1. Jon Campbell, "SUNY Poly's Power Extends into Shadowy World," *Rochester Democrat and Chronicle*, June 11, 2016, http://www.democratandchronicle.com/story/news/2016/06/11/fort-schuyler-fuller-road-suny-polytechnic-investigation/85554264/.

2. New York State Committee on Open Government (COOG), "Advisory Opinion AO-19255," Mar. 3, 2015.

3. Ibid.

4. Jim Heaney, "Suppression of Buffalo Billions Spending Records," *Investigative Post*, Dec. 22, 2014, http://www.investigativepost.org/2014/12/22/stonewalling-spending-buffalo-billion/.

5. Jim Heaney, "State Relents on Buffalo Billion Records," *Investigative Post*, July 28, 2015, http://www.investigativepost.org/2015/07/28/state-relents-on-buffalo-billion-records/.

6. Ibid.

7. New York State COOG, *40 Years of FOIL and the Committee on Open Government* (Albany: COOG, Sept. 2014), 1, http://www.dos.ny.gov/coog/pdfs/Timeline2014.pdf.

8. Bob Freeman, interviewed by Brett Orzechowski, May 18, 2016.

9. New York State COOG, *Committee on Open Government Annual Report to the Governor and State Legislature* (Albany: COOG, Dec. 2016), https://www.dos.ny.gov/coog/pdfs/2016%20Annual%20Report.pdf.

10. Grace Rauh, "Mayor Keeps E-mails with Outside Consultants Secret, Fueling Accusations of a Shadow Government," NY1, May 18, 2016, http://www.ny1.com/nyc/all-boroughs/politics/2016/05/18/mayor-keeps-emails-with-outside-consultants-secret.html.

11. Jon Campbell, "Transparency Watchdog Says de Blasio's 'Agents of the City' Excuse Is Bogus," *Village Voice*, Aug. 3, 2016. https://www.villagevoice

.com/2016/08/03/transparency-watchdog-says-de-blasios-agents-of-the-city
-excuse-is-bogus/.

12. Freeman interview, May 18, 2016.

13. Grace Rauh, "NY1 Sues City Hall in Freedom of Information Battle,"
NY1, Sept. 9, 2016, http://www.ny1.com/nyc/all-boroughs/politics/2016/09/8/ny1
-sues-city-hall-in-freedom-of-information-battle.html.

14. Jon Campbell, "De Blasio on His Agents of the City E-mails: Every
Mayor Does It, Don't Worry about It," *Village Voice*, Nov. 29, 2016, http://www
.villagevoice.com/news/de-blasio-on-his-agents-of-the-city-emails-every-mayor-
does-it-dont-worry-about-it-9400034.

15. Grace Rauh, "NY1 Lawsuit against Mayor over His Emails with Outside
Adviser Moves Ahead," NY1, Dec. 8, 2016, http://www.ny1.com/nyc/all-boroughs
/politics/2016/12/8/ny1-lawsuit-against-mayor-over-his-emails-with-outside-adviser
-moves-ahead.html.

16. Quoted in Rich Calder, "De Blasio Must Release E-mails with Close
Private Advisors," *New York Post*, Mar. 23, 2017, http://nypost.com/2017/03/23
/de-blasio-must-release-emails-with-close-private-advisers/.

17. Freeman interview, May 18, 2016.

18. New York State COOG, *40 Years of FOIL and the Committee on Open
Government*, 1.

19. Hon. Ralph J. Marino, "The New York Freedom of Information Law,"
Fordham Law Review 43, no. 1 (1974): 83, http://ir.lawnet.fordham.edu/flr/vol43
/iss1/3.

20. Robert D. McFadden, "Ralph J. Marino, Former State Senate
Leader, Dies at 74," *New York Times*, Apr. 7, 2002, http://www.nytimes
.com/2002/04/07/nyregion/ralph-j-marino-former-state-senate-leader-dies-at
-74.html.

21. New York State COOG, *40 Years of FOIL and the Committee on Open
Government*, 2.

22. Ibid.

23. *Congress Overrode President Ford's Veto of Court Review*, in *National
Security Archive Electronic Briefing Book No. 142*, Nov. 23, 2004, http://ns
archive.gwu.edu/NSAEBB/NSAEBB142/.

24. New York State COOG, *40 Years of FOIL and the Committee on Open
Government*, 2.

25. Ibid.

26. Ibid., 1.

27. Ibid.

28. Louis Contiguglia, interviewed by Brett Orzechowski, May 24, 2016.

29. US Department of Education, *Legislative History of Major FERPA Provisions* (Washington, DC: US Department of Education, Feb. 11, 2014), http:// www2.ed.gov/policy/gen/guid/fpco/ferpa/leg-history.html.

30. Freeman interview, May 18, 2016.

31. Richard Liebson, "Longtime Editor, Civic Leader Bill Bookman Dies at 92," *Westchester Journal News*, Jan. 28, 2015, http://www.lohud.com/story/news /local/westchester/2015/01/28/bill-bookman-editor-civic-leader-dies/22481051/.

32. Ibid.

33. New York State COOG, *40 Years of FOIL and the Committee on Open Government*, 3.

34. Ibid.; Burke v. Yudelson, 368 NYS2d 779, aff'd 51 AD2d 673, 378 NYS2d 165 (1976); Zuckerman v. New York State Board of Parole, 385 NYS2d 811, 53 AD2d 405 (1976).

35. Dunlea v. Goldmark, 380 NYS2d 496, aff'd 54 AD2d 446, aff'd 43 NY2d 754 (1977); Sheehan v. City of Binghamton, 59 AD2d 808 (1977); Westchester Rockland v. Mosczydlowski, 58 AD2d 234 (1977).

36. New York State COOG, *40 Years of FOIL and the Committee on Open Government*, 3.

37. Bill Mahoney and Jimmy Vielkind, "Cuomo Vetoes Bills for Transparency, Wine Shipping, and CUNY, SUNY Funding," *Politico*, Dec. 12, 2015, http://www.politico.com/states/new-york/albany/story/2015/12/cuomo-vetoes -bills-for-transparency-wine-shipping-and-cuny-suny-funding-029079.

38. Ibid.

39. Casey Seiler, "Cuomo's Executive Order Follows FOIL Vetoes," *Albany Times Union*, Dec. 12, 2015, http://www.timesunion.com/local/article/Cuomo-order -Fast-track-Freedom-of-Information-6693990.php.

40. Diane Kennedy, interviewed by Brett Orzechowski, May 23, 2016.

2. Legacy Media: Choices and Challenge

1. Rick Edmonds, "Newspaper Industry Lost 3,800 Full-Time Editorial Professionals in 2014," *Poynter*, July 28, 2015, http://www.poynter.org/2015/newspaper -industry-lost-3800-full-time-editorial-professionals-in-2014/360633/.

2. Rick Edmonds, "Print Advertising Woes Are Getting Worse," *Poynter*, Oct. 21, 2016, http://www.poynter.org/2016/print-advertising-woes-are-getting -worse/435402/.

3. Jodi Edna, Katerina Eva Matsa, and Jan Lauren Boyles, "America's Shifting Statehouse Press," Pew Research Center, July 10, 2014, http://www.journalism .org/2014/07/10/americas-shifting-statehouse-press/.

4. Brendan Lyons, interviewed by Brett Orzechowski, June 28, 2016.

5. Michael Huber, "Tuffey Had Knowledge of Sticker System," *Albany Times Union*, Mar. 31, 2009, http://blog.timesunion.com/readandreact/440/secret-system -shields-privileged-from-albany-parking-tickets/.

6. Lyons interview, June 28, 2016.

7. Brendan J. Lyons, "'Bull's-Eye' Stickers from Albany Police Union Give 'Pass' on Fines to Hundreds," *Albany Times Union*, Nov. 15, 2008.

8. Jordan Carleo-Evangelist, "Audit: Loss Defies Count," *Albany Times Union*, Aug. 8, 2009, http://www.timesunion.com/local/article/Audit-Loss -defies-count-547149.php.

9. Brendan J. Lyons, "Albany Pays $70,000 to Settle FOIL-Denial Case," *Albany Times Union*, Apr. 4, 2012.

10. Ibid.

11. Brendan J. Lyons and Jordan Carleo-Evangelist, "The Fall of a Police Chief," *Albany Times Union*, Sept. 2, 2009, http://www.timesunion.com/local /article/The-fall-of-a-police-chief-545389.php.

12. Jordan Carleo-Evangelist, "'Ghost Tickets' Had Repercussions," *Albany Times Union*, Dec. 27, 2009, http://www.timesunion.com/local/article/Ghost -tickets-had-repercussions-560678.php.

13. Lyons, "Albany Pays $70,000 to Settle FOIL-Denial Case."

14. Ibid.

15. Lyons interview, June 28, 2016.

16. Ibid.

17. Mark Mahoney, interviewed by Brett Orzechowski, June 8, 2016.

18. "Board Members Should Have Full Access to Schools" (editorial), *Glens Falls Post-Star*, Jan. 16, 2008.

19. "Silencing of Board Members Violates First Amendment Rights" (editorial), *Glens Falls Post-Star*, Dec. 10, 2008.

20. "Comptroller, Whitehall Board Worked Together to Shut Out Public from Audit Meeting" (editorial), *Glens Falls Post-Star*, July 17, 2008.

21. "Public Is Paying for Decisions in Which It Has No Input" (editorial), *Glens Falls Post-Star*, Nov. 13, 2008.

22. Ibid.

23. Pulitzer Prize Board, "The 2009 Pulitzer Prize Winner in Editorial Writing," 2009, http://www.pulitzer.org/prize-winners-by-year/2009.

24. Mahoney interview, June 8, 2016.

25. James T. Mulder, "The Rise and Fall of Dr. David R. Smith, Former Upstate President Accused of Padding His Pay," *Syracuse Post-Standard*, Nov. 10, 2013, http://www.syracuse.com/news/index.ssf/2013/11/post_933.html.

26. John O'Brien, "FBI Investigating Upstate Medical Administrators' Compensation, Sources Say," *Syracuse Post-Standard*, Dec. 11, 2013, http://www.syracuse.com/news/index.ssf/2013/12/upstate_medical_administrators_outside_pay_could_land_them_in_legal_trouble_expe.html.

27. "No Contract for Upstate's Ex-Boss? SUNY's Foggy Answers Do Little to Inspire Confidence" (editorial), *Syracuse Post-Standard*, Mar. 4, 2014, http://www.syracuse.com/opinion/index.ssf/2014/03/no_contract_for_upstates_ex-boss_sunys_foggy_answers_do_little_to_inspire_confid.html#incart_river.

28. "SUNY Responds to Editorial and Story about Upstate President's Contract" (editorial), *Syracuse Post-Standard*, Mar. 5, 2014, http://www.syracuse.com/opinion/index.ssf/2014/03/suny_responds_to_editorial_and_story_about_upstate_presidents_contract.html.

29. John O'Brien, "SUNY Violates the Law by Withholding Upstate's Public Records, Legal Experts Say," *Syracuse Post-Standard*, Mar. 12, 2014, http://www.syracuse.com/news/index.ssf/2014/03/sunys_violating_the_law_by_denying_access_to_records_in_upstate_medical_investig.html.

30. James T. Mulder, "Audit: $33 Million Upstate Medical School Fund Was Ripe for Abuse," *Syracuse Post-Standard*, Mar. 8, 2015, http://www.syracuse.com/health/index.ssf/2015/03/audit_33_million_upstate_medical_school_fund_was_ripe_for_abuse.html.

31. Ibid.

32. John O'Brien, interviewed by Brett Orzechowski, June 8 2016.

33. Haley Viccaro, "Woman: Schenectady Mayor Was Highly Intoxicated during Encounter," *Schenectady Gazette*, May 25, 2016, http://www.dailygazette.com/news/2016/may/25/police-mccarthy-late-night-run-not-criminal/.

34. Paul Nelson, "No Charges against Schenectady Mayor in May Incident," *Albany Times Union*, Jan. 13, 2017, http://www.timesunion.com/local/article/No-charges-against-Gary-McCarthy-in-May-incident-10856326.php.

35. "Has Camera Use Gone Too Far?" (editorial), *Schenectady Gazette*, Feb. 7, 2016, http://www.dailygazette.com/news/2016/feb/07/2007editcameras/.

36. "Can Households Use CCTV to Film the Public Highway as Well as Their Home?" *Guardian*, Aug. 31, 2010, https://www.theguardian.com/commentisfree/libertycentral/2010/aug/31/householders-cctv-public-highway-film.

37. Mahoney interview, June 8, 2016.

38. James M. Odato, "Odato: Meter Running on E-mail," *Albany Times Union*, June 30, 2013, http://www.timesunion.com/local/article/Odato-Meter-s-running-on-email-4639539.php.

39. Jimmy Vielkind, "After Outcry, Cuomo Reverses E-mail Deletion Policy," *Politico*, May 22, 2013, http://www.politico.com/states/new-york/albany /story/2015/05/after-outcry-cuomo-reverses-email-deletion-policy-022371.

40. Lyons interview, June 28, 2016.

3. Digital Media: Access and Denial

1. Jim Heaney, interviewed by Brett Orzechowski, May 25, 2016.

2. Thomas Kaplan, "Cuomo Focuses on Job Creation in 2012 Agenda," *New York Times*, Jan. 4, 2012, http://www.nytimes.com/2012/01/05/nyregion /governor-cuomo-delivers-state-of-the-state-address.html.

3. Jim Heaney, "Cuomo Still Stonewalling on Buffalo Billion," *Investigative Post*, Mar. 24, 2015, http://www.investigativepost.org/2015/03/24/cuomo-still -stonewalling-on-buffalo-billion/.

4. New York State Committee on Open Government (COOG), "Advisory Opinion: SUNY Foundation," Mar. 3, 2015, http://ipost.wpengine.netdna-cdn .com/wp-content/uploads/2015/03/cfrench.pdf.

5. Jim Heaney, "Buffalo Billion Probe Targets Cuomo Insiders," *Investigative Post*, Apr. 29, 2016, http://www.investigativepost.org/2016/04/29/buffalo-billion -probe-targets-cuomo-insiders/.

6. Benjamin Weiser, "Sentencings for Dean Skelos and Sheldon Silver Now Set for Same Day," *New York Times*, Mar. 14, 2016, http://www.nytimes.com /2016/03/15/nyregion/sentencings-for-dean-skelos-and-sheldon-silver-are-now -set-for-same-day.html.

7. Benjamin Weiser, "Dean Skelos's 2015 Corruption Conviction Is Over-turned," *New York Times*, Sept. 26, 2017, https://www.nytimes.com/2017/09/26 /nyregion/dean-skelos-2015-corruption-conviction-overturned.html.

8. Jim Heaney, "Suppression of Buffalo Billion Spending Records," *Investigative Post*, Dec. 22, 2014, http://www.investigativepost.org/2015/07/28/state -relents-on-buffalo-billion-records/.

9. Jim Heaney, "iPost Sues over Suppression of Records," *Investigative Post*, May 19, 2015, http://www.investigativepost.org/2015/05/19/ipost-sues-over -suppression-of-records/.

10. Charlotte Keith, "Tainted Contract Nets LPCiminelli $20 Million," *Investigative Post*, Nov. 9, 2016, http://www.investigativepost.org/2016/11/09 /allegedly-rigged-contract-pays-well-for-ciminelli/.

11. Jim Heaney, "Shenanigans Beset Buffalo Billion," *Investigative Post*, June 22, 2015, http://www.investigativepost.org/2015/06/22/shenanigans-beset -buffalo-billion/.

12. Jim Heaney, "State Relents on Buffalo Billion Records," *Investigative Post*, July 28, 2015, http://www.investigativepost.org/2015/07/28/state-relents-on-buffalo-billion-records/.

13. Heaney, "iPost Sues over Suppression of Records."

14. Ibid.

15. Ibid.

16. Quoted in ibid.

17. Heaney, "Suppression of Buffalo Billion Spending Records."

18. New York State COOG, "Advisory Opinion: SUNY Foundation."

19. Heaney, "State Relents on Buffalo Billion Records."

20. Ibid.

21. Larry Rulison, "Exclusive: SUNY Poly Merging Fuller Road, Fort Schuyler," *Albany Times Union*, Aug. 10, 2016, http://www.timesunion.com/tuplus-local/article/Exclusive-SUNY-Poly-merging-Fuller-Road-Fort-9133695.php.

22. Heaney interview, May 25, 2016.

23. Cezary Podkul and Marcelo Rochabrun, "Landlords Fail to List 50,000 NYC Apartments for Rent Limits," *ProPublica*, Nov. 5, 2015, https://www.ProPublica.org/article/landlords-fail-to-list-fifty-thousand-nyc-apartments-for-rent-limits.

24. Ibid.

25. Ibid.

26. Cezary Podkul, interviewed by Brett Orzechowski, June 8, 2016.

27. Ibid.

28. Ibid.

29. Cezary Podkul and Gregory Korte, "'Earmarks' to Nowhere: States Losing Billions," *USA Today*, Jan. 5, 2011, http://usatoday30.usatoday.com/news/washington/2011-01-04-earmarks_n.htm.

30. Ibid.

31. Podkul interview, June 8, 2016.

32. US Department of Commerce, Economics and Statistics Administration, Office of the Chief Economist, *Economic Impact of Hurricane Sandy: Potential Economic Activity Lost and Gained in New Jersey and New York* (Washington, DC: US Department of Commerce, Sept. 2013), http://www.esa.doc.gov/sites/default/files/sandyfinal101713.pdf.

33. Emmarie Huetteman, "New Jersey Representative, Citing Fraud, Calls on Congress to Investigate FEMA," *New York Times*, Apr. 28, 2016, http://www.nytimes.com/2016/04/29/nyregion/new-jersey-congressman-citing-fraud-calls-on-congress-to-investigate-fema.html.

34. Joaquin Sapien, interviewed by Brett Orzechowski, June 10, 2016.

35. Joaquin Sapien, "Foiled by FOIL: How One City Agency Has Dragged Out a Request for Public Records for Nearly a Year," *ProPublica*, Apr. 21, 2016, https://www.ProPublica.org/article/how-city-agency-dragged-out-request-for-public-records-for-nearly-a-year.

36. Joaquin Sapien, "Violent Crimes Mar Effort at Less Restrictive Homes for Children," *ProPublica*, June 5, 2015, https://www.ProPublica.org/article/violent-crimes-mar-effort-at-less-restrictive-homes-for-children.

37. Ibid.

38. Quoted in Sapien, "Foiled by FOIL."

39. Joaquin Sapien, "Investigation Exposes Failings of Oversight in NYC Group Homes," *ProPublica*, Apr. 13, 2016, https://www.ProPublica.org/article/investigation-exposes-failings-of-oversight-in-nyc-group-homes.

40. Ibid.

41. Sapien interview, June 10, 2016.

42. Joseph Lichterman, "*MuckRock* Is Launching a National Database of FOIA Exemptions," NiemanLab, July 14, 2016, http://www.niemanlab.org/2016/07/MuckRock-is-launching-a-national-database-of-foia-exemptions/.

43. Jie Jenny Zou and Shawn Musgrave, "In Pursuit of Open Records," *New York World*, Aug. 18, 2015, http://www.thenewyorkworld.com/2015/08/18/pursuit-open-records-2/.

44. Jie Jenny Zou, interviewed by Brett Orzechowski, June 6, 2016.

45. Ibid.

46. Jie Jenny Zou and Shawn Musgrave, "FOIL'd: The Pursuit of Open Records in New York: Lost and Unfound in the Empire State," *MuckRock*, Aug. 18, 2015, https://www.MuckRock.com/news/archives/2015/aug/18/ny-foil-assessment/.

47. Ibid.

48. Zou interview, June 6, 2016.

4. Article 78: Last Resort, First Step

1. Danny Hakim, "10 Republicans Dominate Senate's Pet Projects, with Bruno's $6.4 Million Topping the List," *New York Times*, Dec. 8, 2006, http://www.nytimes.com/2006/12/08/nyregion/08pork.html.

2. Capitol Newspaper Division of Hearst Corporation and Robert J. Port v. Bruno, Silver, Boggess, and Walsh, Supreme Court of the State of New York, County of Albany, Oct. 3, 2006, https://www.dos.ny.gov/coog/pdfs/casestudies/cap_news_bruno.pdf.

3. Ibid.

4. David Carr, "Subpoenas and the Press," *New York Times*, Nov. 27, 2006, http://www.nytimes.com/2006/11/27/business/media/27carr.html?_r=0.

5. Eve Burton, interviewed by Brett Orzechowski, Aug. 4, 2016.

6. Capitol Newspaper Division of Hearst Corporation and Robert J. Port v. Bruno, Silver, Boggess, and Walsh.

7. Ibid.

8. Ibid.

9. Ibid.

10. Burton interview, Aug. 4, 2016.

11. Ibid.

12. Hakim, "10 Republicans Dominate Senate's Pet Projects."

13. Robert Gavin, "Bruno Acquitted," *Albany Times Union*, May 19, 2014, http://www.timesunion.com/local/article/Bruno-acquitted-5483377.php; Matthew Hamilton, "Sheldon Silver Sentenced to 12 Years in Prison," *Albany Times Union*, May 3, 2016, http://www.timesunion.com/local/article/Sheldon-Silver -sentenced-to-12-years-in-prison-7391561.php.

14. Michael J. Grygiel, interviewed by Brett Orzechowski, June 17, 2016.

15. Gannett Satellite Information Network, Inc. v. County of Putnam and Office of Putnam County Clerk, New York State Supreme Court, Appellate Division, Second Department, Jan. 5, 2015.

16. James Barron, "Nation Reels After Gunman Massacres 20 Children at School in Connecticut," *New York Times*, Dec. 14, 2012, http://www.nytimes.com/2012 /12/15/nyregion/shooting-reported-at-connecticut-elementary-school.html?_r=0.

17. Jon Campbell, "N.Y. First State to Tighten Gun Laws after Newtown," *USA Today*, Jan. 15, 2013, http://www.usatoday.com/story/news/nation/2013 /01/15/new-york-assault-weapons-guns/1835785/.

18. Becky Bratu and Pete Williams, "New York Passes Major Gun Control Law—First since Newtown Massacre," *NBC News*, Jan. 15, 2013, http://usnews .nbcnews.com/_news/2013/01/15/16515653-new-york-passes-major-gun-control -law-first-since-newtown-massacre?lite.

19. John Dankosky, "Covering Trauma," WNPR, Apr. 29, 2013, http://wnpr .org/post/covering-trauma#stream/0.

20. David J. Goodman, "Newspaper Takes Down Map of Gun Permit Holders," *New York Times*, Jan. 13, 2013, http://www.nytimes.com/2013/01/19/ny region/newspaper-takes-down-map-of-gun-permit-holders.html.

21. Ibid.

22. Gannett Satellite Information Network, Inc. v. County of Putnam and Office of Putnam County Clerk," Supreme Court of the State of New York, Westchester County, Mar. 5, 2014, https://www.dos.ny.gov/coog/pdfs/gannett vputnam.pdf.

23. Ibid.

24. Ibid.

25. Ibid.

26. Abbey Oldham, "2015: The Year of Mass Shootings," PBS, Jan. 4, 2016, http://www.pbs.org/newshour/rundown/2015-the-year-of-mass-shootings/.

27. Gannett Satellite Information Network, Inc. v. County of Putnam and Office of Putnam County Clerk, Mar. 5, 2014.

28. Ibid.

29. Jonathan Bandler, "Putnam Loses Appeal on *Journal News*' Access to Gun Data," *Westchester Journal News*, Sept. 16, 2016, http://www.lohud.com /story/news/local/putnam/2016/09/15/putnam-loses-appeal-newspapers-access /90415762/.

30. Roy Gutterman, interviewed by Brett Orzechowski, June 13, 2016.

31. Grygiel interview, June 17, 2016.

32. Mark Fowler, interviewed by Orzechowski, June 16, 2016.

5. Exemption, Ethics, and the Joint Commission on Public Ethics

1. Karl Sleight, interviewed by Brett Orzechowski, July 26, 2016.

2. Michael Cooper, "Hevesi's Lawyers Take on Ethics Commission," *New York Times*, Nov. 1, 2006, http://www.nytimes.com/2006/11/01/nyregion/01 hevesi.html?_r=0.

3. Ibid.

4. Ibid.

5. Diane Cardwell, "Despite Accusations, Hevesi Is Re-elected New York's Comptroller," *New York Times*, Nov. 8, 2006, http://www.nytimes.com/2006 /11/08/nyregion/08hevesi.html.

6. John Eligon, "Hevesi Sentenced to One to Four Years," *New York Times*, Apr. 15, 2011, http://cityroom.blogs.nytimes.com/2011/04/15/hevesi-sentenced-to -one-to-four-years/.

7. Sleight interview, July 26, 2016.

8. Lawrence Norden, Kelly Williams, and John Travis, "Meaningful Ethics Reform for the 'New' Albany," Brennan Center for Justice Reform, New York University School of Law, Feb. 11, 2011, https://www.brennancenter.org /publication/meaningful-ethics-reform-new-albany.

9. New York State Joint Commission on Public Ethics, *2015 Annual Report* (Albany: New York State, Apr. 7, 2016), http://www.jcope.ny.gov/pubs/POL /2015_%20Annual%20Report_%20FINAL_4_6_16.pdf.

10. Ibid.

11. Bob Freeman, interviewed by Brett Orzechowski, Aug. 4, 2016.

12. Susanne Craig, William K. Rashbaum, and Thomas Kaplan, "Cuomo's Office Hobbled Ethics Inquiries by Moreland Commission," *New York Times*,

July 23, 2014, https://www.nytimes.com/2014/07/23/nyregion/governor-andrew
-cuomo-and-the-short-life-of-the-moreland-commission.html.

13. New York State Executive Department, Office of the Governor, *3.10
Executive Order No. 10: Directing Filing of Financial Statements by Certain
Officers and Employees within the Executive Department,* July 31, 1981, https://
govt.westlaw.com/nycrr/Document/I4ef7fdc5cd1711dda432a117e6e0f345?view
Type=FullText&originationContext=documenttoc&transitionType=Statute
Navigator&contextData=(sc.Default)&bhcp=1.

14. New York State Executive Department, Office of the Governor, *4.3
Executive Order No. 3: Establishing a Board of Public Disclosure,* Jan. 18, 1983,
https://govt.westlaw.com/nycrr/Document/I4ef9f995cd1711dda432a117e6e0f345
?viewType=FullText&originationContext=documenttoc&transitionType
=CategoryPageItem&contextData=(sc.Default).

15. David Howard King, "Investigating the NY Legislature Isn't Easy. Just
Ask Mario Cuomo," *Gotham Gazette* (New York), June 24, 2013, http://www
.gothamgazette.com/index.php/government/4292-investigating-the-ny-legislature
-isnt-easy-just-ask-mario-cuomo.

16. Peter Bienstock, interviewed by Brett Orzechowski, Aug. 2, 2016.

17. Ibid.

18. John D. Feerick, "Reflections on Chairing the New York State Commission on Government Integrity," *Fordham Urban Law Journal* 18, no. 2 (1990):
161, http://ir.lawnet.fordham.edu/cgi/viewcontent.cgi?article=1340&context=ulj.

19. Ibid., 158.

20. Ibid., 163, 170.

21. Associated Press, "Russell Simmons Victorious in Lobbying Case," Aug.
18, 2004, http://www.foxnews.com/story/2004/08/18/russell-simmons-victorious
-in-lobbying-case.html.

22. Andy Soltis, "Vegas Casino Socked over Silver Service," *New York
Post,* Oct. 6, 2005, http://nypost.com/2005/10/06/vegas-casino-socked-over
-silver-ervice/.

23. Danny Hakim, "For Chief Ethics Watchdog in Albany, a Dozen Years
of Conflict Draw to a Close," *New York Times,* Sept. 20, 2007, http://www
.nytimes.com/2007/09/20/nyregion/20grandeau.html?_r=0.

24. Ibid.

25. Chris Bragg, "'Dark Prince' Gets His Revenge," *Crain's New York Business,* Dec. 7, 2014, http://www.crainsnewyork.com/article/20141207/POLITICS
/141209867/dark-prince-gets-his-revenge.

26. Grandeau interview, July 28, 2016.

27. Ibid.

28. Ibid.

29. Celeste Katz, "Vito Lopez Responds to JCOPE Investigation, Says He Faced 'All-Out War'—and Survived," *New York Daily News*, May 15, 2013, http://www.nydailynews.com/blogs/dailypolitics/vito-lopez-responds-jcope-investigation-faced-all-out-war-survived-blog-entry-1.1694641.

30. Casey Seiler, "JCOPE Names Former Cuomo Aide as Executive Director," *Albany Times Union*, May 22, 2016, http://blog.timesunion.com/capitol/archives/247354/jcope-names-former-cuomo-aide-as-executive-director/.

31. Chris Bragg, "Two JCOPE Commissioners Quietly Depart," *Albany Times Union*, Apr. 12, 2016, http://www.timesunion.com/tuplus-local/article/Two-JCOPE-commissioners-quietly-depart-7243678.php.

32. Chris Bragg, "Another JCOPE Commissioner Departs," *Albany Times Union*, Nov. 21, 2016, http://blog.timesunion.com/capitol/archives/269567/another-jcope-commissioner-departs/.

33. Chris Bragg, "JCOPE Chairman Resigns, Replacement Unclear," *Albany Times Union*, Nov. 29, 2016, http://blog.timesunion.com/capitol/archives/269701/jcope-chairman-resigns-replacement-unclear/.

34. Seth Agata, interviewed by Brett Orzechowski, Aug. 12, 2016.

35. Ibid.

36. Ibid.

6. The Legislature: Two FOIL Bills, One Veto

1. Joseph Spector, "NY's Legislative Session: What Was Done, What Wasn't," WGRZ, June 18, 2016, http://www.wgrz.com/news/legislature-works-into-night-to-end-session/247760307.

2. "Troubled NY Lawmakers: A Compilation of Lawmakers in New York State Who Have Faced Legal or Ethical Charges since 2000," *Rochester Democrat and Chronicle*, continuous, http://rochester.nydatabases.com/database/troubled-ny-lawmakers.

3. Mike McAndrew, "Final Day for NY State Legislature: 5 Things Still Unresolved," *Syracuse Post-Standard*, June 16, 2016, http://www.newyorkupstate.com/news/2016/06/final_day_for_ny_state_legislature_5_things_still_unresolved.html.

4. Bill Mahoney and Jimmy Vielkind, "Cuomo Vetoes Bills for Transparency, Wine Shipping, and CUNY, SUNY Funding," *Politico*, Dec. 12, 2015, http://www.politico.com/states/new-york/albany/story/2015/12/cuomo-vetoes-bills-for-transparency-wine-shipping-and-cuny-suny-funding-029079.

5. Casey Seiler, "Cuomo's Executive Order Follows FOIL Vetoes," *Albany Times Union*, Dec. 12, 2015, http://www.timesunion.com/local/article/Cuomo-order-Fast-track-Freedom-of-Information-6693990.php.

6. Amy Paulin, interviewed by Brett Orzechowski, June 23, 2016.

7. David Howard King, "Cuomo's FOIL Order Has More Limited Scope Than Vetoed Bills," *Gotham Gazette* (New York), Dec. 15, 2015, http://www.gothamgazette.com/index.php/government/6039-cuomos-foil-order-has-more-limited-scope-than-vetoed-bills.

8. Paulin interview, June 23, 2016.

9. King, "Cuomo's FOIL Order Has More Limited Scope Than Vetoed Bills."

10. David Buchwald, interviewed by Brett Orzechowski, Aug. 10, 2016.

11. New York State Legislative Bill Search, 2015–16.

12. Patrick Gallivan, interviewed by Brett Orzechowski, June 29, 2016.

13. Ibid.

14. Ibid.

15. Paulin interview, June 23, 2016.

16. Ibid.

17. Ibid.

18. Ibid.

19. Casey Seiler, "Cuomo's Executive Order Follows FOIL Vetoes," *Albany Times Union*, Dec. 12, 2015, http://www.timesunion.com/local/article/Cuomo-order-Fast-track-Freedom-of-Information-6693990.php

20. New York State Office of the Governor, "Governor Cuomo Signs Executive Order Expediting Freedom of Information Law Appeals Process," Dec. 12, 2015, https://www.governor.ny.gov/news/governor-cuomo-signs-executive-order-expediting-freedom-information-law-appeals-process.

21. Buchwald interview, Aug. 10, 2016.

22. Bill Mahoney, "Cuomo Signs Bill to Expedite FOIL Appeals," *Politico*, Nov. 29, 2016, http://www.politico.com/states/new-york/albany/story/2016/11/cuomo-signs-bill-expediting-foil-appeals-107689.

7. Policy: Police Cameras and the Public

1. Gene Demby, "What We See in the Eric Garner Video, and What We Don't," NPR, July 29, 2014, http://www.npr.org/sections/codeswitch/2014/07/29/335847224/what-we-see-in-the-eric-garner-video-and-what-we-dont.

2. Melanie Eversley and Mike James, "No Charges in NYC Chokehold Death; Federal Inquiry Launched," *USA Today*, Dec. 4, 2014, http://www.usatoday.com/story/news/nation/2014/12/03/chokehold-grand-jury/19804577/; Josh Dawsy, "New York City Agrees to Pay Family of Eric Garner $5.9 Million," *Wall Street Journal*, July 13, 2015, http://www.wsj.com/articles/new-york-agrees-to-pay-family-of-eric-garner-5-9-million-1436833250.

3. Pervaiz Shallwani, "NYPD Prepares to Expand Body Camera Use," *Wall Street Journal*, Mar. 2, 2016, http://www.wsj.com/articles/nypd-wrapping-up -body-camera-pilot-program-1456916402.

4. Rocco Parascandola, "60 NYPD Cops Set to Begin Wearing Body Cameras in Pilot Program," *New York Daily News*, Sept. 5, 2014, http://www.nydaily news.com/new-york/50-nypd-cops-set-wearing-body-cameras-pilot-program -article-1.1927876.

5. Jake Pearson, "NYPD Plans 23,000 Body Cams. Number on Streets Now: 0," Associated Press, Feb. 11, 2017, https://apnews.com/317bedda27c64dbca52e6 aefcfa5344a/nypd-plans-23000-body-cams-number-streets-now-0.

6. Brian Curran, interviewed by Brett Orzechowski, June 13, 2016.

7. David Riley, "RPD Officers to Be Equipped with Body Cams," *Rochester Democrat and Chronicle*, Dec. 18, 2014, http://www.democratandchronicle.com /story/news/2014/12/18/rochester-police-body-cameras/20604723/.

8. City of Rochester poll, 2015, http://www.cityofrochester.gov/RPDBody WornCamera/.

9. Kevin Oklobzija, "Rochester Cops Get Grant for Body Cameras," *Rochester Democrat and Chronicle*, Sept. 22, 2015, http://www.democratandchronicle .com/story/news/2015/09/22/rochester-cops-get-grant-body-cameras/72592660/.

10. Patrick Lohmann, "Why Didn't Syracuse Win Grant for Body Cameras?" *Syracuse Post-Standard*, Jan. 14, 2016, http://www.syracuse.com/news/index.ssf /2016/01/why_didnt_syracuse_police_win_grant_for_body_cameras.html.

11. Kevin Oklobzija, "Rochester Cops Get Grant for Body Cameras," *Rochester Democrat and Chronicle*, Sept. 22, 2015, http://www.democratandchronicle .com/story/news/2015/09/22/rochester-cops-get-grant-body-cameras/72592660/.

12. Will Cleveland, "ME: Man's Death by Police Taser a Homicide," *Rochester Democrat and Chronicle*, Mar. 31, 2016, http://www.democratandchronicle .com/story/news/2016/03/30/me-man-tased-death-ruled-homicide/82451264/.

13. Will Cleveland, "Grand Jury Reviews Death, Says Police Taser Use Justified," *Rochester Democrat and Chronicle*, May 24, 2016, http://www.democrat andchronicle.com/story/news/2016/05/24/grand-jury-police-use-taser-justified /84879888/.

14. Michael Ciminelli, interviewed by Brett Orzechowski, July 1, 2016.

15. Quoted in Steve Miletich and Jennifer Sullivan, "Costly Public-Records Request May Threaten SPD Plan for Body Cameras," *Seattle Times*, Nov. 20, 2014, http://www.seattletimes.com/seattle-news/costly-public-records-requests -may-threaten-spd-plan-for-body-cameras/, and in Jennifer Sullivan, "Man Drops Massive Records Request, Will Help Seattle Police with Video Technology," *Seattle Times*, Nov. 20, 2014, http://www.seattletimes.com/seattle-news/man-drops -massive-records-requests-will-help-seattle-police-with-video-technology/.

16. Jennifer Sullivan, "'Hackathon' Asks Techies to Aid on Sensitive-Video Issue," *Seattle Times*, Dec. 14, 2014, http://www.seattletimes.com/seattle-news /lsquohackathonrsquo-asks-techies-to-aid-spd-on-sensitive-video-issues/.

17. Ibid.

18. Ibid.

19. Ansel Herz, "Programmer Tim Clemans Resigns from Police Department after a Challenging Six Months," *Seattle Stranger*, Oct. 29, 2015, http://www.the stranger.com/blogs/slog/2015/10/29/23084403/programmer-tim-clemans-resigns -from-police-department-over-turf-battle.

20. Curran interview, June 13, 2016.

8. Public-Information Officers: Boards and the Bored

1. Mikale Billard, interviewed by Brett Orzechowski, June 15, 2016.

2. Ibid.

3. Ibid.

4. Elizabeth Cooper, "County Searches for Options for Homeless Sex Offenders," *Utica Observer-Dispatch*, Apr. 24, 2013, http://www.uticaod.com /x94498369/County-searches-for-options-for-homeless-sex-offenders.

5. Elizabeth Cooper, "Area Motels No Longer House Sex Offenders," *Utica Observer-Dispatch*, Dec. 20, 2014, http://www.uticaod.com/article/20141220 /NEWS/141219418.

6. Billard interview, June 15, 2016.

7. Jonathan Lin, "Former Mob Hit Man from Bayonne, Harold Konigsberg, Dies at 89 in Florida," *Jersey Journal*, Dec. 4, 2014, http://www.nj.com/hudson /index.ssf/2014/12/former_bayonne_hit_man_dies_at_89_is_buried_in_florida _cemetery.html.

8. Konigsberg v. Coughlin III, Commissioner, New York State Department of Correctional Services, Court of Appeals of New York, Oct. 16, 1986.

9. "Mayor Erastus Corning 2nd Papers," Albany County Clerk's Office, n.d., http://www.albanycounty.com/Government/Departments/AlbanyCountyHallof Records/TheMayorErastusCorning2ndPapers.aspx.

10. Christa Schafer, interviewed by Brett Orzechowski, Aug. 16, 2016.

11. Ibid.

12. Cheryl Ketchum, interviewed by Brett Orzechowski, June 16, 2016.

13. Ibid.

9. The Business of FOIL

1. Michele Zilgme, interviewed by Brett Orzechowski, June 28, 2016.

2. Ibid.

3. Charles Kenny, "Taking The Mystery out of Government Contracting," *Wall Street Journal*, Nov. 27, 2014, http://www.wsj.com/articles/charles-kenny -taking-the-mystery-out-of-government-contracting-1417123926.

4. Office of the United States Trade Representative, "Government Procure-ment," n.d., https://ustr.gov/issue-areas/government-procurement, accessed Aug. 22, 2016.

5. Jeff Rubenstein, interviewed by Brett Orzechowski, Aug. 19, 2016.

6. Ibid.

7. Kenny, "Taking the Mystery out of Government Contracting."

8. Lauren Dyson, "The State of Local Government Procurement," Code for America, Sept. 27, 2013, https://www.codeforamerica.org/blog/2013/09/27/the -state-of-local-government-procurement/.

9. Jeff Rubenstein, "Hacking FOIA: Using FOIA Requests to Drive Govern-ment Innovation," in *Beyond Transparency: Open Data and the Future of Civic Innovation*, ed. Brett Goldstein, with Lauren Dysen (San Francisco: Code for America Press, 2013), 81–92.

10. Rubenstein interview, Aug. 19, 2016.

10. The Citizen: George and Helen of Troy

1. League of Women Voters, "The League of Women Voters: Making Democracy Work—History," n.d., http://lwv.org/history.

2. Helen Bayly, "From Dancing in Australia as a Kid, 40s, to Masters Diving in USA in 70s," Masters Diving, Mar. 2008, http://www.mastersdiving.org /articles/article%20from%20Helen%20Bailey.htm.

3. "Rensselaer Open in Full to Women," *New York Times*, Oct. 19, 1960.

4. "State Legislature Honors SPAC's 50th Anniversary," *Saratogian* (Sara-toga, NY), Aug. 15, 2016, http://www.saratogian.com/article/ST/20160615 /NEWS/160619854.

5. Helen Bayly, interviewed by Brett Orzechowski, May 26, 2016.

6. Joseph Horowitz, *Artists in Exile: How Refugees from 20th-Century War and Revolution Transformed the American Performing Arts* (New York: Harper-Collins, 2008).

7. SPAC, "About SPAC; the Official Site of the Saratoga Performing Arts Center," n.d., http://spac.org/aboutspac.cfm.

8. Ibid.

9. Amy Biancolli, "SPAC Concerts, Finances a Balancing Act," *Albany Times Union*, May 5, 2014, http://www.timesunion.com/entertainment/article/SPAC -concerts-finances-a-balancing-act-5451436.php.

10. Matt Leon, "Whitney, Pataki Endorse New SPAC," *Glens Falls Post-Star*, May 19, 2005, http://poststar.com/news/local/whitney-pataki-endorse-new -spac/article_116559ce-2854-57aa-a535-d1d992c79854.html.

11. Jim Shahen Jr., "SPAC a Place Performers Like to Play," *Albany Times Union*, July 6, 2016, http://www.timesunion.com/tuplus-features/article/SPAC-a -place-performers-like-to-play-8343640.php.

12. New York State Office of Parks, Recreation, and Historic Preservation, "Final Audit: Saratoga Performing Arts Center (SPAC)," Mar. 17, 2005; the figures given in the text come from this audit.

13. Ibid.

14. Ibid.

15. Jason McCord, "State Audit Faults SPAC Managers," *Glens Falls Post-Star*, Nov. 24, 2004, http://poststar.com/news/local/state-audit-faults-spac -managers/article_24d177ca-9730-53e5-b080-f1d6e1616b90.html.

16. Jason McCord, "State to Conduct Audit of SPAC Bookkeeping," *Glens Falls Post-Star*, Feb. 28, 2004, http://poststar.com/news/local/state-to-conduct -audit-of-spac-bookkeeping/article_c8f86777-f316-52d2-bebc-a90618088c1e.html.

17. "NYC Ballet to Return to SPAC in 2005," *Albany Business Review*, Apr. 1, 2004, http://www.bizjournals.com/albany/stories/2004/03/29/daily40.html.

18. George Neary, interviewed by Brett Orzechowski, June 3, 2016.

19. New York State Office of Parks, Recreation, and Historic Preservation, "Final Audit."

20. Neary interview, June 3, 2016.

21. Bayly interview, May 26, 2016.

22. Ibid.

23. Quoted in Jason McCord, "State Audit Faults SPAC Managers," *Glens Falls Post-Star*, Nov. 24, 2004, http://poststar.com/news/local/state-audit-faults -spac-managers/article_24d177ca-9730-53e5-b080-f1d6e1616b90.html.

24. New York State Office of Parks, Recreation, and Historic Preservation, "Final Audit."

25. Ibid.

26. Jason McCord, "SPAC's New Director Begins Tenure," *Glens Falls Post-Star*, Mar. 5, 2005, http://poststar.com/news/local/spac-s-new-director-begins -tenure/article_e43ea760-56ec-5740-ab59-d9751a32550c.html.

27. Ibid.

28. Steve Barnes, "Former SPAC Director Herb Chesbrough Dies at 67," *Albany Times Union*, Sept. 19, 2014, http://www.timesunion.com/local/article /Former-SPAC-director-Chesbrough-has-died-5762503.php.

29. New York State Office of Parks, Recreation, and Historic Preservation, "Final Audit."

30. George Neary, FOIL request submitted to the New York State Office of Parks, Recreation, and Historic Preservation, Dec. 7, 2004.

31. Jason McCord, "SPAC Membership Approves New Board," *Glens Falls Post-Star*, May 26, 2005, http://poststar.com/news/local/spac-membership -approves-new-board/article_3bcea4f1-1dba-5ae2-8fd3-fc011c4b5c86.html.

32. Rick Karlin, "Marcia White to Retire from SPAC after 2016," *Albany Times Union*, Feb. 19, 2016, http://www.timesunion.com/local/article/Marcia -White-to-step-down-from-SPAC-6842742.php.

33. Neary interview, June 3, 2016.

11. Watchdogs: Transparency and Civil Liberties

1. Tim Hoefer, interviewed by Brett Orzechowski, July 19, 2016.

2. Ibid.

3. Ibid.

4. Jennie Grey, "Six-Figure Salaries Up 48 Percent since 2008–09," *Saratogian* (Saratoga, NY), Oct. 9, 2014, http://www.saratogian.com/article/ST/2014 1009/NEWS/141009611.

5. "New York State Public Payroll," *Albany Times Union*, Aug. 8, 2008, http://www.timesunion.com/payroll/.

6. Hoefer interview, July 19, 2016.

7. Ibid.

8. Empire Center for New York State Policy v. New York State Teachers' Retirement System, Court of Appeals of New York, 23 N.Y.3d 438, May 6, 2014.

9. Hagan v. the City of New York, Supreme Court of the State of New York, County of Kings, Cal. No.: 35-37 012574/2014, Apr. 2, 2015.

10. Empire Center for Public Policy Inc. v. MTA New York City Transit, Supreme Court of the State of New York, County of Kings, Index No. 6681/2015, Aug. 6, 2015.

11. Hoefer interview, July 19, 2016.

12. Kaela Sanborn-Hum, "New York City's Evolving Approach to Open Data," *Gotham Gazette* (New York), Apr. 11, 2016, http://www.gothamgazette .com/index.php/city/6272-new-york-city-s-evolving-approach-to-open-data.

13. Laura Nahmias and Sally Goldenberg, "Heavy Redactions Mark de Blasio's Latest 'Agents' E-mail Release," *Politico*, Feb. 27, 2017, http://www.politico .com/states/new-york/city-hall/story/2017/02/de-blasio-releases-more-agents -emails-109895.

14. Bill Mahoney and Jimmy Vielkind, "Cuomo Vetoes Bills for Transparency, Wine Shipping, and CUNY, SUNY Funding," *Politico*, Dec. 12, 2015,

http://www.politico.com/states/new-york/albany/story/2015/12/cuomo-vetoes
-bills-for-transparency-wine-shipping-and-cuny-suny-funding-029079.

15. John Kaehny, interviewed by Brett Orzechowski, July 25, 2016.

16. Ibid.

17. As explained in ibid.

18. Office of Bill de Blasio, Public Advocate for the City of New York, *Breaking Through Bureaucracy: Evaluating Government Responsiveness to Information Requests in New York City* (New York: Office of the Public Advocate, Apr. 2013).

19. Chester Soria, "A Lukewarm Report for City Government Transparency," *Gotham Gazette* (New York), Apr. 24, 2013, http://www.gothamgazette.com /index.php/government/4229-a-lukewarm-report-card-for-city-government -transparency.

20. Ibid.

21. Kaehny interview, July 25, 2016.

22. Reinvent Albany, *Listening to FOIL: Using FOIL Logs to Guide the Publication of Open Data* (Albany: Reinvent Albany, July 23, 2014), http:// reinventalbany.org/wp-content/uploads/2014/07/Final-DEC-FOIL-Analysis.pdf.

23. Kaehny interview, July 25, 2016.

24. William K. Rashbaum and Al Baker, "50 Bullets, One Dead, and Many Questions," *New York Times*, Dec. 11, 2006, http://www.nytimes.com/2006/12 /11/nyregion/11shoot.html.

25. Jonathan Allen, "NYPD Forces Out Four Officers in Sean Bell Shooting," Reuters, Mar. 24, 2012, http://www.reuters.com/article/us-newyork-police -idUSBRE82O00G20120325.

26. Juan Forero, "Serial Rapist Gets 155 Years; Judge Suggests His Crimes Contributed to Diallo Shooting," *New York Times*, Aug. 2, 2000, http://www .nytimes.com/2000/08/02/nyregion/serial-rapist-gets-155-years-judge-suggests -his-crimes-contributed-diallo.html.

27. Greg Ridgeway, *Analysis of Racial Disparities in the New York Police Department's Stop, Question, and Frisk Practices* (Santa Monica, CA: RAND Corporation, sponsored by the New York City Police Foundation, 2007), http:// www.rand.org/pubs/technical_reports/TR534.html.

28. Christine Hauser, "Police Told to Give Street-Stop Data," *New York Times*, May 31, 2008, http://www.nytimes.com/2008/05/31/nyregion/31frisk.html.

29. New York Civil Liberties Union, "NYPD Stop-and-Frisk Data: 2002– 2015," n.d., http://www.nyclu.org/content/stop-and-frisk-data.

30. Chris Dunn, interviewed by Brett Orzechowski, Aug. 3, 2016.

31. Colin Moynihan, "New York Police Agree to Take Public Records Requests via Email," *New York Times*, June 29, 2017, https://mobile.nytimes

.com/2017/06/29/nyregion/new-york-police-agree-to-take-public-records-requests
-by-email.html.

32. C. J. Ciaramella, "Secrets of the NYPD," *Salon.com*, May 8, 2013,
http://www.salon.com/2013/05/08/why_is_ray_kellys_schedule_more_secret
_than_president_obamas/.

33. Dunn interview, Aug. 3, 2016.

12. Data: Numbers In, Some Numbers Out

1. Coulter Jones, interviewed by Brett Orzechowski, June 17, 2016.

2. David Howard King, "Transparency in Albany? No Joke: Technology
Helping to Pry Open Government," *Gotham Gazette* (New York), Mar. 11, 2013,
http://www.gothamgazette.com/index.php/government/4186-transparency-in
-albany-no-joke-technology-helping-pry-open-govt.

3. Stacey Higginbotham, "The White House Opens the Data Floodgates, and
Now the Real Work Will Begin," *GIGAOM*, May 9, 2013, https://gigaom.com
/2013/05/09/the-white-house-opens-the-data-floodgates-and-now-the-real-work
-will-begin/.

4. Bill Mahoney, interviewed by Brett Orzechowski, June 8, 2016.

5. Danny Hakim and William K. Rashbaum, "Spitzer Is Linked to Prostitution Ring," *New York Times*, Mar. 10, 2008, http://www.nytimes.com/2008/03
/10/nyregion/10cnd-spitzer.html?_r=0.

6. Gabrielle Levy, "How Citizens United Has Changed Politics in 5 Years,"
U.S. News & World Report, Jan. 21, 2015, http://www.usnews.com/news
/articles/2015/01/21/5-years-later-citizens-united-has-remade-us-politics;
Citizens United v. Federal Election Commission 558 U.S. 310 (2010).

7. New York State Joint Commission on Public Ethics, *2015 Annual Report*
(Albany: New York State, Apr. 7, 2016), http://www.jcope.ny.gov/pubs/POL
/2015_%20Annual%20Report_%20FINAL_4_8_16r.pdf.

8. Mahoney interview, June 8, 2016.

9. Jones interview, June 17, 2016.

10. Ben Wellington, *How We Found the Worst Place to Park in New York
City—Using Big Data*, TEDx Talk, video, Nov. 2014, https://www.ted.com/talks
/ben_wellington_how_we_found_the_worst_place_to_park_in_new_york_city
_using_big_data?language=en.

11. Ben Wellington, interviewed by Brett Orzechowski, Aug. 19, 2016.

12. Ibid.

13. Ibid.

14. Daniel Prendergast and Rebecca Harshbarger, "Misleading Fire Hydrant
Costing City Drivers $33K in Tickets," *New York Post*, Apr. 28, 2014, http://

nypost.com/2014/04/28/misleading-fire-hydrant-costing-city-drivers-33k-in
-tickets/.

15. Quoted in Jon Campbell, "New York's King of Open Data Says City
'Can Do Better' in TEDx Talk," *Village Voice*, Jan. 21, 2015, http://www.village
voice.com/news/new-yorks-king-of-open-data-says-city-can-do-better-in-tedx
-talk-6700446.

16. Max Galka, "How an Open Data Blogger Proved the NYPD Issued Parking Tickets in Error," *Guardian*, July 26, 2016, https://www.theguardian.com
/cities/2016/jul/26/open-data-blogger-parking-tickets-new-york-nypd.

17. Ben Wellington, "Uber Isn't Causing New York City's Traffic Slowdown,"
New Yorker, Aug. 14, 2015, http://www.newyorker.com/tech/elements/uber-isnt
-causing-new-york-citys-traffic-slowdown.

18. Wellington interview, Aug. 19, 2016.

19. Ibid.

13. State and Fed: Different Levels, Same Issues

1. The Waterston video is captured in "FOIA@50 Conference Day 2,"
Columbia Journalism School, June 3, 2016, video, YouTube, https://www.youtube
.com/watch?v=71D6z2YQzIM.

2. Joseph Bernstein, "Can an Algorithm Do the Job of a Historian?"
BuzzFeed, June 15, 2015, https://www.buzzfeed.com/josephbernstein/can-a
-computer-algorithm-do-the-job-of-a-historian?utm_term=.mqjG2r0Y0#.xc8VN
jWmW.

3. "FOIA@50 Conference Day 2."

4. Erin Siegal, "To Sue or Not to Sue? The First Two Years of OGIS,"
Columbia Journalism Review, Feb. 1, 2012, http://www.cjr.org/behind_the_news
/to_sue_or_not_to_sue.php.

5. Ibid.

6. Josh Gerstein, "FOIA Reform Bill Headed to Obama," *Politico*, June 13,
2016, http://www.politico.com/blogs/under-the-radar/2016/06/foia-reform-bill
-headed-to-obama-224293.

7. Jason Leopold, "It Took a FOIA Lawsuit to Uncover How the Obama
Administration Killed FOIA Reform," *VICE News*, Mar. 9, 2016, https://news
.vice.com/article/it-took-a-foia-lawsuit-to-uncover-how-the-obama-administration
-killed-foia-reform.

8. Ibid.

9. Ibid.

10. Ibid.

11. Ibid.

12. Ibid.

13. Ibid.

14. Ted Bridis and Jack Gillum, "U.S. Government Sets Record for Failure to Find Files When Asked," Associated Press, Mar. 18, 2016, http://bigstory.ap.org /article/697e3523003049cdb0847ecf828afd62/us-govt-sets-record-failures-find -files-when-asked.

15. Rudy Takala, "Report: Obama Denied a Record 77 Percent FOIA Requests," *Washington Examiner*, Mar. 18, 2016, http://www.washingtonexaminer .com/report-obama-denied-a-record-77-percent-of-foia-requests/article/2586257.

16. Josh Gerstein, "Obama Signs FOIA Reform Bill," *Politico*, June 30, 2016, http://www.politico.com/blogs/under-the-radar/2016/06/obama-signs-foia -reform-bill-225010.

17. Jason Leopold, "In a Victory for Government Transparency, Obama Is Set to Sign FOIA Reform Bill into Law," *VICE News*, June 14, 2016, https://news .vice.com/article/obama-to-sign-foia-reform-bill-into-law-foia-improvement-act.

18. "FOIA@50 Conference Day 2."

19. Ibid.

20. Ibid.

21. Ibid.

22. Ted Brindis, "Emails: Insiders Worried over Political 'Meddling'?" Associated Press, Mar. 28, 2011, https://www.yahoo.com/news/emails-insiders -worried-over-political-meddling-20110328-002019-663.html.

23. "FOIA@50 Conference Day 2."

24. From the data at FOIA.gov used to compile the totals given in table 1.

25. "FOIA@50 Conference Day 2."

26. Ibid.

27. Ibid.

14. Transparency: Defining the Future of "Open"

1. "Personal Democracy Forum Open Government Workshop 6/6," June 6, 2014, video, YouTube, posted by Benjamin Kallos, June 10, 2014, https://www .youtube.com/watch?v=jmfI9L8P3NM.

2. Ibid.

3. Ben Kallos, interviewed by Brett Orzechowski, July 5, 2016.

4. Ibid.

5. Michael Grass, "Open Gov Backers Launch 'Free Law' Group," Government Executive, July 16, 2014, http://www.govexec.com/state-local/2014/07/free -law-founders-open-data-nyc-san-francisco-dc-chicago-boston/88858/.

6. Kallos interview, July 5, 2016.

7. Samar Kurshid, "As Problems Persist, City Council to Examine Board of Elections," *Gotham Gazette* (New York), Apr. 25, 2016, http://www.gotham gazette.com/index.php/city/6297-as-problems-persist-city-council-to-examine -board-of-elections.

8. A. J. Vicens, "The Story of the Great Brooklyn Voter Purge Keeps Getting Weirder," *Mother Jones*, Apr. 22, 2016, http://www.motherjones.com/politics /2016/04/new-york-primary-voter-purge.

9. Rashed Aqrabawi, "Is New York City Ready for Digital Voting?" *Vice*, Aug. 9, 2013, http://motherboard.vice.com/blog/is-new-york-city-ready-for -digital-voting.

10. Kallos interview, July 5, 2016.

11. David Sobel, interviewed by Brett Orzechowski, July 8, 2016.

12. Parker Higgins, *Who Has Your Back? 2015: Protecting Your Data from Government Request*, white paper (San Francisco: Electronic Frontier Foundation, July 2, 2015), https://www.eff.org/wp/who-has-your-back-2015-protecting -your-data-government-requests.

13. Sobel interview, July 8, 2016.

14. Sunlight Foundation, "Open States: Open Legislative Data Report Card," n.d., http://openstates.org/reportcard/.

15. Emily Shaw, interviewed by Brett Orzechowski, July 18, 2016.

16. Ibid.

17. Ibid.

18. Ibid.

19. Ibid.

20. Rebecca Kheel, "The Pentagon Needs to Update FOIA Policies," *The Hill*, Aug. 18, 2016, http://thehill.com/policy/defense/291841-watchdog-pentagon -needs-to-update-foia-policies.

21. Dan Bevarly, interviewed by Brett Orzechowski, Aug. 22, 2016.

22. Mary Ellen Klas, "Gov. Rick Scott Agrees to Pay $700,000 to End Public Records Lawsuit," *Tampa Bay Times*, Aug. 7, 2015, http://www.tampabay.com /news/politics/stateroundup/gov-rick-scott-agrees-to-pay-700000-to-end-public -records-lawsuit/2240461.

23. Mary Ellen Klas, "Legislators Weigh Whether Change Will Gut Florida Public Records Law or End Abuses," *Tampa Bay Times*, Feb. 2, 2016, http:// www.tampabay.com/news/politics/stateroundup/legislators-weigh-whether -change-will-gut-florida-public-records-law-or/2263804.

24. Jim Saunders, "FL Supreme Court Rules Agencies Must Pay Attorneys' Fees When Violating Public Records Law," *Tampa Bay Times*, Apr. 14, 2016, http://www.tampabay.com/blogs/the-buzz-florida-politics/fl-supreme-court-rules -agencies-must-pay-attorneys-fees-when-violating/2273251.

25. Quoted in Rachel Silberstein, "For Second Time, Legislature Sends FOIL Penalty Bill to Cuomo," *Gotham Gazette* (New York), June 9, 2017, http://www .gothamgazette.com/state/6982-for-second-time-legislature-sends-foil-penalty -bill-to-cuomo.

26. Tom Precious, "New York's Freedom of Information Law Gets a Boost," *Buffalo News*, Dec. 13, 2017, http://buffalonews.com/2017/12/13/new-yorks -freedom-of-information-law-gets-a-boost/.

15. The Administration

1. Jesse McKinley, "Cuomo to Halt State Business with Groups That Back Boycott of Israel," *New York Times*, June 5, 2016, http://www.nytimes.com /2016/06/06/nyregion/cuomo-new-york-israel-boycott-bds-movement.html.

2. Alphonso David, "Statement from Counsel to the Governor," New York State Governor's Press Office, July 15, 2015, https://www.governor.ny.gov/news /statement-counsel-governor-alphonso-david.

3. Alphonso David and Bart M. Schwartz, "Statements from Governor's Counsel," New York State Governor's Press Office, Apr. 29, 2016, https://www .governor.ny.gov/news/statements-governor-s-counsel-alphonso-david-and-bart -m-schwartz.

4. Karen DeWitt, "Behind the Buffalo Billion: Kaloyeros No Longer at Center of Decision-Making," WRVO, June 9, 2016, http://wrvo.org/post/behind -buffalo-billion-kaloyeros-no-longer-center-decision-making#stream/0.

5. Jimmy Vielkind, "Schneiderman Examining Phone of SUNY Poly President," *Politico*, June 8, 2016, http://www.politico.com/states/new-york/albany /story/2016/06/eric-schneiderman-alain-kaloyeros-phone-suny-poly-102613.

6. Jimmy Vielkind, "Lobbyist at Center of Inquiry Advised SUNY Poly and Its Contractors," *Politico*, May 2, 2016, http://www.politico.com/states/new-york /albany/story/2016/05/lobbyist-at-center-of-inquiry-advised-suny-poly-and-its -contractors-101281.

7. Jesse McKinley and Vivian Yee, "How Joseph Percoco, Cuomo's Problem-Solver, Became a Problem," *New York Times*, June 13, 2016, http://www.nytimes .com/2016/06/14/nyregion/how-cuomos-problem-solver-became-a-problem-for -the-governor.html.

8. Joseph Spector and Jon Campbell, "Ten Charged in Sweeping NY Corruption Case," *Rochester Democrat and Chronicle*, Sept. 22, 2016, http://www .democratandchronicle.com/story/news/politics/blogs/vote-up/2016/09/22 /percoco-top-cuomo-ally-indicted/90825902/.

9. Quoted in Benjamin Weiser, William K. Rashbaum, and Vivian Yee, "Ex-Cuomo Aides Charged in Federal Corruption Inquiry," *New York Times*, Sept.

22, 2016, http://www.nytimes.com/2016/09/23/nyregion/cuomo-former-aides
-charges.html.

10. Marty Steinberg, "Top Cop of Wall Street, Preet Bharara, Fired After Refusing Trump's Call to Resign," CNBC, Mar. 11, 2017, http://www.cnbc.com /2017/03/11/preet-bharara-says-he-was-fired-moments-ago.html.

11. Tom Precious, "New York's Freedom of Information Law Gets a Boost," *Buffalo News*, Dec. 13, 2017, http://buffalonews.com/2017/12/13/new-yorks -freedom-of-information-law-gets-a-boost/.

12. Alphonso David, interviewed by Brett Orzechowski, Aug. 30, 2016.

13. Ibid.

14. Josefa Velasquez, "State D.A.s Call Cuomo Special Prosecutor 'Gravely Flawed,'" *Politico*, July 13, 2015, http://www.politico.com/states/new-york/albany /story/2015/07/state-das-call-cuomo-special-prosecutor-gravely-flawed-000000.

15. Eliot Brown, "Lawmakers to Revisit Debate over Visa Program," *Wall Street Journal*, Apr. 12, 2016, http://www.wsj.com/articles/lawmakers-to-revisit -debate-over-visa-program-1460480134.

16. Ibid.

17. Ibid.

18. Eliot Brown, "Expiration of Visa Program Nears," *Wall Street Journal*, Sept. 20, 2016, http://www.wsj.com/articles/expiration-of-visa-program-nears -1474399593.

19. Kate Briquelet, "Upper West Condo Has Separate Entrances for Rich and Poor," *New York Post*, Aug. 18, 2013, http://nypost.com/2013/08/18/upper-west -side-condo-has-separate-entrances-for-rich-and-poor/.

20. Eliot Brown, interviewed by Brett Orzechowski, Nov. 8, 2016.

21. Ibid.

22. New York State Governor's Press Office, "Governor Cuomo Announces Establishment of Clean Energy Standard That Mandates 50 Percent Renewables by 2030," Aug. 1, 2016, https://www.governor.ny.gov/news/governor-cuomo -announces-establishment-clean-energy-standard-mandates-50-percent-renewables.

23. Ibid.

24. Town of Somerset, website, http://www.townofsomerset.org/.

25. T. J. Pignataro, "Winds of Discontent Blow over Lake Ontario Towns Eyed for Turbines," *Buffalo News*, July 30, 2016, http://buffalonews.com/2016/07 /30/winds-of-discontent-blow-over-lake-ontario-towns-eyed-for-turbines/.

26. Ibid.

27. Benjamin Wisniewski, interviewed by Brett Orzechowski, Nov. 10, 2016.

28. Dennis C. Vacco, "Don't Trample Rights of Localities," *Albany Times Union*, Sept. 28, 2016, http://www.timesunion.com/tuplus-opinion/article/Don-t -trample-rights-of-localities-9390378.php.

29. Wisniewski interview, Nov. 10, 2016.

30. As reported in Wisniewski interview, Nov. 10, 2016.

31. Tom Prohaska, "Town of Somerset Budgets Big Money to Fight Windmills," *Buffalo News*, Nov. 11, 2016, http://buffalonews.com/2016/11/11/somerset -budgets-big-money-for-wind-power-fight/.

16. FOIL Analysis and Review: In Their Words

1. Eve Burton, interviewed by Brett Orzechowski, Aug. 4, 2016.

2. John Kaehny, interviewed by Brett Orzechowski, July 25, 2016.

3. Bill Mahoney, interviewed by Brett Orzechowski, June 8, 2016.

4. Brian Curran, interviewed by Brett Orzechowski, June 13, 2016.

5. Michael J. Grygiel, interviewed by Brett Orzechowski, June 17, 2016.

6. Patrick Gallivan, interviewed by Brett Orzechowski, June 29, 2016.

7. Brendan Lyons, interviewed by Brett Orzechowski, June 28, 2016.

8. Jim Heaney, interviewed by Brett Orzechowski, May 25, 2016.

9. Cezary Podkul, interviewed by Brett Orzechowski, June 8, 2016.

10. Wayne Barrett, "The Truth behind Troopergate," *Village Voice*, Sept. 25, 2007, http://www.villagevoice.com/news/the-truth-behind-troopergate-6424250.

11. David Grandeau, interviewed by Brett Orzechowski, July 28, 2016.

12. Drew Kerr, "Saratoga Businessmen Could Face More Than 50 Years in Prison," *Glens Falls Post-Star*, Dec. 1, 2007, http://poststar.com/news/latest /saratoga-businessmen-could-face-more-than-years-in-prison/article_95f57234 -c7f9-5575-993a-e0e11034700f.html.

13. Karl Sleight, interviewed by Brett Orzechowski, July 26, 2016.

14. Peter Bienstock, interviewed by Brett Orzechowski, Aug. 2, 2016.

Index

Abel, Elie, 13–17

Agata, Seth, 85–88

Albany Common Council, 27

Albany County, 129, 130

Albany Police Officers Union, 26

Anti-SLAPP Law, 71

application programming interface (API), 167, 194, 197–202

Arroyo, David, 85

Article 10 of the Public Service Law, 223–24. *See also* Lighthouse Wind

Article 78, 6; attorneys' fees, 92–94; Community Projects Fund investigation, 60; Hearst, City of Albany, and no-fine ghost tickets, 27; *Investigative Post* and Fort Schuyler, 42; *Journal News* v. Town of Putnam, 63–65; *New York Post*, NY1, and agents of the city, 10; *Observer-Dispatch* and Oneida County, 121; *Post-Standard* and Upstate Medical, 24; preserving requests, 36; purpose, 59–60; risk, 67, 71; SeeThroughNY project, 153–55; *Village Voice* and agents of the city, 10

Barnette, Betty (Albany city treasurer), 27–28

Bayly, Helen, 140–48

Bell, Sean, 161

Bevarly, Dan, 205

Bharara, Preet (US attorney for the Southern District of New York), 40–42, 211–12

Bienstock, Peter, 80–81, 239–40

Billard, Mikale, 117–22

Bing, Jonathan (New York State assemblyman), 197

Bloomberg, Michael, 170

Board of Public Disclosure, 80

Body Worn Camera (BWC) Project: and City of Rochester, 109–16

Boehner, John (US speaker of the house), 183

Bogardus, T. Elmer, 13

Bookman, William "Bill," 17

Brandeis, Louis (justice), 182

Breaking Through Bureaucracy, 158

Brennan Center for Justice at NYU, 77

Brewer, Gale A. (Manhattan borough president), 194

Brown, Eliot, 218–21

Brown Institute for Media Innovation, 180

Bruno, Joseph L. (New York Senate majority leader), 57–62, 77, 83, 237

Buchwald, David (New York State assemblyman), 94–95, 101–4, 106
Buffalo Billion, 39–41, 210–11
Buffalo Common Council, 39
Buffalo Municipal Housing Authority, 39
Buffalo News, 6, 38–39
Burke v. Yudelson, 18
Burton, Eve, 59–62, 227–28
Bush administration, 181

Carey, Hugh (New York governor), 7, 16, 18, 79
Carter, Zachary (New York City corporation counsel), 158
Castro, Bernadette (State Parks and Recreation commissioner), 144–46
Catt, Carrie Chapman, 139
Center for Public Integrity, 54
Center for Responsive Politics, 202
Central Intelligence Agency, 180
Charter Revision Commission, 74
Chesbrough, Herb (SPAC president), 142–47
Ciminelli, Louis, 41
Ciminelli, Michael (Rochester police chief), 111–12
Citizens United, 169
Clemans, Timothy A., 114
Clinton, Hillary, 217
Clinton Correctional Facility, 214–16
Code for America, 134, 159
Colleges of Nanoscale Science and Engineering (SUNY), 40
Colonie, Town of, 127–33
Columbia University Graduate School of Journalism, 13, 52, 180–85

Commission on Government Integrity (Feerick Commission), 80–82
Commission on Judicial Conduct, 73
Committee on Open Government (COOG): and Buffalo Billion, 40–42; and ethics, 78–79; and function, 4–9; and government oversight, 206; and operation, 17–22; and SPAC 126, 144–45
Committee on Public Access to Records (COPAR), 7, 13, 15–18
Common Cause, 102
Conflict of Interest Board (COIB), 74
Connelly, Dr. Matthew, 180
Contiguglia, Louis, 14
Corning, Erastus, 2nd (Albany mayor), 122
Covello, Joe, 85
Cuomo, Andrew (New York governor): and campaign contributions, 41; and Commission to Investigate Public Corruption, 79; and ethics reform, 88–90; and Fort Schuyler Management Corp., 6–7; and JCOPE, 78–79, 85; and SAFE Act, 63–65; 2015 FOIL veto, 19, 21, 91–95, 96–98, 157; and Troopergate, 237
Cuomo, Mario (New York governor): and Executive Order No. 3, 80; and Moreland Act and Feerick Commission, 81; as secretary of state, 7
Curran, Brian (City of Rochester corporation counsel), 109–16

David, Alphonso, 210–14
Davis, Brian (Buffalo Common Council member), 39

Davis, Richard, 110
de Blasio, Bill (New York City mayor): and agents of the city, 9–10; and email correspondence, 228; as public advocate, 93, 156–60, 174
Declassification Engine, 180
Delaware County, 122
Delray Beach Police Department, 131
DelTek, 133
Diallo, Amadou, 161
Digital Millennium Copyright Act (DMCA), 200
Dignan, Caroline R. (Monroe County medical examiner), 110
DiNapoli, Thomas P. (New York State comptroller), 27
Dingley, Sarah, 35
Dunlea v. Goldmark, 18
Dunn, Chris, 161–63

EB-5 (employment-based fifth preference visa), 218–21
Egan, John C., Jr. (Appellate Division justice), 238
Eisenhower administration, 180
Electronic Communications Privacy Act of 1986, 200
Electronic Frontier Foundation (EFF), 198–201
Empire Center for Public Policy, 149–56
Empire State Development (Corporation), 40–42, 216, 220
Executive Order No. 147, 216
Exemption 2 (FOIA), 191
Exemption 5 (FOIA), 183

Exemption 5 (or B5) (FOIA), 182
Exemption 6 (FOIA), 191
Exemption 7 (FOIA), 191
Extell Development Company, 220

Family Educational Rights and Privacy Act (FERPA), 16, 21
Farrell, Mark, 196–97
Federal Emergency Management Agency (FEMA), 48–49
Feerick, John, 80–83
Feerick Commission (Commission on Government Integrity), 80–82
First Amendment, 25, 31, 59
Florida First Amendment Foundation, 208
Florida Supreme Court, 208
FOIA@50 conference, 181–92
FOIA Machine, 206
FOIA Oversight and Implementation Act of 2014, 182
Ford, Gerald, 12
Fort Edward School District, 31
Fort Schuyler Management Corporation (FSMC), 5–6, 22, 40–42
Fowler, Mark, 63, 71
Freedom of Access Act (FOAA) (Maine), 207
Freedom of Information Advisory Council (Virginia), 206
Freedom of the Press Foundation, 183
Free Law Founders, 196
Freeman, Robert (Bob) J.: COOG involvement, 4–10; and COPAR, 11–17; and FOIL exemption and ethics, 78–79; and FOIA@50 Conference, 184–85
Fuller Road Management Corp., 42

Galef, Sandy (New York State assemblywoman), 99
Gallivan, Patrick M. (New York senator): and future FOIL legislation, 232–33; and 2015 attorneys' fees bill, 96–98; and 2017 attorneys' fees bill, 209
Gannett Satellite Information Network, Inc., 63
Garner, Eric, 107–9
Gazette (Schenectady), 29–35
Goldstein, Brett, 134
Google, 172, 228
Grandeau, David, 82–84, 236–37
Granicus, 194–95
Grygiel, Michael J., 62, 68–70, 231–32
Gutterman, Roy, 68

Hasson, Janet, 65
Health Insurance Portability and Accountability Act (HIPAA), 21, 119
Heaney, Jim: and Buffalo Billion investigation, 38–43; and *Investigative Post* and Article 78, 6; and strength of FOIL, 235
Heinlein, Robert, 4
Hevesi, Alan G., 74–76
History Lab, 180
Hoefer, Tim, 149–56
Holder, Eric (US attorney general), 182
Holzerland, William, 184–88
Horwitz, Daniel J., 85
Howe, Todd, 211–12
Hudson Yards, 218
Hurricane Sandy, 48, 98

Infausto, Felix, 15–16
Investigative Post (Buffalo), 6, 38–42
Investigative Reporters and Editors, 205
Iowa Public Information Board, 207
I Quant NY, 170, 174

Jacksonville Police and Fire Pension Fund, 208
Jennings, Jerry (Albany mayor), 26
Joint Commission on Public Ethics (JCOPE): and campaign contributions and expenditures, 169; and ethics reform, 86–89; and exemption, 78–82; formation, 74, 78; and integrity, 82–85
Jones, Coulter, 165, 170, 206
Journal News (Westchester), 62–71

Kaehny, John, 157–160, 228–29
Kallos, Ben (New York City Council member), 168, 194–98
Kaloyeros, Alain E., 6, 40–41, 211–12
Kaplan, Thomas, 215
Kelly, Raymond, 161
Kennedy, Diane, 22–23
Ketchum, Cheryl, 125–26
Knickerbocker News (Albany), 122–23
Knight Foundation, 206
Konigsberg, Harold, 122–23

Lanza, Adam, 63
Laudato, Paul L. (NYOPRHP chief counsel), 145

League of Women Voters, 99, 102,
139
Legistar, 194–96
Lemann, Nicholas, 185
Lesser, Benjamin, 52
Lighthouse Wind, 223–24
Listening to FOIL, 160
Lobis, Joan (Manhattan Supreme
Court judge), 10
LPCiminelli, 40–42
Lyons, Brendan, 24–29, 37, 233

MacArthur Foundation, 180
Mahoney, Bill, 166–69, 229–30
Mahoney, Mark, 29–33, 335–36
Marino, Ralph J. (New York State
senator), 12–14
Mauro, Dominic, 158
McCarthy, Gary (Schenectady
mayor), 35
McGuire Development, 41
McKenna, Meghan, 112
Melton, Dan, 194
Metropolitan Transportation Author-
ity (MTA), 5, 155
Moreland Commission to Investigate
Public Corruption, 79
MuckRock, 51–54
Musgrave, Shawn, 52–53
MySQL, 197

National Declassification Center, 180
National Freedom of Information
Coalition (NFOIC), 205–7
Neary, George, 143–48
Neary, Robert A. (New York
Supreme Court justice), 63

New England First Amendment
Coalition, 205
Newtown, 18, 63–64
New York City Administration for
Children's Services (ACS), 49–51
New York City Ballet (NYCB),
141–48
New York City Council, 44, 158, 161
New York City Council Technology
and Government Operations Com-
mittee, 158
New York City Department of Hous-
ing Preservation and Development,
43–45
New York City Department of Inves-
tigation, 50
New York City Department of Trans-
portation, 171
New York City Fire Department Pen-
sion Fund, 155
New York City Office of Chief Medi-
cal Examiner, 107
New York City Police Foundation,
108
New York Civil Liberties Union
(NYCLU), 161–63
New York Civil Rights Law (50-a),
73, 163
New York Clean Energy Standard,
222
New York Daily News, 9, 62, 215
New Yorker, 174
New York News Publishers Associa-
tion, 23, 92–94, 102
New York Police Department
(NYPD), 107–9, 155, 159, 161–67,
172
New York Public Interest Research
Group (NYPIRG), 168

New York State Association of Clerks of County Legislative Boards conference, 120, 122

New York State Association of Tax Receivers and Collectors, 130

New York State Board of Electric Generation Siting and the Environment, 224

New York State Commission on Public Integrity, 77

New York State Constitution, 14, 60

New York State Court of Appeals, 28, 59, 66–67, 69, 80, 122, 155

New York State Department of Correctional Services, 122

New York State Department of Corrections and Community Supervision, 122, 167

New York State Department of Environmental Conservation (DEC), 160, 225

New York State Department of Labor, 220

New York State Department of Public Service (DPS), 224–25

New York State Homes and Community Renewal (NYSHCR), 44–45

New York State Office of Parks, Recreation, and Historic Preservation, 143

New York State Office of the Attorney General, 149

New York State Public Integrity Reform Act of 2011 (PIRA), 78, 86, 169

New York State Public Service Commission, 222

New York State Society of Newspaper Editors, 17

New York State Supreme Court, 59, 62

New York State Teachers' Retirement System (NYSTRS), 155

New York State Thruway Authority, 39

New York Temporary State Commission on Lobbying, 77, 82

New York Times, 168, 214–15

New York World, 52

Nineteenth Amendment, 139

Nisbet, Miriam, 184–85, 193

Nordstrom Tower, 220

NYC OpenData (portal), 171, 174

NYC Open Data Law, 158

NYC OpenFOIL Law, 158

NYC Transparency Working Group, 159–60

NY1, 9–10

NY OpenGovernment, 149

Oakland, City of, 159

Obama, Barack, 13, 47, 166, 181–82, 188, 197

O'Brien, John, 33–35

Observer Dispatch (Utica), 121

Odell, MaryEllen, 65–66

Office of General Services, 7

Office of Government Information Services, 181

Office of Information Policy of the United States Department of Justice, 181–82

Office of Management and Budget (US), 183

Office of Open Government (Washington, DC), 207

Office of Open Records Counsel (Tennessee), 207

Office of the New York State Comptroller, 149

Office of the United States Trade Representative, 132
Oneida County, 117–21
Oneida County Board of Legislators, 118
Oneida County Department of Social Services, 121
Open Book New York, 149
Open Data: State of New York (portal), 171
Open Data for All, 157
Open Door Law or Access to Public Records Act (Indiana), 206
OPEN Government Act of 2007, 181
Open Meetings Law (OML), 4, 7, 17, 22, 40, 79, 89, 99, 118, 139

Pataki, George (New York governor), 8, 57–58, 234
Paterson, David (New York governor), 32, 86
PATRIOT Act, 200–201
Paulin, Amy (New York State assemblywoman): on public information laws, 98–101; on 2015 attorneys' fees bill, 91–94; on 2017 attorneys' fees bill, 209
Pentagon, 204
Percoco, Joseph, 212, 220
Perlin, Mark, 234
Personal Democracy Forum, 194–96
Personal Privacy Protection Law (PPPL), 4
Podkul, Cezary, 43–47, 235–36
Police Benevolent Association of the New York State Troopers, 32
Politico, 166, 169, 214–15
Port, Bob, 24, 58
Post-Standard (Syracuse), 33–34

Post-Star (Glens Falls), 29–32
proactive disclosure, 5, 23, 70, 87, 93, 115, 118–19, 123, 130, 156–59, 160–62, 182, 186, 198, 202–3
ProPublica, 44–47, 48–51
Public Employee Ethics Reform Act (PEERA), 77
Pulitzer Prize, 32–33
Pustay, Melanie Ann, 181–83, 191
Putnam County, 65–66

Racette, Steve, 216
RAND Corporation, 161
Ranzenhofer, Michael (New York State assemblyman), 94
Rath, Mary Lou, 85
Rauh, Grace, 9–10
Rehabilitation Act of 1973 (Section 508), 192
Reinvent Albany, 91–92, 102, 157–61
Rochabrun, Marcelo, 45
Rochester, City of, 109–16
Rockefeller, Nelson (New York governor), 14, 140–41
Rockland County, 64–65
Rosen, Jonathan, 9–10
Rubenstein, Jeff, 131–35

Sackett, Robert A. (New York State Supreme Court justice), 61
Sadler, Frederick, 184–87, 190, 192–93
Sanders, Bernie (Vermont senator), 197
Sandy Hook, 64–65, 96
Sant, Dennis (Putnam County clerk), 65

Sapien, Joaquin, 48–51

Saratoga Performing Arts Center (SPAC), 140–48

Saxton, Richard, 238–39

Scarsdale Village Board, 99–100

Schafer, Christa, 122–24

Scheindlin, Shira (US District judge), 108

Schneiderman, Eric (New York State attorney general), 212

School Tax Relief (STAR), 129

Schwartz, Bart M., 211

Schwartz, Lawrence, 220

Scott, Rick (Florida governor), 208

Seattle Police Department, 113–14

Seattle Times, 113–14

Second Amendment, 64–66

Secure Ammunition and Firearms Enforcement (SAFE) Act, 62–66, 210

SeeThroughNY, 151–56

September 11 (9/11), 18, 199–200

Shaw, Emily, 202–4

Sheehan v. City of Binghamton, 18

Silver, Sheldon (former speaker of the New York State Assembly), 40, 57, 82, 85, 90

Sirota, David, 215

Skelos, Dean G. (former majority leader of the New York State Senate), 40, 85, 90

Sleight, Karl J., 72–77, 237–39

SmartProcure, 132–35

Smith, Dr. David R., 33–35

Sobel, David, 198–201

SolarCity, 39, 211

Somerset, Town of, 221–26

Speech and Debate Clause, 60

Spitzer, Eliot (attorney general), 61, 77–79, 82–83, 168, 237

Startup NY, 32

State Ethics Commission, 72–77, 82, 237

State Investigation Commission, 73

State University of New York (SUNY Polytechnic Institute), 5–6, 22, 40–42, 211

State University of New York Research Foundation, 39–41, 139

stop-and-frisk, 108, 161–62

Sunlight Foundation, 102, 201–4, 206

Sunshine Law (Florida), 206–8

Sunshine Week, 30, 32, 183

SUNY Upstate Medical University (Syracuse), 33–35

Tagliafierro, Letizia, 85

Taylor, Donald (New York State assemblyman), 12–14

Teachers' Retirement System of the City of New York (TRS), 155

Times-Union (Albany), 58–60

Tomson, Lou, 15–16

Troopergate, 237

TrueAllele, 234

Tuffey, James W. (Albany police chief), 26–28

United States Citizen and Immigration Services (USCIS), 189

United States Customs and Border Protection (CBP), 190

United States Department of Education, 167

United States Department of Homeland Security (DHS), 185, 189

United States Department of Justice (DOJ), 110, 181

United States Department of State, 180, 236
United States Fish and Wildlife Service, 225
United States Food and Drug Administration (FDA), 184–88, 192
United States Immigration and Customs Enforcement (ICE), 189
USA Today, 47

Vacco, Dennis C. (former New York State attorney general), 223–24
Velasquez, Josefa, 216
Vice News, 183
Vilensky, Mike, 216

Wachtler, Sol (New York State Supreme Court chief judge), 122
Wall Street Journal, 214, 218–21
Warren, Lovely (Rochester mayor), 109–10
Warrensburg Board of Education, 31
Washington Public Records Act, 113
Watergate, 7, 11, 14

Wellington, Ben, 170–75
Werner, Stephen, 43–44
Westchester County, 65, 99
Westchester Rockland v. Mosczydlowski, 18
WGRZ, 6, 42
Whitehall Town Board, 31
Wilson, Malcolm (New York governor), 7, 14
Wisniewski, Benjamin, 223–26
Witkoff, Steve, 219
WNYC, 165, 170
Worley, Dwight, 65–66
Wyoming County Board of Supervisors, 125

Yates, Town of, 222–23

Zakroczemski, Daniel, 4
Zilgme, Michele, 128–31
Zimpher, Nancy (SUNY chancellor), 34–35
Zou, Jie Jenny, 52–54
Zuckerman v. NYS Board of Parole, 18

Photograph by

Brett Orzechowski is an assistant professor of management and media at Utica
College, where he also teaches entrepreneur-
ship and data-related courses. He joined
the faculty at Utica in 2015 after serving
as CEO and publisher of the *Connecticut
Mirror*/Connecticut News Project, Inc., a
public-policy news organization in Hartford
and Washington, DC, and after teaching at
Quinnipiac University, with an emphasis on
public-affairs reporting and interactive digital media.